$22.50
56A

European Communities Information
Its use and users

European Communities Information
Its use and users

Edited by
Michael Hopkins

Mansell Publishing Limited
London and New York

First published 1985 by Mansell Publishing Limited
(A subsidiary of The H.W. Wilson Company)
6 All Saints Street, London N1 9RL, England
950 University Avenue, Bronx, New York 10452, U.S.A.

British Library Cataloguing in Publication Data

European Communities information: its use and users.
   1. European Communities—Bibliography
   2. European Communities—Information services
   I. Hopkins, Michael, *1945*–
382.9′142′07   HC241.2

   ISBN 0-7201-1701-1

Library of Congress Cataloging in Publication Data

European communities information, its use and users.

   Includes index.
   1. European communities—Information services.
I. Hopkins, M. (Michael), 1945–
JN15.E815 1984   354.1′819   84-20138
ISBN 0-7201-1701-1

Printed in Great Britain at the University Press, Cambridge

Contents

Part 2: Sources of European Communities Information and their use

List of Contributors

Paul Bongers

Executive Secretary of the International Union of Local Authorities and Council of European Municipalities and Regions. Previously on the staff of the Council of Europe, worked in local government in the United Kingdom and was an Assistant Secretary at the Association of Metropolitan Authorities.

Maria Collins

Librarian of the Statistics and Market Intelligence Library since 1978. Previously held library posts in the British Geological Survey and elsewhere in the Department of Trade and Industry.

Anthony Crombie

Information Officer at the International Union of Local Authorities and Council of European Municipalities and Regions and Editor of the *European Information Service*. Previously worked for the Central Office of Information.

Dermot Englefield

Deputy Librarian of the House of Commons since 1976, Secretary of the IFLA Parliamentary Libraries Section and Chairman of the Libraries Group of the European Centre for Parliamentary Research and Documentation. His publications include *Parliament and information: the Westminster scene* (1981), and he has edited *Commons Select Committees — catalysts for progress* (1984) and *Information sources in politics and political science — a survey worldwide* (1984).

Eric Gaskell

Head of the Central Library of the Commission of the European Communities since 1973. Previously Librarian of the Wellcome Institute for the History of Medicine. Author of various contributions on librarianship, medical history and Dickens.

John Michel Gibb

Head of the Department for Scientific and Technical Communication in Directorate-General XIII (Information Market and Innovation) in the

Commission of the European Communities in Luxembourg. Previously assistant to the Director-General in Directorate-General XIII and Editor of *Eurospectra*.

Jim Hogan

A Special Writer with *Your business* magazine. Formerly European Community News Editor of *British business*, for which magazine he compiled a number of special businessmen's guides to the European Community. His publications also include *EEC contacts* (1984).

Michael Hopkins

Sub-Librarian at Loughborough University of Technology, Chairman of the Association of EDC Librarians and Chairman of the Library Association Working Party on European Communities Publications. Previously Official Publications Librarian at Leicester University. His publications include *Policy formation in the European Communities: a bibliographical guide to Community documentation 1958–1978* (1981) and *Publications, documents and means for their dissemination in the Commission of the European Communities* (1981).

John Jeffries

Assistant Librarian at the University of Kent at Canterbury, currently Chairman of the British and Irish Association of Law Librarians and past Treasurer of the Association of EDC Librarians. Author of *A guide to the official publications of the European Communities* (2nd edn., 1981) and of various other contributions to the professional press.

Simon O'Sullivan

Member of the European Communities Group at the Ministry of Agriculture, Fisheries and Food. Previously Economics Librarian at the Ministry of Agriculture, Fisheries and Food.

Giancarlo Pau

Head of the Information Unit at the London Office of the Commission of the European Communities. Previously worked in both Brussels and Luxembourg in various documentation and information posts, including the 'cabinets' of both the President and Vice-President of the Commission. His publications include the annual *Index to documents of the Commission of the European Communities* (3rd edn., 1984).

David Perry

Senior manager at the Office for Official Publications of the European Communities in Luxembourg with particular responsibility for marketing and distribution. Previously Marketing Director at Her Majesty's Stationery Office and a commercial law publisher with Butterworths in the United Kingdom and overseas.

Edward Phillips

Member of the Scientific and Technical Communication Department of Directorate-General XIII (Information Market and Innovation) in the Commission of the European Communities in Luxembourg. Previously with Macmillan Journals Ltd, where he was on the editorial staff of *Nature*.

Anthony Reid

Head of Division in charge of the Library, and of the Reference, Information and Documentation Services in the European Parliament in Luxembourg. Previously Manager of Library and Information Service of Reckitt and Colman.

Gay Scott

Director of Eurofi (UK) Ltd, and a specialist in information and consultancy work on European Communities issues. Previously worked in the Greater London Council European Unit and the House of Commons Library. Her publications include *A guide to European Community grants and loans* (4th edn., 1984) and *The European Economic Community: a guide to sources of information* (1979).

Walter Verheyden

Director of the Office for Official Publications of the European Communities in Luxembourg and President of the Consultative Committee on Publications in the Commission of the European Communities. His earlier posts include those of Director of the Secretariat-General of the Commission and Secretary of the High Authority in the European Coal and Steel Community.

List of Abbreviations

ACP	African, Caribbean and Pacific States
ADAS	Agricultural Development and Advisory Service
AMIS	Agricultural Management Information Systems
BOTB	British Overseas Trade Board
BTN	Brussels Tariff Nomenclature
CAP	Common Agricultural Policy
CBI	Confederation of British Industry
CCCN	Customs Cooperation Council Nomenclature
CCP	Consultative Committee on Publications
CCT	Common Customs Tariff
CEM	Council of European Municipalities
CFP	Common Fisheries Policy
COM	Commission of the European Communities
COPA	Committee of Agricultural Producer Organizations
COREPER	Committee of Permanent Representatives
COST	Coopération Scientifique et Technique
DEP	Depository Library
DG	Directorate-General
DoI	Department of Industry
DTI	Department of Trade and Industry
EAEC	European Atomic Energy Community
EAGGF	European Agricultural Guidance and Guarantee Fund
EC	European Community
ECE	Economic Commission for Europe
ECHO	European Commission Host Organization
ECOSOC	Economic and Social Committee
ECR	European Court Reports
ECSC	European Coal and Steel Community
ECU	European Currency Unit

EDC	European Documentation Centre
EDG	European Democratic Group
EDP	Electronic data processing
EEB	Exports to Europe Branch of the BOTB
EEC	European Economic Community
EFTA	European Free Trade Association
EIB	European Investment Bank
EIS	European Information Service
EIS	Export Intelligence Service
ERDF	European Regional Development Fund
ERG	Exchange Risk Guarantee
ESA	European System of Integrated Accounts
ESF	European Social Fund
ESSPROS	European System of Integrated Social Protection Statistics
FAO	Food and Agriculture Organization
FAST	Forecasting and assessment in the field of science and technology
FEOGA	Le Fonds européen d'orientation et de garantie agricole (*See also* EAGGF)
GATT	General Agreement on Tariffs and Trade
GDP	Gross domestic product
GLC	Greater London Council
HS	Harmonized System
ILO	International Labour Organization
ISBN	International Standard Book Number
ISIC	International Standard Industrial Classification of all Economic Activities
IULA	International Union of Local Authorities
JET	Joint European Torus
JRC	Joint Research Centre
KAU	Kind of activity unit
MAFF	Ministry of Agriculture, Fisheries and Food
MCA	Monetary compensatory amount
MEP	Member of the European Parliament
NACE	General Industrial Classification of Economic Activities within the European Communities
NCI	New Community Instrument
NFU	National Farmers' Union
NIMEXE	Nomenclature of Goods for the External Trade Statistics of the Community and Statistics of Trade between Member States
NIPRO	Common Nomenclature of Industrial Products
NTB	Non tariff barrier
OECD	Organization for Economic Cooperation and Development
OGIL	Open General Import Licence
OJ	*Official journal of the European Communities*

PACO	Agricultural prices and the economic accounts of agriculture and forestry
PDB	Preliminary draft budget
SAUS	School for Advanced Urban Studies (University of Bristol)
SCAD	Central Documentation Service
SDI	Selective dissemination of information
SEC	Secretariat
SEPD	Scottish Economic Planning Department
SIGLE	System for Information on Grey Literature in Europe
SITC	Standard International Trade Classification
SMIL	Statistics and Market Intelligence Library
SNA	System of National Accounts
SOEC	Statistical Office of the European Communities
TED	Tenders Electronic Daily
TEPSA	Trans-European Policy Studies Association
THE	Technical Help to Exporters
UACES	University Association for Contemporary European Studies
UDC	Universal Decimal Classification
UK	United Kingdom
UN	United Nations
UNCTAD	United Nations Conference on Trade and Development
UNESCO	United Nations Educational, Scientific, and Cultural Organization
USDA	United States Department of Agriculture
VAT	Value added tax
WOID	Welsh Office Industry Department
ZPAI	Supply balance sheets and production statistics

Introduction

MICHAEL HOPKINS

As a member of the European Community (EC) the United Kingdom has pledged its allegiance to the principles and policies embodied in the Treaty of Rome and has granted to Community institutions the power to make laws which can override existing national legislation. The influence of the European Community on the socio-economic and political fabric of the United Kingdom has been considerable. Many activities now take place exclusively within a Community framework; others have a clear Community dimension or are directly affected by action taken on a Community plane. At the highest levels of national life the machinery of government has been modified to take account of new decision-making processes, parliamentary procedures have been altered and the work of many government departments has been significantly changed. Other levels of public administration and professional activity have been similarly affected. Business life too has had to adjust not only to the application of the many rules and regulations governing economic and commercial activity in the Common Market but also to the challenges and opportunities afforded by the much expanded domestic market. The consequence is that people in many walks of national life now need regular access to EC information in the conduct of their daily business.

The purpose of this book is to consider the nature and use of EC information from a number of contrasting viewpoints. In the first part of this book senior Community officials contribute chapters in which they explain the policies and practices adopted by Community institutions regarding the provision of information and the arrangements made for its dissemination and use. Special attention is devoted to the role of the European Community as an official publisher. The factors that determine the characteristics of Community publishing, the institutional arrangements made for executing a publishing

1

programme and the part played by publications in general Community information policy are discussed. Consideration is also given to the library and information systems that have been developed in response to internal demand for information in Community institutions. By way of contrast, the second part of the volume is concerned with EC information from the external user's point of view. It includes chapters that examine the way in which EC membership has impinged upon the information needs of important groups in society and which describe the sources of information that best match those needs. In view of their importance for many groups of users, chapters of a mainly bibliographical nature are also included on such topics as Community law and statistics.

The very publication of this book serves to underline the fact that the library and information profession is itself one of those groups whose activities have been directly affected by Community membership. This is not surprising in that libraries reflect the needs of their users in terms of both stock and services. The chapters of this book illustrate how Members of Parliament and civil servants, local government officers and public administrators, business managers and manufacturers, lawyers and lecturers, farmers and fishermen and many more besides are all to varying degrees affected in their daily work by the European Community. The impact of their consequent information requirements on library and information services has been considerable. Such is the pervasive influence of the organization and the nature of its legal order that libraries of many descriptions are now called upon to stock literature by and about the European Community and to have staff whose familiarity with Community documentation is sufficient to answer an infinite variety of questions of varying degrees of complexity.

In fact, the library and information profession has a key role to play in the information process as it relates to the European Community. Many people are either intimidated by the prospect of using official documents and legislative texts, have neither the time nor the inclination to become familiar with often complicated and sometimes confusing publications or simply are ignorant of the information resources available to them. Without ready access to appropriate texts and expert guidance, many people will be deprived of the information they require. In the Community context this lack of information can have significant practical consequences. It can mean lost business contracts, failure to take full advantage of both the financial resources and the commercial opportunities afforded by the Common Market and lack of awareness and observance of legal obligations imposed by Community rules and regulations. The accelerating use of information technology serves only to make the role of the intermediary even more crucial.

Librarians have not found it easy to come to terms with the consequences of Community membership. When the United Kingdom entered the European Community in 1973 librarians were confronted on the one hand by a mass of unfamiliar documentation produced by a system whose practices were very different from anything they had previously known, and on the other by a public whose ignorance of Community affairs was such that a high level of assistance was necessary if its information needs were to be satisfied. These problems were compounded by the manifest inadequacies in the bibliographic apparatus available to those who wished to consult Community sources of information.

In some respects little has changed in the past ten years. Despite the fact that British membership of the European Community has never ceased to be a live political issue and as such has received constant media attention, the general level of understanding of Community aims, activities and institutional processes in the population as a whole has remained disappointingly low. For the majority of ordinary people the European Community remains a remote and bureaucratic organization whose activities provoke general interest only when they seem to pose a threat to yet another aspect of the British way of life. The consequence for libraries is a continuing need for high levels of reader service in this important area of activity.

The contrast with 1973 is that ten years on librarians are much better placed to provide the level of service that is required. They have at their disposal superior printed products and improved means of bibliographical control. Specialized and sometimes commercial information services and sources have been developed and a fund of expertise and experience has been accumulated. Within the library and information profession itself initiatives have been taken at a national level to provide a platform and a focus for professional activities relating to the European Community. In 1979 the Library Association established a Working Party on European Communities Publications for the purpose of creating a dialogue with Community institutions on matters of mutual concern and in 1981 an Association of EDC Librarians was created to represent the special interests of those librarians responsible for European Documentation Centres (EDCs) and Depository Libraries (DEPs) in the United Kingdom. These professional bodies have provided a particularly valuable service in the fields of education and training. As a result of their efforts in organizing conferences, seminars and workshops many librarians have had the opportunity to hear about Community publications and to learn how best to exploit them.

Both the Library Association Working Party on European Communities Publications and the Association of EDC Librarians have acted as pressure groups, expressing the British user's point of view and making suggestions for improvements which conform with the best standards of the English-speaking world. It may well be that some demands have derived too closely from the British tradition of government and administration and have taken insufficient account of the very different nature of the European Community and the constraints under which it operates. In the first chapter of this book Verheyden points out that there are perfectly understandable reasons why Community publishing activities have developed in the way they have and he explains why it has proved difficult to respond positively or quickly to some of the suggestions advanced by British librarians. He draws attention to the fact that the European Community is still a very recent creation whose principal concern so far has been to develop its policies and political influence rather than to refine and rationalize its internal organization and methods — which themselves, not surprisingly, reflect Continental rather than Anglo-Saxon practice. The differing traditions of each of the three separate Communities, the largely autonomous existence and differing constitutional roles of each of the main institutions make it difficult to establish a uniformity of approach on such matters as publications policy. Moreover, the major upheavals caused first by the merger of the institutions and then successive enlargements have allowed little time and opportunity for the consolidation of procedures and the evolution of consistent and coordinated policies in those areas, including publications policy, which transcend institutional responsibilities.

However, despite these problems it is also clear from Verheyden's chapter that considerable progress has been made in the coordination and control of publishing activities both within institutions, particularly through the Consultative Committee on Publications (CCP) in the Commission, and between institutions, through the increasingly prominent role played by the Office for Official Publications. Perry deals with this subject in much more detail in his chapter. His full description of the constitutional position of the Office and of its precise relationship with other Community institutions provides an answer for those who ask why the Office does not exert more central control over Community publishing activities. The Office's power of influence over Community publishing policy is strictly limited; it depends upon the support and approval of other Community institutions for many of its actions. That there has been a noticeable expansion of the role of the Office over the past decade is a measure of its success in exploiting the benefits of new technology to improve operating procedures, in introducing new and improved products, particularly in the field of bibliographical control, and generally in adopting a much more businesslike attitude towards Community publishing. Although sales revenue is still not the principal motivating factor, it is clear from what Perry has to say that the placement of Community publishing activities on a more commercial basis has inevitably introduced the concept of value-for-money and a more professional approach to the production, promotion and distribution of publications.

Many of the improvements that have been made in the provision and dissemination of information have occurred as a result of the application of information technology. Verheyden and Perry explain how automated systems have been employed in the Office for Official Publications to speed up and sophisticate publishing processes and to improve the accessibility of information by the development of electronic storage and delivery facilities and by machine-based indexing systems. In his chapter Gaskell describes the computer-based information retrieval systems that have been designed to improve general efficiency and performance in the Commission by providing officials with rapid and highly specific access to the many thousands of documents produced by both the Commission and other institutions. He also refers to the ways which computer applications have made possible significant improvements in both housekeeping routines in the Central Library and in the quality of service offered to readers. Reid too mentions data processing, although the involvement of the European Parliament has been modest as compared with that of the Commission and has mostly concentrated upon the development of tools to assist the management of parliamentary procedures.

Many of the data bases described by Gaskell are available for internal use only. Members of the public benefit only indirectly from such services — from the more efficient conduct of Community business, the occasional printed by-product of an automated system and from indirect access to the information contained in a data base through the services of a privileged intermediary. However, some important files are open to the public, the most important of which are described in this book. Jeffries describes the CELEX system which provides online access to Community law in the form of both treaties and secondary legislation. There are plans to extend its coverage to include preparatory documents from both the Commission and the European Parliament. Gibb and Phillips describe the EABS and SIGLE data bases, the latter of which is intended to cover 'grey' or 'non-conventional' literature and which will include some of the considerable amount of grey literature produced by the institutions of the European Communities themselves. Collins draws attention to the major initiatives taken by the Statistical Office of the European Communities in the use of data banks to promote the rapid transmission of data. The increasing size and scope of the CRONOS and COMEXT data banks, supported by the distribution of detailed results on magnetic tape and in microfiche, means that users can have speedier access to current data than was previously possible through conventional printed publications and also have the opportunity to manipulate it to their convenience. O'Sullivan also mentions CRONOS and COMEXT along with other more specialized online systems in his discussion of sources of information on agricultural policy. It is clear that these and other information retrieval systems mentioned in this book, such as POLIS and EUROLEX, have made an enormous impact on the availability and accessibility of EC information in the past ten years.

However, despite the expanding contribution of online services and the impending impact of electronic document delivery the printed word continues to have a major part to play in the transmission of EC information. Indeed, it is still conventional printed publications that receive most attention from the authors of the chapters in this book, even in those areas where important online developments have occurred. Jeffries provides a concise introduction to the main elements of the Community legal order, with particular reference to the instruments and sources of Community law. In their chapter Gibb and Phillips show how integral to the Community scientific and research effort is the dissemination of published information. They describe the research activities and programmes of Community institutions and draw attention to the various ways in which research results are made available. They explain the publishing philosophy of Directorate-General XIII and well illustrate the point made by Verheyden regarding the nature and diversity of Community publishing practices. Collins describes the work of the Statistical Office of the European Communities, with particular reference to its efforts to provide Community officials with data of a comparable nature and to the main statistical serials that are published. In a very comprehensive survey of sources of information on agricultural policy O'Sullivan describes not only the sources but also the context from which they emanate. He explains the main features of the Common Agricultural Policy (CAP), discusses the information needs that arise and provides expert guidance on a wide variety of both official and commercial sources of information.

The value of printed sources of information varies considerably from one user group to another. As Hopkins explains in his chapter, the academic community works in an environment in which the written word plays an important part in the communication process, in which printed sources of information are widely used in many subject disciplines to support both teaching and research, and in which output in terms of publications is one of the criteria used to measure the standing of its members. It is not surprising, therefore, that the publications and documents described by Hopkins should have such value for the academic community, a fact well recognized by the Commission in its generous provision of documentation free of charge to those institutions engaged in the study of European integration.

For other groups, however, it is not specific publications or whole texts that are required but discrete pieces of information or advice. Hogan illustrates this well in his provocative chapter on the information needs of British business and its relationship with Europe. Business men and women do not generally have the time or inclination to keep abreast of general Community developments. Unlike the academic community, for instance, they do not form a homogeneous group whose information and documentation needs can be anticipated. Their work is not usually literature based and they are not library oriented. They are interested in European Community information, as Hogan notes, only if and when the Community impinges upon their business activities and profitability. Moreover, they have little interest in the sources of information or in the process of acquiring information; they want immediate answers to practical questions. In this context publications are not always an ideal source of assistance: the information they contain is impersonal, it may need expert interpretation or be presented in an unhelpful way and it may even be out-of-date. For these reasons personal contacts are often more productive. In view of the numerous ways in which EC legislation impinges upon business practices and the general environment within which business operates, government departments and other official agencies are particularly important contact points. It is sources of this kind that are emphasized by Hogan in his wide-ranging discussion of business attitudes towards Europe and of their implications for information provision.

The nature of library and information services provided for various user groups is often indicative of the relative importance of different types of information. As Hopkins explains in his chapter, many academic disciplines are book-based; the library is largely a place for the satisfaction of the literature needs of the academic community. In other contexts the purpose of the library is to provide research support for staff whose primary function is to supply information. This is the case in the London Office of the Commission where the library and data room, as Pau illustrates, provide essential support for the information services offered by the Office. In a chapter in which he considers the nature of European Parliament information and the way in which parliamentary information services are organized, Reid describes how the library forms an integral part of a larger administrative whole whose general task is to provide research and documentation services for both Members and staff. The situation is somewhat different in the Commission of the European Communities where, in the strength of its stock and the range of its services, the Central Library resembles a specialized academic library. As Gaskell indicates, while the Central Library is best placed to satisfy the literature needs of Commission officials many of their daily information needs are met by two related but separate agencies, the Division for Integrated Information and the Central Documentation Service.

It is sometimes said that British companies that wish to exploit the opportunities offered by an enlarged domestic market are often disadvantaged because foreign competitors have better contacts and greater access to information. An area of concern in the past has been the reluctance of British firms, public authorities, research institutions and others to take full advantage of the financial opportunities offered by Community membership. In view of the continuing ignorance in some quarters of the scope and potential of Community financial aids, this book includes a chapter in which Scott provides a brief and practical guide to the various grants and loans that emanate from Community institutions and the provisions concerning their use. As Bongers and Crombie point out in their chapter, local government has been one of the biggest customers of both the regional and social funds. Indeed, it was the prospect of financial aid for local improvements that first stimulated the interest of local government in the European Community and which in turn encouraged the development of the information services Bongers and Crombie describe.

If both business community and local government are to make best use of Community membership then they need timely information. Immediacy is not a vital consideration for the academic community, whose interests often span several decades of Community activity. Practitioner groups however, need current information early enough to be able to turn it to practical effect, whether it be to take business decisions, win contracts or to make applications for Community funds. It is in this respect that current awareness services, which monitor Community developments and allow subscribers to keep abreast of Community developments as they happen, are of particular value. Several such alerting services are mentioned in this book. Bongers and Crombie describe the news and information service which the British Sections of the International Union of Local Authorities (IULA) and the Council of European Municipalities (CEM) provide for local government staff. O'Sullivan describes some of the press agency services of both general and agricultural interest, all of which provide a valuable service but which are simply too expensive for all but a few libraries to acquire.

Early access to information is of particular importance to those groups who wish to participate in the policy-forming process, who wish to obtain early warning of official thinking on a specific issue or who want an opportunity to defend or promote a viewpoint before irrevocable decisions are taken. International pressure and special-interest groups have an important part to play in policy formation, a fact reflected in the presence of several hundred such organizations in Brussels. O'Sullivan briefly describes the work of the Committee of Agricultural Producer Organizations (COPA), an important and powerful umbrella organization formed to promote the interests of agricultural producers and traders in the Community. Bongers and Crombie also discuss the methods used by local government officers to gain timely access to relevant information.

One rather privileged group whose need for information at the policy-forming stage has led to the establishment of elaborate procedures to keep them informed are Members of Parliament. Englefield describes the arrangements that have been made in both the House of Commons and the House of Lords to allow the British Parliament to monitor the legislative activity of Community institutions and to give it an opportunity to express its opinion to Government before decisions are taken in the Council. Englefield describes in some detail the various types and series of parliamentary publications which are published as a result of this exercise and he clearly illustrates how British government publications can themselves be a mine of information on the affairs of the European Community.

The chapters of this book reveal the richness and variety of sources available to those who require information on the European Community. They describe the wealth of both general and specialized literature published by EC institutions, government agencies, private publishers and others; they illustrate how the increasing use of data bases and data banks has significantly improved the availability and accessibility of information; they highlight library and information services and generally draw attention to the sources of expertise and assistance that are available in the United Kingdom. It is surprising, therefore, that people still talk about a lack of information on the European Community. No doubt many information sources and services could be improved and new ones usefully introduced. However, the basic lack is not one of information but of awareness of what already exists. Such is the nature of EC information provision that many information services and sources were designed for a specific audience and are little known or used outside the specialist circles for which they were first intended. What is required is better coordination of effort between information providers and more general exploitation of existing resources. This book is prepared as a contribution to that end.

Part One

The Nature of
European Communities Information

1

The Publications Policy and Programme of the European Communities

WALTER VERHEYDEN

Introduction

Each year the European Communities publish approximately one thousand titles in the form of books, periodicals and other publications. Most of these are produced through the Office for Official Publications of the European Communities and can therefore be found in the Office's catalogue and be obtained through its network of sales outlets. However, this is not always the case: some publications or language versions of them are issued by private publishers; some information publications are published and distributed by the information offices; the European Investment Bank does not use the Publications Office channels; and so on.

Another distinctive feature of the European Communities' distribution system is the fact that many publications are distributed free, thus either competing with existing sales outlets or forming an alternative way of distribution. There are always understandable political or administrative reasons for free distribution, but it is obvious also that alternative channels frustrate uniform access to the publications in question.

Finally, it is characteristic of the Communities that they distinguish between publications and documents. Now, if what constitutes a 'publication' is open to question then the risks of confusion are multiplied when one talks about 'documents'. Documents may be authorized and official texts which reflect the opinion of the institution involved; or they may be texts which are equally official, but form part of the dialogue between the institutions such as the COM documents; they may be the results of studies which are considered to be of interest by a department but which do not necessarily represent a final point of view; or they may quite simply be internal documents which find their way to a limited external audience more or less by chance.

Obviously, Community institutions will treat one document differently from another depending on the circumstances. But it is equally obvious that the outside user is not necessarily aware of such distinctions. He or she sees only that distribution methods vary from one case to another, giving an impression of inconsistency or confusion. It is curious to note that English-language users have always found this more confusing than Continentals. Is this because the latter have had a longer acquaintance with Community affairs, or because they have somewhat different customs?

Users in the United Kingdom have long been accustomed to very high standards from their librarians and documentalists. Furthermore, as regards official publications, the United Kingdom can feel justly proud of Her Majesty's Stationery Office (HMSO), which is a well-structured and well-established publishing organization working against a background of a long-established political and administrative system supplying it with material for publication and distribution. Compared with the UK, the European Communities as a publisher, as in many other fields, is still in its infancy. The first of the Communities, the European Coal and Steel Community, began its activities scarcely thirty years ago, with a very small administrative staff whose main concern was to create and run the common market in coal and steel, rather than to worry about methods of day-to-day administration. Euratom and the European Economic Community — usually referred to as the Common Market — joined the European Coal and Steel Community in the late fifties. Euratom's management methods derived substantially from its scientific background and objectives, while in the Common Market the administrative tradition had strongest influence. The merger of the three only took place as recently as 1967, and even then it was not the three Communities themselves that merged, but merely their institutions; this explains the names currently used: *the* Commission and *the* Council of the European Communi*ties*.

The attempt to achieve uniform policies and practices with regard to publications could start only after this merger. It is also interesting to note that the very establishment of the Office for Official Publications of the European Communities, a sort of Community HMSO, dates also from after 1967. It was from this time that the new single Commission of the European Communities began to organize its publishing procedures, to centralize its resources and to define its publications policy. The new Office for Official Publications was given the task of printing or having printed all publications on behalf of the institutions, and its sales office set up a distribution system. To distribute what? *Official publications* of the Communities, not 'documents', and publications intended for *sale*, not publications or copies distributed free of charge.

These two distinctions are important, because in addition to the relatively late attempt at overall coordination and the six different national administrative traditions against which it had to be made, they were to hamper access to

Community publications for some time to come. We shall now see in what way they did so.

The origins of the European Communities' publishing activities

The need for each of the three Communities to organize its own individual publishing activity arose from several factors.

(i) The institutions' legislative work made it necessary from the very beginning to publish an *Official journal*. The treaty establishing the European Coal and Steel Community (ECSC) laid down that the legal acts of the High Authority would take effect by the mere fact of publication. In theory, the High Authority could have made do with making its decisions known through announcements in the press. However, it wisely proceeded to set up its own *Official journal of the European Coal and Steel Community* which was first issued on 31 December 1952.

In view of the existence of this *Official journal*, the Treaties of Rome laid down more explicitly that regulations should be published in 'the' Official journal of 'the' Community. Strictly speaking, the *Official journal of the European Coal and Steel Community* should thus have been joined by a second Official journal of the European Economic Community, and then by a third Euratom Official journal.

Fortunately, it was agreed to publish a single *Official journal of the European Communities* which would contain all the acts and communications of all the institutions[1] of the three Communities, and which would have the same layout as the *Official journal of the European Coal and Steel Community*. The task of compiling this *Official journal* in the four official languages of the time was entrusted to the publications department of the High Authority of the European Coal and Steel Community until the merger, after which, in 1969, the joint Office for Official Publications of the European Communities took over the task, which remains one of its principal activities even now.[2]

(ii) Furthermore, treaties or associated texts laid down that the institutions had to produce a number of obligatory publications. For instance, the High Authority and the two Commissions each had to publish an annual general report on the Community's activity. The Parliament also had to publish its acts, but it chose to use the *Official journal* rather than issue a separate publication.

Parliament also publishes the Community budget in the *Official journal*, since becoming responsible for the final adoption of the General Budget in 1975. The Court of Justice is also obliged to publish the decisions it reaches concerning the interpretation and application of treaties.

(iii) Other obligations, which were less explicit in writing but mandatory in fact, gave rise to other types of publication. For instance, the technical and scientific research financed by the European Coal and Steel Community and the rules for the dissemination of information from Euratom were to lead to the publication of research results under specific conditions. In the field of economics and statistics, certain data collected by the Statistical Office of the European Communities or forwarded to it by national statistical offices for processing and publishing in a Community context, are no longer published at national level, and have therefore become the special responsibility of the Community.

(iv) In certain fields, where Community activity does not have a legislative function, studies and publication of their results represent an important step towards integration. In this case publication is valuable in itself. The same thing can be said, to some extent, for publications whose aim is to inform the public of the work of the institutions and the aims of European integration. As regards information and comment, the printed word is still a privileged medium, even in this audio-visual age.

(v) Finally, the departments of an organization which has general economic responsibilities inevitably accumulate, as a by-product of their normal activities, a mass of information and data of interest to industry, labour and management, local authorities, research workers, etc. Although there is strictly speaking no obligation to pass on this information, it is obvious that publication may satisfy the needs of these groups. It is thus the duty of a public institution to publish such information as well.

Guidelines established by the Commission

This summary of the origins of Community publications shows that, leaving aside the *Official journal*, the vast majority of all publications originate within the Commission. Naturally, the other institutions also issue a number of publications of their own each year, and they may also participate in joint publications. In one case, *Report of cases before the Court*, the institution confines itself to issuing a single publication, though one of importance and size. Nevertheless, it is the publications of the Commission which are most varied in their subject matter, origin and destination.

The fact that all the institutions contribute to the publications programme of the Community,[3] each retaining a certain independence in its choice of subject matter, expression and presentation, obviously makes the task of drawing up a publications policy difficult. However, the brunt of the task necessarily fell upon the Commission which was obliged to set up the most elaborate procedures to organize its publications.

The most important step was the establishment in 1972 of the Consultative Committee on Publications (CCP). The Committee is composed of representatives of the various directorates-general to whom budget appropriations are available for publications — the Statistical Office, the Directorate-General for Information (DG X), the Directorate-General for Information Market and Innovation (DG XIII), the Directorate-General for Personnel and Administration (DG IX) and, of course, the Secretariat-General. The Committee is chaired by a president who preferably does not belong to this group of 'owners of appropriations', and who is assisted by the representatives of the departments which are the 'authors' of the material to be published. Its responsibility is to draw up an internal Commission publication programme every year for the following financial year.

The first programmes submitted by the CCP for the Commission's approval were necessarily confined to channelling the flood of requests for publication originating from every Commission department, to establishing a number of essential procedures, and to seeing that the demand for publishing did not exceed the appropriations set aside or the production capacity available.

In the first stage of planning, which was rather passive, a large share of the responsibility for deciding which material to publish remained with the 'author' departments. However, this was soon followed by the establishment of certain priorities and selection criteria which made it easier to provide a policy for the annual programme. Very soon, reading committees were set up to assess already published texts with a view to setting guidelines for future publications. For several years now, there has been a preliminary reading committee working at DG IX which has given the CCP valuable advice, passed on editorial recommendations to the 'author' departments and brought an awareness of writing standards to authors who, being administrators and technicians, do not always have the journalist's touch.

This is the foundation, achieved in less than ten years, upon which the CCP must now build in order to go beyond efficient administration and embark upon a genuine publications policy based on an awareness of which subjects must have priority and of the sort of quality needed for the publications to reach their target through the sales channels.

This makes it essential to strive towards greater clarity and improved access for the public. For this reason the CCP proposes gradually to arrange all publications in series under general headings. Economic and monetary subjects are covered by the periodical entitled *European economy*. Material originating from the Directorate-General for Employment, Social Affairs and Education has been brought together in a single journal entitled *Social Europe*. Similar journals or series dealing with particular subjects will follow in due course. The 'horizontal' series entitled *European perspectives* will systematically bring together high-quality publications providing an overall view of Community issues for a wide public.

This organizational effort to make the Commission's publication programme much more selective and more easily intelligible to readers will be accompanied by an improvement in the indexing system, which will also achieve a more extensive coverage than in the past.

The role of the Publications Office

The Publications Office is not an institution provided for in the treaties. As mentioned previously, it is an organization jointly created by all the institutions as a rationalization measure after the 1967 merger. Its task is to produce and market publications on their behalf.

Although the 'production' side is responsible for employment of the majority of the Office's staff and absorbs most of its efforts, that point is not relevant in this context. However, it is worthwhile briefly mentioning the specific constraints under which the 'publishing' side has to function.

Since each institution is basically master of its own publication programme — apart from a certain amount of inter-institutional coordination to avoid duplication and to ensure adequate coverage — the Office is a publishing house which cannot itself decide on grounds of profitability what should be made available to its customers. Furthermore, the production and marketing costs of each publication are considerable because it must generally be printed in several languages. Instead of being able to enlarge the range of publications, the Office has to invest money in marketing the same publication in several languages, some of which will have only limited circulation.

A third difficulty already mentioned in the introduction lies in the distinction made by the Community, often somewhat arbitrarily, between a 'publication' and a 'document'. In this context, a publication is a work presented in durable form and catalogued. The number of copies are fixed in advance on the basis of a known target market, and are distributed by the sales network. A document, on the other hand, always begins as an internal text and is neither planned by the Consultative Committee on Publications nor catalogued, and is therefore, by definition, outside the influence of the Publications Office.

These definitions are certainly borne out by the institutional practice of the Community. The division of executive power between the Commission and the Council means, for example, that a document originating with the Commission, and approved by it, is not automatically a 'government paper'. The Commission is therefore obliged to restrict distribution. Nevertheless, the fact remains that, sooner or later, the restrictions on certain documents disappear, and these then become official, semi-official or information documents. They begin to circulate among the public, either in an organized way through the Commission or by the initiative of various directorates-general.

Doubtless a mistake has been made in not following the example of the documentalists and librarians of the Anglo-Saxon school, for whom a document that is released to the public thereby becomes a publication and is treated as such. Instead, the Continental practice prevailed and a text that begins life as a document continues to be treated as such unless it is republished in the form of a publication as a result of a specific decision. This gave rise to a number of distinctions quite disconcerting for the user: between publications and documents, documents which are public and documents which are not, and a mass of grey and unpublished literature. However, due particularly to the contacts which Community organizations have had in recent years with British documentalists the tide is beginning to turn. The systematized distribution of COM documents and 'public documents' reflects this.

Future prospects

Four points emerge from the Commission's new publication policy:

— the 'publication' treatment will not be confined to books, but will be extended to documents which are available to the public;

— the publications will normally be sold to the public and not distributed free of charge;

— documents on electronic data processing (EDP) media (magnetic tapes and data bases) which are made accessible to the public will also be considered as publications;

— awareness and delivery systems must be perfected so as to improve availability to the public and to achieve the circulation for which the publications are intended.

These four points need further comment.

(i) The distribution mechanism for COM documents has already been set up by the Publications Office. The Economic and Social Committee and the European Parliament will use it to broadcast their opinions and resolutions. In this way, a subscription with the Publications Office will cover the whole range of official papers, which are catalogued and sent at regular intervals either as hard copy or in microform. It will be possible to take out a partial subscription on profiles.

Furthermore, the Publications Office will include in its monthly catalogue of publications the 'public documents' to be available on order. The Commission intends as far as possible to give 'public document' status to all 'documents' which are released for public distribution. This clearance will be a simple administrative operation, the material costs will be low, the Publications Office will provide the appropriate cover bearing the title, catalogue number and ISBN (International Standard Book Number) and the whole will be made available to the customer very swiftly (in the languages available) as hard copy or in microfiche.

All this will involve some effort, but it will put an end to the discrimination between the 'publication', which is selected for official publication, and the 'document', which an outsider could usually obtain only by a rather indirect means — and only then if aware of the existence of the document.

(ii) Although the Commission has opted to sell its publications as far as possible, this is not merely for the sake of making money. A book purchased is more likely to be read than a book given away. Sale will also oblige the author departments and publishers to be mindful of quality and will eventually allow the concept of publication in the traditional sense of the term to be reserved for works which are of interest to a wider public. More specialized texts of interest to a smaller section of the public will then be treated as 'public documents' while still remaining perfectly accessible to the reader as a consequence of the measures taken by the Publications Office.

Documentation centres and depository libraries will obviously continue to receive free supplies. But from now on these will be provided by the Publications Office. This will rationalize the system, avoid duplication and allow these users to benefit from the 'added value' of indexing and cataloguing.

Finally, another form of marketing which could be used more frequently would be the co-publication of certain works, or certain language versions of a work, by a private publisher and the Publications Office. Such titles would figure in the Office's catalogue and its sales outlets.

(iii) The marketing of electronic publications is entrusted systematically to the Publications Office. This will benefit the user, who will be able to deal with the same supplier for a traditional publication, a microfiche, a magnetic tape, or a data base.

The number of Community data bases commercially available to the public is bound to increase gradually. At the present time, there are:
the CELEX law base and the EURODICAUTOM multilingual data bank belonging to Directorate-General IX of the Commission; the COMEXT and CRONOS bases of the Statistical Office of the European Communities; and the TED (Tenders Electronic Daily) base of the Publications Office, which reproduces the 'S' series of the *Official journal* (notices of invitation to tender).

(iv) As already mentioned, considerable efforts have already been made to extend the indexing system and to make the Community literature more readily available to the public. The Publications Office is, however, aware that there is still scope for increasing the coverage (for any given subject a research worker likes to find in a single index not only the publications and documents issued by the institutions of the Community but also those published by private publishers, research institutes, universities, etc.) *and* for an in-depth analysis of the texts, for example in the form of extracts.
Here there is room for cooperation with the private sector. The Commission and the Publications Office consider such an agreement a next step which might be taken for the benefit of the public.

The technical aspects of some of the Publications Office's projects

The Publications Office relies on the services of printers in the private sector for more than 95% of the works it publishes. These printers are currently equipped with third generation photocomposition equipment. This allows scope for several interesting developments.

First of all, programmed photocomposition is used, or is being prepared for a number of works obtained from data banks (in particular, statistics). Text management and automated synoptic typesetting are also used for works which are partly repetitive. The printing of the Community budget is a striking example of the flexibility of these automated systems. The European Parliament voted on the 1984 budget just before Christmas 1983. By 16 January 1984 the first printed copies were being released, and a few days later all the copies of this impressive edition of the *Official journal*, numbering 1,130 pages in each of seven languages, had been distributed.

The Publications Office has developed a standard exchange format for all its typesetting on EDP media, and its use is obligatory for printers with contracts for such work. This makes it easier to reprocess certain texts, such as oft-consolidated versions of legal instruments which are subject to frequent amendments. Who has not had occasion to fume at the need to consult a large number of *Official journals* in order to reconstitute the current text of a particular regulation from all its amendments and corrigenda! Another consequence of introducing a Publications Office exchange format is that typeset texts can be fed directly into data bases, either as full texts for consultation or as files of titles for indexing.

The TED data base, which is the world's first online journal in seven languages, is one of the full text data bases. The Supplement to the *Official journal* (bulletin of notices of invitations to tender) is typeset and immediately fed into a data base; the notices can then be consulted by the firms concerned on the very morning that the printed versions are posted, which is sometimes several days before they reach their destination. For the moment notices of invitations to tender published in TED relate to works and supplies contracts put out to tender by the national and local authorities of the member states of the Community. Notices from the European Development Fund and Community institutions are also included. Before the spring of 1984 the scope will be extended to Japanese public supply contracts in accordance with the Government Procurement Agreement signed in 1979 under the General Agreement on Tariffs and Trade (GATT).

The next stage will be to include invitations to tender from other countries who have signed this agreement. Now that an online *Official journal* is established, the Publications Office is thinking of setting up the same system for the 'L' series of the *Official journal*. The printing and dispatch of the series have been rationalized to the utmost. When compared to the speed of these operations, to deliver the journals by post is becoming hopelessly slow. When legal texts are made available online, this will greatly improve the public service. The Publications Office will, for the sake of speed, provide only copies of the texts that appear in the hard copy edition; the more refined documentary processing of these texts will remain the responsibility of the CELEX base, and the plain texts will be withdrawn from the Publications Office's base as soon as they are accessible through CELEX. The CELEX base can also be fed faster because standardized exchange format is available.

Considerable progress is also being made in the field of indexing. For example, it will be possible to speed up considerably the preparation of the monthly and annual tables for the *Official journal*, since it will be possible to retrieve the titles of published texts. This will also be true for the *Register of current Community legal instruments*. This excellent cumulative index, which provides references for all Community legal instruments in force on a key date, normally 1 January of each year, has not yet realized its full potential because of the relative lateness of its publication. It would be to the great advantage of all those practising Community law for publication to be speeded up. Generally speaking, the Publications Office has broken down the subjects of its indexes and catalogues into the seventeen fields covered by the *Register*. Even when Commission publications are assembled to form collections they will be grouped in more or less the same way, except that some fields have been combined, so as to give ten instead of seventeen collections.

The most significant step forward will, however, be the introduction of machine-aided indexing on the basis of the Eurovoc multilingual thesaurus. This thesaurus was developed on the initiative of the Publications Office on the basis of work already carried out by Directorate-General XIII B and the Secretariat of the European Parliament. Representatives of the European Parliament and of various departments of the Commission, especially the Integrated Information Systems Division, the Brussels Central Library, the Terminology and Computer Applications Service in Luxembourg and DG XIII, cooperated in this major project. The Eurovoc macrothesaurus consists of a list of standardized terms constituting a controlled vocabulary covering the various fields of Community language. This standardized vocabulary comprises descriptors and non-descriptors.

As from the beginning of 1984, the Publications Office will be using Eurovoc to index the *Official journal*. The main advantage will be to reduce the indexing work to one language version; this rationalization will be made possible through the use of a semi-automatic system which, based on one language version, will then provide speedy equivalent indexes for the other Community languages. The same method will be adopted when using Eurovoc for other indexes, such as the various catalogues of publications produced by the Office. The European Parliament is already using Eurovoc on an experimental basis. Because Eurovoc provides fairly specific coverage of the fields in which the Community is involved, and because it will adapt as the Community language evolves, it is a documentary tool which all institutions and outside organizations may, if they so wish, use for information management.

References and notes

1 During this 'pre-merger' period, these were: the High Authority of the European Coal and Steel Community, the two Commissions of the European Economic Community and the European Atomic Energy Community; the three Councils which shared a single General Secretariat; the Assembly, which was already common to the three Communities; and the Court of Justice, which was also common to all three (plus the Economic and Social Committee). After the merger in 1967 there was a single Council and a single Commission for all three Communities, besides other institutions already common to the three.

2 In 1983 35,000 pages of *Official journal* were published in each of the seven languages.

3 The singular 'Community' will be used whenever it is not necessary to specify its legal basis under the three treaties of Paris and Rome.

2

The Role of the Office for Official Publications of the European Communities

DAVID PERRY

Introduction

The Office for Official Publications of the European Communities — referred to informally in this chapter as the Publications Office — is generally regarded as a publisher, and accorded the description of official publisher to the Communities.[1] A common service department of the six principal institutions of the Communities, it operates under their joint management and without derogation from their ultimate responsibilities. In conventional order of precedence the six institutions are the European Parliament, the Council, the Commission, the Court of Justice, the Economic and Social Committee and the Court of Auditors. It is confusing that the term 'institutions' is often applied to a larger number of bodies — including the European Investment Bank — which are neither managing institutions of the Publications Office, nor otherwise related to it; and that the term is applied in the treaties to include only the first four bodies mentioned above. However, the use of the term to apply exclusively to the six bodies, apart from being legitimized by the Publication Office's own statute, corresponds with the régime and usage of the General Budget of the European Communities. It also recognizes as a single group the six regular contributors to the *Official journal*, who are therefore so to speak conscripted associates in the Publications Office.

The Office's services have been used primarily by those institutions and their departments, but are available to other Community bodies too. Those services — somewhat extended in the case of the *Official journal of the European Communities* — include the design, preparation for press, manufacture and distribution (principally by sale) of the publications entrusted to it.

As this implies, the European Communities' obligations — statutory, conventional or occasional — to publish for the benefit of the Community citizen devolve directly upon the individual institutions and other Community bodies under the treaties or other instruments of their foundation. This principle has always been applied — to the extent that the costs incurred and revenue received by or through the Publications Office are apportionable to the institutions individually, not just publication by publication, but, if necessary, text by text within publications to which several institutions contribute matter. There is no general fund to pay the costs of Community publishing, only the budgets allocated to individual institutions, and there is no single body in overall control of their information and publishing activity.

Before the Publications Office was established in 1969 the principle was that each institution ran its external information and publishing activities independently as an extension of its internal communications. They were able to develop and use their autonomous facilities for reproduction, warehousing and distribution, supplementing them at their own discretion by independently purchasing printing capacity on the open market and by licensing publication by commercial publishers of texts in which copyright was vested in the Communities.

This autonomy was subject to two important qualifications. The *Official journal* was compiled and produced by the Publications Service of the High Authority of the European Coal and Steel Community (ECSC) in Luxembourg (absorbed since 1967 into the single Commission); and there was under the same management a Sales Office, administering sales of priced publications of all the institutions. In the case of the *Official journal*, which combined the contributions of all the institutions, coordination was of course mandatory, and in the case of sales — dominated by the *Official journal* itself — virtually obligatory too. But sale was not at the time a significant element in distribution, even of priced publications: free distribution was the rule, and it was administered by the institutions individually.

It was of course in a sense anomalous that any single institution should directly administer activities for which the ultimate responsibility was shared by others. It was evidently accepted too that if inter-institutional cooperation in publishing was to be extended, as seemed necessary, a new organization, independent of any single institution, but jointly responsible to them all, would have to be created. The opportunity to found one arose in the context of the extensive rationalization and relocation of services set in train by the Merger Treaty of 8 April 1965, establishing a single Council and a single Commission of the European Communities.[2] The creation of the Publications Office under joint inter-institutional control, absorbing the ECSC High Authority's Luxembourg based Publications Service and Sales Office staff and resources, was provided for, if somewhat obliquely, by an instrument linked to the Merger Treaty and signed on the same date: the Decision of the Representatives of the

Governments of the Member States on the Provisional Location of Certain Institutions and Departments of the Communities, the eighth of the thirteen articles of which reads:

> An Official Publications Office [*sic*] of the European Communities with a joint sales office and a medium- and long-term translation service attached shall be located in Luxembourg.[3]

As already suggested, the motive for the creation of the Publications Office was not simply to continue existing forms of inter-institutional cooperation in a novel structure.

During the 1960s there had emerged an irresistible case for extending cooperation to cover print buying. Purchasing from commercial printers by individual institutions showed them to be unequally equipped for the task, and in competition for the same capacity. Of course, these problems grew more serious as the Communities became more active and their output increased. Take the *Official journal* for example. The number of printed pages of text in the then four official languages of the Communities multiplied more than thirteen times between 1958 and 1968 (though the output of some 36,600 pages in 1968 is modest compared with the 247,400 pages in seven languages published in 1983). These growing demands upon printing trade suppliers made it desirable that the institutions should coordinate their orders and schedules. Also their expenditure had reached a level which obliged them to adopt standard and publicly justifiable purchasing methods based upon a system of competitive tendering. This would ensure that printers throughout the Communities would have an equal opportunity of competing for the business, and that public money would be seen to be well spent.

There was also a strong and connected case for the institutions to improve and standardize the presentation of their publications. It was clearly both convenient and economical that a single organization should establish common standards approved by the institutions and take responsibility for seeing that these standards were applied. Thus arose the extension of the Publications Office's functions to include the design, preparation for press and overseeing of manufacture generally. The argument in favour of this was made doubly compelling by the convenience and economy of concentrating technical and linguistic skills in one area. In the context of the Community of six, it was already impractical for each institution individually to maintain a personnel able to sub-edit, mark up for press and proof read publications produced simultaneously in four languages.

But in reality the need to extend the range of inter-institutional activity was no more pressing than the need to make more effective provision for continuing established types of cooperation. Reference has already been made to the rapid increase in the volume of matter published in four languages in the *Official journal.* This had in effect already been transformed by events into a daily newspaper, operating under similar constraints as to deadlines for the reception of copy for publication and as to timely appearance, but with added difficulties: the continuous actual and prospective increase in the volume of matter to be published; the administrative complications caused by publishing simultaneously in four languages (increased to six in 1973 and to seven in 1981, with a further increase to nine in prospect on the expected accession of Spain and Portugal to the Communities); the provision of adequate current and cumulative indexes to the growing mass of published material; and by no means least, the challenge of coordinating daily delivery within acceptable and reasonably equivalent schedules to users in all corners of the Community. All these were urgent problems which needed to be tackled together by all the institutions who shared ultimate responsibility for a periodical whose regularity of appearance and timeliness is crucial to the effectiveness of the Communities.

A further motive for the establishment of the Publications Office was the need to rationalize distribution policy and practice. The Office naturally took responsibility on behalf of the institutions generally for the already centralized sales function, including the management of a network of agents in the member states and elsewhere, and the warehousing and distribution of stock for sale. It was accepted that for the *Official journal* its functions would be extended to the control and warehousing of all stocks, and to the direct dispatch of all subscriptions, paid or free. Apart from the more general considerations of improved efficiency, centralization was intended to allow the application of uniform rules to restrain the growth of free circulation, which had become over-generous. There was a predominant view also that the creation of the Office should contribute to coordination of practice as to whether publications should or should not be priced, and, where they were priced, to standardization of the rules on free distribution. For the conviction was growing within the institutions that, except in the case of literature aimed at persuading or informing public opinion on an extensive scale, free distribution was an ineffective and extravagant method of dissemination, and should be more strictly controlled than in the past. The corollary was that sales facilities and activities should be reinforced. But, perhaps surprisingly, it seems not to have been thought necessary to bring together facilities for free and sales distribution other than in the case of the *Official journal*. However, the Publications Office's distribution facilities were to be available in support of the individual institution's facilities for free distribution in case of need.

Such were the major ideas behind the creation of the Publications Office as part of the information and publishing system of the Communities.

Foundation and relationship with the institutions

As we have seen, the creation of the Publications Office and its location in Luxembourg were the subject of a prospective statutory provision in 1965. That provision was formally implemented on 28 January 1969. On that date there came into force the Decision of 16 January 1969 establishing the Office for Official Publications of the European Communities.[4] It was a joint Decision of the European Parliament, the Council, the Commission, the Court of Justice and the Economic and Social Committee. All five bodies were termed institutions for the purposes of the Decision, the preamble to which records *inter alia* that the Publications Office 'must be run in such a way as to allow all the institutions to participate in its management, and each of the institutions to benefit from the services that it is required to supply'. The Decision of 16 January 1969 in effect provided the Publications Office with its written constitution, specifying its purpose and its tasks and providing for its management, staffing and financing. The Decision has been amended on one occasion, by the Decision of 7 February 1980[5]; its most significant effect was to add the Court of Auditors as a sixth managing institution.

The Publications Office did not of course spring into existence fully equipped and operational, with a definitive set of policies and procedures. The Decision of 16 January 1969 has served to provide a statutory framework within which the organization's role has developed, first to meet the challenges perceived at the time of its creation, and subsequently in response to new influences. The paragraphs which follow will refer both to the outline of statutory rules within which the Publications Office works, and show how within these rules its functions have developed.

STATUS

The Publications Office is functionally a common service department of the six managing institutions named above. Though it may now serve other Community bodies as well, its primary purpose and the overwhelming substance of its activity remains the provision of services to those institutions and their departments, and those institutions jointly manage the Office through its Management Committee. However, for formal reasons the Publications Office has to be treated for administrative and budgetary purposes as part of one institution, in practice the Commission, subject to various procedural acknowledgements of the Office's inter-institutional nature. For example, while members of the Publications Office's staff are treated as staff of the Commission, appointments and other procedures are subject to the approval of all the institutions through the Management Committee. Furthermore, while the maintenance costs of the Publications Office are entered under a special heading in the Commission's annual budget, the total amount is also prorated between the institutions, pro forma appropriations being entered by way of memoranda in each institution's budget. But where the Publications Office contracts for services with suppliers, it does so on behalf of the institutions, and they individually are required to authorize expenditure and, directly or indirectly, to settle contractors' invoices from their individual budgetary resources. The general principle is that in all its activities the Publications Office is the instrument of the managing institutions; and all the costs and revenues connected with its activities are attributable either to one of those institutions or to other clients.

The Decision of 16 January 1969 establishing the Publications Office did not in its original form contemplate the use of the Publications Office's services by bodies other than the managing institutions. But since the amendments introduced by the Decision of 7 February 1980 it is clear that the Publications Office may handle the production and distribution of 'any publications from independent bodies set up by Community act'.[6] There is no obligation on such independent bodies to publish through the Publications Office; indeed even the managing institutions do not regard themselves as bound exclusively to the Office. The only 'independent body' that makes regular use of the Publications Office's production and distribution service is the European Centre for the Development of Vocational Training, which is established in Berlin.

RELATIONS WITH THE INSTITUTIONS THROUGH
THE MANAGEMENT COMMITTEE AND OTHERWISE

The Management Committee governing the Publications Office was set up by article 3(1) of the Decision of 16 January 1969. Each of the six managing institutions is represented on it, exercising one vote each. The Committee's rules of procedure emphasize the equality of the institutions, by providing that the chairmanship should rotate among the members every six months, though in recent practice there has been a long period of continuous chairmanship by the representative of the Court of Auditors. The Publications Office does not have express membership of the Committee, nor exercise any right to vote. But the Director of the Publications Office, who is of course directly responsible to the Committee for the development and running of the organization, provides its secretariat and is naturally in practice the source of the majority of submissions to it. The Management Committee is a body of great weight; its titular members have, since the Publications Office's establishment, always been the Secretaries-General of the European Parliament, the Council and the Commission, the Director-General of Personnel and Administration of the Commission, the Registrar of the Court of Justice and the Secretary-General of the Economic and Social Committee, and, since 1980, a Member of the Court of Auditors. In recent years the titular members have met annually, regular business being dealt with at meetings of alternates — a situation in sharp contrast with that of the Publications Office's early years, when twenty-three meetings of titular members, and none of alternates, were held in the period 1969 to 1972. But those were the years in which the structures of the Publications Office were still being established and the lines of policy first laid down; they also led up to the first enlargement of the European Communities in 1973, with an increase in the number of member states from six to nine, the number of official languages from four to six, and they saw rapidly growing demands on the Publications Office's capacities at a time when its facilities were still being set up. Indeed it was not until the end of 1973 that the organization was brought together in a single building at its present address,[7] having previously been housed at six different addresses.

The Management Committee's functions are spelt out in detail in the Decision of 16 January 1969. The provisions emphasize the distinction in the relations between the institutions and the Publications Office depending upon whether the area at issue is considered to be of proper inter-institutional interest, or the concern of each one individually. The Management Committee exercises the general management of the Publications Office as a production, procurement and distribution facility, and sets the general policies and rules for access to it, but otherwise stands between the institutions and the Publications Office only so far as the institutions publish through a common vehicle, principally the *Official journal*, or otherwise undertake joint action. Thus the Decision of 16 January 1969 contains separate provisions as to the general management of the Publications Office by the Management Committee, and as to its role as a publishing and editorial committee for the *Official journal* —one in which the committee's functions are broadly parallel with those of the internal publishing control structures of the Commission, headed by its Consultative Committee on Publications (CCP), or with the internal but less formalized structures of other individual institutions through which they establish their publishing policies and programmes of publications which, unlike the *Official journal*, have no inter-institutional element.

But if the institutions generally, acting through the Management Committee, do not seek to control each other's individual publishing policies and programmes, nevertheless the Committee plays an important role in the exchange of views and experiences between the institutions, and therefore indirectly in the coordination of individual institutions' approaches to similar questions.

Official publications of the European Communities

We have seen that the relationships of the Publications Office with the institutions and other bodies of the European Communities may in theory, but do not yet in practice extend far beyond those with the six managing institutions. This is an aspect of the decentralization of the Communities' publishing system which seems to cause problems for regular users who seek methodically to acquire a large range of its output, even though those six institutions, and in particular the Commission, are overwhelmingly the predominant source of Community information. Such decentralization seems to conflict with the ostensible purpose of the Publications Office, whose full title is 'Office for Official Publications of the European Communities' which implies an ability to supply if not to produce any publicly available material from a Community source.

But there are limitations on the Publications Office's activity as a producer and distributor of information material from the six managing institutions. The exceptions under the Office's founding statute relate to publications of the external offices: the Commission's Press and Information Offices in cities 'other than the provisional locations of the Communities', which may be handled independently;[8] publications in which the involvement of the Publications Office would appreciably increase costs or make it impossible for an urgent publication to be produced and distributed within the time available (an exception which has resulted principally in direct recourse by the institutions to commercial publishers);[9] and to material which the institutions have classed as 'internal documents' rather than publications.[10]

EXTERNAL OFFICES

The independence of the Press and Information Offices in the production and distribution of their publications simply recognizes the logistical as well as intellectual futility of attempting to control from a geographically and culturally remote centre every aspect of a programme of information aimed at a member state or third country. But some interesting side issues arise, and these may affect the organization of the Community publishing systems in future.

The publishing activity of the external offices shows that the institutions realise the need to conduct their publishing activities at two levels — that of the individual member state, and that of the Community as a whole. Most publishing is carried out at the level of the Community. Publications are conceived, designed and written principally in Brussels and Luxembourg to a notional Community standard and as a general rule translated into every official language of the Community, with all versions published simultaneously, each identical in meaning, authority, accessibility and price. The coordination of the writing, translation, production and distribution of a multilingual mass of centrally produced material is the principal problem of the publishing systems of the institutions, because of the costs and delays that are inherent in it. And as the Community embraces a larger number of member states, official languages and cultures, it seems likely that the value to the individual citizen of a centrally directed, uniform multiple language publishing programme will become more limited. It is already apparent that one factor that has constrained the effectiveness of Community publishing policy is the presumption that what is published in one Community language should not only be published in them all, but that the form in which the information is presented and the terms of access to it should be identical for each language of publication, and that, correspondingly, production and distribution should be centrally organized rather than decentralized by language and member state. While the presumption is valid up to a point, most obviously for legislative and other primary texts, its validity is not so evident for secondary and interpretative material. The implication is that as the Community continues to develop there may need to be a progressive decentralization in its publishing system to improve efficiency at the expense of uniformity.

COMMERCIAL PUBLISHING

The direct licensing by the institutions of the publication of their copyright manuscripts is foreseen in the Publications Office statutes. It is a procedure justified by article 3(4) of the Decision of 16 January 1969, which reads:

> At the request of an institution, the Management Committee may, under exceptional circumstances, authorise the printing of publications otherwise than through the [Publications Office] ... where [its] involvement ... would appreciably increase costs or where, for technical reasons [it] is unable to act with the urgency required in order to print and distribute a publication with the minimum of delay ...

From the point of view of the Commission, the already well established practice of Directorate-General XIII (DG XIII) of licensing the publication of scientific and technical texts by commercial publishers was confirmed as a policy to be extended to other areas of publishing in a notice published in the *Official journal* in 1979.[11] In 1981 the Court of Auditors noted that 'since 1975 DG XIII of the Commission has had about 150 scientific and technical works published in this way': further the Court observed that 'in the Commission, only DG XIII has had works published in this way, and ... other institutions have rarely used this method of publication ... the [Publications Office] was involved neither in the decisions nor in the arrangements made with private publishers'.[12]

There are a number of reasons why an institution may license a commercial publisher in preference to publishing directly through the Publications Office. Financial motives are practically always present, since recourse to a commercial publisher will virtually always benefit the institution in budgetary terms, if not the Communities on a true balance of cost and revenue over time. Specialist works may benefit from the attention of publishers with specialized publishing and marketing skills. But there are disadvantages. Such publications will be omitted from the catalogues of official publications, with the result that they may be overlooked by those who collect publications by reference to their source. And almost inevitably they will not be supplied by the institutions free of charge to the Depository Libraries, European Documentation Centres and European Reference Centres to which many directly published publications are supplied.

As the institutions respond to the pressures of publishing budgets that tend constantly to diminish in real terms, it would be logical to suppose that recourse to commercial publishers will increase. On the other hand, the institutions have recently approved proposals by the Publications Office that may reduce the problems to which the practice has given rise. These proposals, which have already been applied in a limited number of cases, envisage co-publication of some works under the joint publishing imprints of the Publications Office and a commercial publisher, on such terms that the work may be offered for sale in parallel by both publishers. It remains to be seen whether it will in practice be possible to substitute co-publishing agreements for grants of exclusive licenses to commercial publishers on a substantial scale.

If it is thought to be preferable that publications of Community origin should be published through the Publications Office, the main problem may lie in the way that publishing is financed. For while the institutions publish through the Publications Office their output is always limited by an annual cost ceiling set by their budget. To publish through a commercial publisher is to extend the institution's real publishing resources. It is an anomaly that the institutions should be penalized financially for using official publishing channels, but financing generally is an aspect of the Community system that may need review by reference to the practice of other more developed systems.

INTERNAL DOCUMENTS

At the time of its establishment the Publications Office derived its functions from the managing institutions, but in such a way that each institution preserved its own reproduction, warehousing and distribution services. For they retained direct responsibility for printing and distributing material for internal, inter-institutional and other official use, and also in practice for free distribution of their 'publications', the production and sale of which became the Publications Office's task. The Decision of 16 January 1969 provided for this retained responsibility in article 2(3):

> . . . the internal publications of each institution and limited editions for a known number of recipients may be printed in the reproduction workshops of the institutions concerned and distributed directly.

When a new article was introduced by the amending decision of 7 February 1980, the terminology changed, though not the practical significance or the obscurity of the provision. Instead of referring to 'internal publications ... and limited editions for a number of recipients' it introduced the expression 'internal documents of each institution'. The problem for the user of Community literature has been that the terms 'official publication' or 'publication' on the one hand, and 'internal publication' or 'internal document' on the other, have not in the institutions' usage corresponded precisely to categories of material accessible (or inaccessible) to the public. An 'internal document' in the current terminology came to mean no more than an item reproduced principally for internal, inter-institutional or other official use, for the category included material which might be made available systematically to members of the public as well as that of which circulation was restricted.

It must in fact be doubted whether 'internal documents' as a class could be said to have any characteristic by which the user might distinguish them from publications, except their relative elusiveness. For the rule has been that all 'internal documents', whether or not accessible to the public, should be excluded from the monthly and annual catalogues of publications of the European Communities — unless of course, the same matter is subsequently reproduced or produced in the form of a publication. A publication, in the institutions' usage, has signified matter in which public interest is thought to be sufficient to justify a significant effort and expenditure on the part of the originating institution to ensure that it is presented and promoted in such a way as to maximize its dissemination.

Thus a publication almost by definition corresponded with material which required to be produced through the Publications Office by virtue of the print procurement duties assigned to the Office by the institutions under its statute.

Confusion arising from these distinctions has been compounded by the fact that the text of 'internal documents' and 'publications' is often the same. Many publications reproduce in a more sophisticated form texts previously issued as 'internal documents'. This can have the unfortunate consequence that matter in document form, though less easy of access, is more valuable to the user than the same matter in published form because the appearance of the latter may be delayed.

A certain conflict has thus developed between the terminology and the concepts used by the institutions and the natural language of users. The artificiality of institutional concepts has spilled over into the structure of the publishing services on which the user depends for Community information. The reasons for the conflict are not far to seek. In the first place, the conversion of documents produced cheaply for internal use into conventional publications appropriate for widespread public circulation is especially laborious and costly within the Community context, since every single publication is likely to need to be typeset and processed in parallel in at least several, if not all of the official languages. There is a consequent tendency to weigh carefully the potential public interest — which may be especially difficult to judge on a Community wide basis — before an institution commits itself to issue texts as 'publications'. It may often seem preferable, and indeed necessary, given the growing pressure on publishing budgets, simply to circulate copies of 'internal documents' of a specialized nature on demand. Secondly, institutional criteria for the selection of matter for publication have inevitably lagged behind developing specialist interest. This has been affected by the growth of the Communities' influence generally, and also by the impact of new cultural traditions following each enlargement. But whatever the reasons for the conflict, the problems caused for users by the institutions' distinctions between publications and internal documents have been recognized, in that they are developing a terminology and a practice which users are likely to find more rational.

The solution from the user's point of view might seem to be that 'internal documents', in so far as they are actually available to the public, should be processed, announced, catalogued and distributed in such a way as to eliminate the distinctions between them and 'publications'. The challenge to the institutions and to the Publications Office has been to find means of achieving that result within the limits allowed by the institutions' resources, and the low potential interest of the bulk of the material.

This category of material is currently referred to generically as 'public documents', and it is seen to be composed of two classes, which for present purposes may be labelled 'official documents' and 'departmental documents'.

The first class is represented by the non-confidential parts of series of documents issued or tabled with full institutional approval, and which are selectively reproduced in the *Official journal*: for example, the Commission's COM final documents, the European Parliament's *Working documents*, and the Economic and Social Committee's opinions. The second class consists largely of studies or compilations commissioned by or produced within the departments of the institutions in the process of information gathering and assessment prior to decision making.

As to the first class, the pattern for a general system by which these may be economically assimilated to publications has already been set by the subscription and individual document delivery services for COM final documents introduced in 1983 through the Publications Office, and further developed in 1984. These documents are announced and cumulatively indexed through a system of monthly and annual catalogues available both to subscribers for documents as they are released to the public and to those who prefer to order documents individually. Subscriptions or individual orders may be for paper copies of documents or for microfiche, the latter being substantially cheaper owing to the lower cost of production and dispatch. In the case of paper copies only, subscriptions may be limited by subject area. The services available for COM final documents are being extended to Economic and Social Committee opinions during 1984, and to *European Parliament working documents* thereafter.

As to the second class of public documents — those referred to above as departmental documents — a procedure has been devised which will permit them to be offered to the public on sale by decision of the departments in which they originate, though their form will be simplified as compared with traditional publications, and the range of languages in which they are offered will be reduced. They will be announced in the monthly catalogues of publications of the European Communities and by virtue of that their formal status as publications — even if internally of a particular class — will not be at issue.

The production of publications

Article 1 of the Decision of 16 January 1969 states the Publications Office's purpose to be the 'publication, printing and distribution of the publications of [the] institutions and their departments'. The meaning of the words 'publications of [the] institutions' has been explored; 'production' is the natural global term to apply to the functions of the Office outside the area of distribution. 'Publication' as a description of an activity has an uncertain significance; and printing has long since ceased to be the only method of manufacture of Community publications. Indeed it is well established in principle as well as in practice that the Publications Office's functions are not limited by reference to method of manufacture or medium of distribution of information. The word 'production' is appropriate to the Publications Office's functions because, with limited exceptions, it does not act as author or editor. It provides manufacturing capacity by contract with external firms or from its in-house facilities, and sees to the physical processing of matter for publication from the receipt of an author's manuscript (or its equivalent) to the delivery of finished products by the manufacturer to the Publications Office's warehouse or to the other principal distributors.

The notable exceptions to the rule that the organization does not act as an author or editor arise in the indexing of the *Official journal* and the preparation of certain catalogues. The first exception is the corollary of the fact that the *Official journal* is compiled by the Publications Office from texts supplied from different sources; the second is a consequence of its functions as publisher and distributor of publications.

The most obviously exceptional characteristic of the publishing system of the Communities as compared with other official publishing systems, whether national or of international organizations, lies in the degree of its multilingualism. While multilingualism is present in other official publishing systems, the Communities' system is unique in requiring that primary texts are simultaneously published in so many languages. The requirement carries substantial practical consequences, especially where traditional editorial and production methods are used — extended production schedules; greatly increased production costs and reduced print runs; multiplication of the number of titles that have to be held in stock; and considerable complications in the preparation of indexes and catalogues.

It has for a long time been plain that the most effective way to deal with these is by the rapid development of computer assisted methods of information processing, production and dissemination. The Publications Office has both initiated developments of this sort and responded to initiatives from within institutions. The principal projects in which the Publications Office is involved have been described in Chapter 1. They imply improvements in the quality of indexes and catalogues and in the speed with which they, and the primary materials to which they relate, are published. They also imply new and quicker means of access to current information than is possible by means of paper: the extension of parallel publication on microfiche, the substitution on a larger scale of microfiche for original paper copies as a means of maintenance in print of back list material, and of course extended availability of full text and documentary data bases to online search and indirect access.

The distribution of publications

After the production of publications, or, as the statute prefers it, their publication and printing, distribution is the second of the two statutory purposes assigned to the Publications Office under article 1 of the Decision of 16 January 1969. Distribution includes but is not restricted to the management of sales, for which the statute makes special provision, since it is the separately prescribed duty of the Publications Office 'to manage the Sales Office'[13] an expression which refers to the 'joint sales office' which was to be attached to the Publications Office under article 8 of the Decision of 8 April 1965.[14] In reality, however, the 'Sales Office' does not have a distinct existence. The sales functions are performed within the Publications Office and are divided among its various services, being principally in the hands of the sales and accounting service.

Though the statute seemed to foresee that the Publications Office might be responsible for the distribution of everything produced under its control, whether priced or free of charge, and, vice versa, would have no such responsibility for that which it did not produce, the main development has been of its sales activity. The administration of free distribution of publications produced through the Publications Office has remained largely with individual institutions and their departments, for two reasons: it is difficult, if not impossible, actively to promote the dissemination of that which is sold alongside that which is free; and free distribution of publications produced through the Publications Office is more conveniently handled by the institutions and their machinery for the distribution of 'internal documents'. There are two notable exceptions to this rule: distribution of the *Official journal* is administered entirely by the Publications Office, in principle because it is a publication of all the managing institutions, and not of any single one, and in practice because the maintenance of its rigorous dispatch schedules compel it; while since 1983 the Publications Office has administered a system of consolidated dispatches of publications and documents supplied free of charge on the institutions' instructions to libraries designated as Depository Libraries, European Documentation Centres, or European Reference Centres.

In the sales field, however, the Publications Office's responsibility is largely unchallenged, and a number of factors have led to an increase in its scope. First, the institutions, especially the Commission, have taken the view that the practice of free distribution, other than of information publications, should be significantly reduced, and the number of priced titles and the promotional support given to them correspondingly increased. Second, means have been found to assimilate 'internal documents', previously distributed free, to publications — a development exemplified not only by the recent introduction of subscription and individual document delivery services for COM final documents and prospectively for other series, but also by older practice in the publication of much specialized scientific and technical matter. Third, co-publication contracts are now negotiated in preference, where possible, to the direct licensing of the publication of texts to commercial publishers. And, finally, the institutions have accepted the principle that data bases and their products, being forms of publication, should be offered for sale and marketed through the Publications Office on principles analogous to those which apply in the case of publications in more traditional form, whether or not the Office is directly involved in their creation. The Publications Office may fairly be said to present itself to the outside world as a distributor by way of sale, since its overt involvement in free distribution is essentially accessory to that.

COMMERCIAL ASPECTS AND PRICING

Public service, not profit or any specific balance of cost and revenue, must always be the central objective of official publishing systems. It is certainly so to the extent that much of their output appears as the result of an obligation, and that the obligation extends to making what is published reasonably accessible even where the public interest is limited. Nevertheless, in many national government systems it has been found useful and practical to place official publishers in a commercial or quasi-commercial environment of financial targets, systems and accounts. In any such system pricing becomes a key element. In the Community system, however, official publishing is not subject to such controls, but to a financial régime based on annual budgets. The function of price in the Community system is not to produce a particular balance of costs and revenue in the hands either of the Publications Office or of the institutions but chiefly to contribute to effective dissemination, in three main ways: first, publications need to bear an economic price so that they may be accessible through the commercial channels upon which dissemination of publications largely depends; secondly, so that their quality and usefulness can be tested by the criterion of the public's willingness to buy (bearing in mind of course that such publications can ultimately always be inspected free of charge); and, thirdly, to prevent waste.

The role of the Publications Office in price fixing is to make recommendations to the institutions represented by its Management Committee in the case of the *Official journal*, and to the individual institutions in the case of other publications, as to what the prices of new publications should be, final decisions being in the hands of the institutions.

It being a principle of Community publishing that information should be available to all citizens as far as possible on equal terms, it is the general rule that every language version of every publication should so far as possible be equally priced. Prices are nominally fixed in the European Currency Unit (ECU), and directly converted at exchange rates current at the time of price fixing into published prices, excluding value added tax, in each of the currencies of the member states, and in United States dollars. Subject to the addition to these prices of any value added tax or other taxes which may be applicable in particular countries, these are the uniform prices at which publications are offered for sale by the Publications Office and by the agents and sub-agents for the sale of the publications of the European Communities in the member states.

Fixing or recommending prices always involves an element of judgement apart from the cost-based mathematical formulae on which price fixing mechanisms tend to rely. In the case of the *Official journal*, the Management Committee chiefly takes into account the price levels of similar publications in the member states, attempting to find a fair mean, while also looking for a reasonably constant internal relationship between unit production costs and prices. For other publications preliminary price calculations are based on the average unit production cost of all the language versions of any publication, and a multiplier of two for popular publications and three for more specialized ones. But mechanical rules of this sort can be no more than guidelines. The Court of Auditors has found that the prices of a sample of 53 publications represented on average a multiplier of 2.2, with a minimum of 1.1 and a maximum of 3.8.[15] These multipliers are low in comparison with those applied by commercial publishers, and by national official publishers as well, though the comparison is substantially falsified by the high costs for the institutions of originating publications in a number of parallel language versions. But the general view appears to be that prices for Community publications are competitive by reference to their local counterparts, whether of commercial or official origin.

THE SALES NETWORK

The system for the distribution of the priced official publications of the European Communities has been constructed on the assumption they should be as physically accessible to the citizens of each member state, and as easily heard of and acquired as the publications published from within its own national boundaries. Indeed it is presumed that the official publications of the Communities, in the language versions appropriate to the case, are properly considered as domestic publications of each member state, and that it is to the convenience of the public that they should, where possible, be promoted and distributed with the official publications of national governments.

Except in Luxembourg, where the Publications Office is located, the institutions have therefore sought to distribute their priced publications indirectly through a network of general sales agents for the sale of the publications of the European Communities, in some cases supported by sub-agents and special agents. It is the Publications Office's task to maintain and support this network, rather than to seek to deal directly with buyers in each country. When the Publications Office receives orders from customers in countries where there are sales agents it will normally ask the sales agent to supply them.

General sales agents are publishers or distributors on their own account, most usually of national official publications. Often they are retail booksellers as well. They maintain stocks of all priced publications which are in significant demand in that country, and supply them both direct to the individual purchasers and through booksellers. They also obtain for customers on demand items which they do not hold in stock. In the case of periodicals, general sales agents administer subscriptions for which copies are sent direct from Luxembourg to subscribers, as well as offering individual issues from their own stock.

The responsibilities of general sales agents include promotion. They are expected to announce and publicize Community publications on the same basis as they promote their own publications, and they are supported in this with financial and material aid from the Publications Office and the institutions.

In a few countries within the Community sub-agents have been appointed. These are normally retail booksellers with specialist interests in European affairs who are able to offer comprehensive information and supply services complementing those of the general sales agents. Special agents also exist in a few countries alongside the general sales agents. These are distributors or booksellers dealing in a specialized section of Community literature.

The system of general sales agencies has been extended outside the Community to include candidate countries as well as others where demand is strong. In other countries, publications may be ordered direct from the Publications Office.

It is thus normally unnecessary for citizens of member states, and indeed of a number of other countries, to go outside their national borders for supplies of priced publications. And where they need advice that the sales agents are unable to provide, such advice is also available in each member state and in a number of third countries where the Commission maintains information and press offices or delegations with information services. Information and press offices normally work in liaison with general and other sales agents, but with the single exception of the United States, where the European Community Information Service in Washington DC also acts as sales agent, it has not been considered desirable to combine the information and agency functions.

CATALOGUING AND PROMOTION

While the promotion of priced publications carried out by individual sales agents is invaluable in extending knowledge about the availability of priced publications, it is essentially ancillary to and substantially dependent upon the action of the Community institutions and the Publications Office. So far as the promotion of individual publications and small groups of publications is concerned, the Publications Office has a general responsibility to carry out, either directly or through the sales agents, publicity programmes for priced publications, to which the Publications Office itself, the institutions and the sales agents may all contribute proposals and material. Conventional methods of promotion are used, including the sending of publications for review, press advertising in the institutions' own media and in the general and specialist press, attendance at exhibitions and fairs, and, most of all, direct mail. But the most important form of promotion for official publications is the systematic, comprehensive and prompt announcement of new publications, priced or free, as they become available, and their cumulative cataloguing and indexing. The concern which exists within the institutions and the Publications Office about the inadequacy of the awareness systems currently available has been expressed in the previous chapter, where some important current developments and prospects for the future have been described.

At the present time the Publications Office produces a number of bibliographical aids similar to publishers' catalogues. These include:

(i)   The monthly and annual catalogues of publications of the European Communities. These are free lists which in recent years have covered all matter published directly by the institutions and the Publications Office on their behalf and classed by them as publications. All priced items offered for sale through the Publications Office are of course included, and also a number of unpriced publications available directly from the institutions or the external offices of the Commission. These catalogues are essential for any serious collector of Community information, and among other things include full details of where to obtain Community publications, priced and free of charge. Their value will grow as they increasingly list as priced publications items previously classed as internal documents. These catalogues are published in all the official languages of the Communities and the monthlies are bound into the monthly issues of the *Bulletin of the European Communities*, as well as being available separately. Though 'unilingual' the catalogues are also complete — where a publication is not available in the language of the catalogue, it is listed in another language. For example, in the English versions publications not available in English will be listed in French; if there is no French version also, in German, and so forth.

  These monthly catalogues are normally circulated during the second month after the period to which they relate, and the annuals by the early summer of the succeeding year.

(ii) The monthly and annual catalogues of COM documents. This series of catalogues began publication in 1983. They are sales publications offered to subscribers to the Commission's series of COM final documents, as well as separately, with versions in each official language. These catalogues will be the model for the catalogues of the documents of the Economic and Social Committee and the European Parliament. Though sales publications, and with specific links to subscription services, nevertheless these catalogues have at the same time the characteristics of publishers' catalogues supplementary to the monthly and annual catalogues of publications of the European Communities.

(iii) *The European Community as a publisher* is a free catalogue produced every year, though not necessarily in all the official languages of the Community. It aims to cover the principal publications of the institutions, both priced and free, which are of current interest irrespective of the year of publication.

While the catalogues referred to above have to a greater or lesser degree the character of publishers' catalogues, in official publishing there is not necessarily a clear distinction to be drawn between such matter and other works of bibliographical reference, a number of which are published as sales or free publications by the Publications Office on behalf of the institutions and their departments.

These include *Publications and documents of the E.C. received by the Library*, a multilingual catalogue, cumulative from 1978 and reissued annually with periodic supplements during the course of each year, derived from the complete catalogue of holdings of the Central Library of the Commission in Brussels. Since the Library attempts to collect *inter alia* all accessible literature of Community origin, whether priced or free, classed as publications or documents, or directly or commercially published, it is a listing of an unique comprehensiveness for its period. It is a priced publication available from the Publications Office.

In the statistical field, the bare announcements of Eurostat publications in the monthly and annual catalogues of publications of the European Communities are greatly expanded in *Eurostat news*, a quarterly periodical produced by the Publications Office for the Statistical Office of the European Communities, and distributed free of charge in English, French and German versions. Similarly the monthly periodical *Euro abstracts*, published as a priced publication, with English as its principal language, by the Publications Office for Directorate-General XIII of the Commission, enlarges both in depth and range on the coverage of scientific and technical publications in the EUR reports series given by the monthly and annual catalogues of publications, *inter alia* by abstracting material of Community origin published commercially, as well as directly. Apart from the monthly periodical, there also now exists a useful *Catalogue of EUR documents 1968–1979*, also published as a sales publication for Directorate-General XIII by the Publications Office, which it is planned to update with periodic supplements and cumulative editions.

PRINT QUANTITIES, REPRINTS, CONTROL AND RELEASE OF STOCK

It is natural to expect of publishers that they will fix print and reprint quantities, manage stocks and control their release. However the expectation coincides with the assumption that the publisher will pay the printer's bill, and will be in ultimate control of distribution. These conditions are met in the Publications Office's case only for the *Official journal*, and then by a devolution of responsibility from the institutions to the Office. The need for devolution of responsibility in this case seems self-evident. There are six institutions ultimately responsible, and the day-to-day administration of dispatch of a periodical which is so frequent, linguistically complex and time critical, can scarcely be divided. Nor can the administration of stock, which must be managed with the flexibility and speed of decision imposed by the unpredictability and urgency of demand. It is a noticeable result of the central control of dispatch and warehousing of the *Official journal* that it has in fact been possible to achieve a remarkably close approximation to simultaneous publication of all its seven parallel language versions throughout the Community, despite certain problems of delivery to those areas of the Community most remote from Luxembourg.

Publications other than the *Official journal* are normally publications of a single institution. The conventional role of the Publications Office in these cases is to make recommendations to the institution as to the quantity to be printed for sales purposes, and receiving and managing that element of the printing number.

The individual institutions determine total print quantities, having regard to their own plans for internal and free external distribution, and, of course, to their obligation to finance costs of production from their budgetary resources. It is usual that institutional requirements are larger than those of the Publications Office for sales purposes, and that they are holders of reserve stocks for sales or any other purposes. Experience will show whether adaptations of practice may be required both so as to bring the timing of release of new publications under closer control, and so as to avoid uneven application of rules for free distribution as the institutions develop more fully distribution policies based firmly on sale.

COPYRIGHT AND PERMISSIONS

The Publications Office has been expressly authorized by the institutions to deal on their behalf with applications for copyright licences and permissions relating to their publications, subject to their agreement with the course of action proposed. It is the practice of the institutions to treat matter published in the *Official journal* as in the public domain; that implies freedom to quote without express permission, but not of course to make facsimile reproductions without permission except to the extent provided by copyright law. A number of publications of the institutions contain express limited authorizations to quote from them. But where copyright is claimed without reserve, or where it is sought to reproduce matter to an extent not covered by a limited authorization, it is the institutions' general practice to grant gratuitous permissions except where substantial quantities of matter are involved and the proposed reproduction is for a commercial purpose, when payment of royalties or fees may be sought.

In practice the Publications Office is increasingly asked by the institutions to negotiate on their behalf co-publication and other agreements associating commercial publishers and other bodies external to the institutions with the publication of the institutions' original manuscripts. However, the principal role in the negotiation of publishing agreements is played by Directorate-General XIII, by virtue of its responsibility for the publication of the Commission's scientific and technical works.

An additional area of copyright responsibility for the Publications Office, in which of course it acts in concert with the originating services in the institutions, is the licensing of hosts and brokers in the course of marketing electronic data bases.

ELECTRONIC PUBLICATIONS

The institutions' publishing and marketing policies in this new field have been described in Chapter 1, which has mentioned all the Community data bases at present commercially available, and refers to the developments that are likely in the near future. The Publications Office has overall responsibility for the commercial marketing of Community data bases, as it has for that of publications in traditional form. At present it is actively involved in the marketing of the COMEXT and CRONOS data bases of the Statistical Office of the European Communities, and its own TED data base (an electronic version of the S Series of the *Official journal*, publishing notices of invitations to tender).

Quite clearly, the emergence of these new types of publication calls for new thinking about distribution practices and the roles of the parties to traditional publishing and distribution. In the case of COMEXT and CRONOS, current policy is to give access to the public exclusively through hosts (licensees who hold copies of the data bases to which they offer online access together with other services). In the case of TED the Publications Office directly markets the service and gives subscribers direct access to its own data base, and at the same time will license hosts and brokers (licensees who republish information to their customers other than online) to the extent that they seem able to enhance the value or accessibility of the information offered by the Publications Office direct. It has yet to be seen whether the traditional distributors of European Communities publications will have an active role to play in making their electronic publications accessible to users in the member states.

There is no doubt that the development of electronic publishing will over the next few years require the publishing systems of the Communities to be at least as adaptable to changing circumstances as they have had to be since the foundation of the Publications Office.

References and notes

[1] But see J. Jeffries, *A guide to the official publications of the European Communities*, 2nd edn, Mansell, 1981, p. 9.

[2] *OJ*, No 152, 13 July 1967, p. 2, but not in English. For the English version see *Treaties establishing the European Communities: treaties amending these treaties: documents concerning the accession*, Office for Official Publications, 1978, p. 785. The Merger Treaty came into force on 1 July 1967.

[3] *OJ*, No 152, 13 July 1967, p. 18, but not in English. For the English version see the edition of the treaties referred to in note 2 above, p. 837. 'Official Publications Office' is not the organization's correct title, but 'Office for Official Publications': see Decision 69/13/Euratom/ECSC/EEC establishing the Office for Official Publications of the European Communities, and especially article 1 thereof (*OJ*, L13, 18 January 1969, p. 71, but not in English, which is at *OJ*, L107, 25 April 1980, p. 47). As to the reference to a translation service, the attachment was effected by an agreement of 8 December 1972 between the Commission and the Publications Office, represented by its Management Committee: the Commission's own translation service in Luxembourg is attached to the Publications Office to the extent that the Commission guarantees resources sufficient to meet the translation requirements of the Publications Office on its own behalf and on behalf of the institutions.

[4] For references see note 3 above.

[5] Decision 80/443/EEC, Euratom, ECSC, *OJ*, L107, 25 April 1980, p. 44.

[6] See the Decision of 16 January 1969 as amended, arts. 2(1) and 7(5).

[7] Office for Official Publications of the European Communities, 5 rue du Commerce, L-2985 Luxembourg.

[8] Decision of 16 January 1969, art. 2(2). The 'provisional locations' are, of course, Luxembourg, Brussels and Strasbourg.

[9] Ibid, art. 3(4).

[10] Ibid, art. 2(3) as amended.

[11] *OJ*, C89, 5 April 1979, p. 5.

[12] Court of Auditors, *Special report concerning publishing, printing and reproduction practices ...*, para 3.6, (*OJ*, C150, 19 June 1981, p. 1).

[13] Decision of 16 January 1969, art. 2(1).

[14] See note 3, supra.

[15] Court of Auditors, *Special report concerning publishing, printing and reproduction practices ...*, para 9.5, (*OJ*, C150, 19 June 1981, p. 1).

3

The General Information Policy of the European Communities

GIANCARLO PAU

Introduction

The United Kingdom has been a member of the European Community (EC) for more than a decade and yet the EC remains for the majority of people remote, intangible and bureaucratic. One major reason for this is that there are so few occasions when ordinary people come into direct contact with the European Community or feel themselves directly and personally affected by or involved in its activities. It is also apparent that many people still do not understand how the Community works and still have difficulty in obtaining the information they require on Community affairs. Now that some time has elapsed since the United Kingdom joined the European Community it is worth taking a fresh look at the Community's information policy and at the means employed by the main institutions both to fulfil their treaty obligations and to ensure that the general public is kept well informed. Consequently, the purpose of this chapter is to consider the basic elements of information policy and to suggest ways in which the general public can find out about the Common Market.

Why a Community information policy?

It is clear that without the support of the people of Europe for its policies and actions the European Community cannot hope to attain the goals established in the founding treaties. Information policy has an essential role to play in supporting and promoting Community initiatives and activities. Its task is to inform and to explain and thereby to establish and maintain understanding between the Community and its citizens. Moreover, the citizens of Europe have a right to know about the various measures and decisions taken in their name and which can have a direct impact upon their private or professional lives. They need information if they are to understand why certain actions are necessary, and to understand the impact of Community policies if they are to derive benefit from the measures introduced. Information policy is also directed at audiences outside the Community. Considerable resources are devoted to the task of explaining the activities and achievements of the Community in non-member countries all over the world.

The institutions of the European Community

The European Community, or Common Market as it is commonly known in the United Kingdom, does not 'govern' in the sense that national governments and parliaments do. Community policy emerges from a legislative process which involves the participation of Community institutions according to procedures established in the founding treaties and which also involves long and often tortuous negotiations between representatives of member countries. The system which has evolved is based on the achievement of consensus; to be effective it needs a good working relationship between individual institutions and constant political will on the part of member governments. However, members of the public still find it difficult to comprehend the roles played by Community institutions and the complexities of Community legislation. Since knowledge of the way in which the Community works is a prerequisite of a full understanding of the information and documentation produced by Community institutions, the institutional structure is briefly described in the following paragraphs.

THE COMMISSION OF THE EUROPEAN COMMUNITIES

The main role of the Commission is to initiate Community law, to propose Community action to the Council of Ministers and to ensure that what the ministers decide is carried out. The Commission is the guardian of the treaties in the sense that it has responsibility for making sure that treaty provisions are upheld. It is also the exponent of Community as distinct from national interests in the Council.

The Commission is composed of fourteen members, two from the United Kingdom, appointed for a term of four years by agreement between the governments of the member states. Once appointed, members are entirely independent of their governments and are subject only to the supervision of the European Parliament, which alone has the power to remove them from office. Commission decisions are taken collectively, although each Commissioner is responsible for one or more portfolios, or areas of policy. The Commission has a permanent staff, which is in effect a European civil service. Concentrated mostly in Brussels and Luxembourg, it consists of about 9,500 officials working in some twenty departments (directorates-general).

THE COUNCIL OF THE EUROPEAN COMMUNITIES

The Council of the European Communities is the principal decision-making body and the one in which national interests are represented. It is composed of ministers from each member state who change according to the subject under consideration. When, for instance, the Common Agricultural Policy (CAP) is under discussion, ministers of agriculture attend, and when financial matters are under review the relevant ministers of finance attend. Member governments take it in turns to act as President of the Council for six-monthly periods.

The Council is assisted in its work by the Committee of Permanent Representatives (COREPER), which coordinates its work and prepares its agenda. It is composed of senior national civil servants based in Brussels.

Three times a year the heads of state and government of member states meet as the European Council. The idea is to give national leaders an opportunity to discuss general policy and matters to do with political cooperation. The European Council has also become a forum to which is referred particularly important and complex matters on which it has not been possible to find agreement in the Council of the European Communities.

THE EUROPEAN PARLIAMENT

The European Parliament has 434 members, of which 81 are from the United Kingdom, elected by direct suffrage throughout the Community. The composition of the European Parliament makes it a fully integrated Community institution in the sense that there are no national sections, only Community level political groups. The European Parliament does not have the same legislative powers as a national parliament. In fact, it is the Commission which initiates and drafts proposals for legislation and the Council which enacts most Community legislation. The main task of the European Parliament is to monitor the work of the Commission and the Council; it has to be consulted on most Commission proposals before the Council makes its final decision. It also has the power not only to reallocate items of expenditure in the Community budget but also, in agreement with the Council, to increase its volume or to reject it as a whole.

THE COURT OF JUSTICE OF THE EUROPEAN COMMUNITIES

This supreme court of appeal, composed of eleven independent judges assisted by five advocates-general, ensures that in the interpretation and application of the treaties the law is observed. The court is the final arbiter on all legal questions relating to the treaties and it rules on disputes between member states, Community institutions, companies or individuals. Its decisions are binding. The Court, however, has no jurisdiction over national civil and constitutional law, which remains entirely the responsibility of each individual member state.

THE COURT OF AUDITORS

The operation of the Community budget is supervised by the Court of Auditors, which has extensive powers to verify the legality and regularity of Community revenue and expenditure.

THE ECONOMIC AND SOCIAL COMMITTEE

Mention should also be made of the Economic and Social Committee (ECOSOC). This is not an institution but a consultative body which considers and expresses an opinion on Commission proposals for legislation. ECOSOC consists of representatives of government, both sides of industry and others concerned with the economic and social activity of the Community and provides a forum for the discussion of Community actions which affect these interests.

Information infrastructure

The tasks of individual institutions in the field of information vary according to their respective responsibilities. All, however, have the same basic objective: to draw public attention to their activities and achievements in order to stimulate interest in and support for Community ideals.

The European Commission, being the initiator of Community legislation, generates large quantities of information every day and is by far the greatest source of oral and written information about the work of the Community and its institutions. It is the Commission which largely fulfils the treaty obligation to inform the citizens of Europe about the principles, procedures and objectives of the Community.

To perform these informational tasks efficiently and effectively the Commission has developed a complex infrastructure and specialized services in Brussels — the provisional headquarters of the Community — and a presence in the capitals of the member states. Responsibility for the implementation of information policy rests primarily on the shoulders of two Commission departments, the Directorate-General for Information (DG X) and the Spokesman's Group, which work closely together. The latter is responsible for briefing the 300 or so press, radio and television reporters accredited to the Community institutions in Brussels and elsewhere and for providing them with 'hot news' on the day's decisions and activities. The task of DG X is to spread understanding of the Community and its policies among the citizens of Europe and in third countries. It does this in a variety of ways including the preparation of publications, audio-visual aids and background reports, the organization of fairs, exhibitions and information visits and the development of specialized information services for priority audiences.

The Commission's information policy has been decentralized so that it can correspond more closely to the needs and interests of individual member states and third countries. For this purpose, press and information offices have been established in the capitals of the ten member countries and regional sub-offices in other locations whose special regional differences need to be taken into account. In the United Kingdom sub-offices have been established in Scotland (Edinburgh), Wales (Cardiff) and in Northern Ireland (Belfast). Diplomatic missions of the European Commission in major third countries or accredited to international organizations, also have units responsible for information. The

Commission's delegations in African, Caribbean, Pacific, Maghreb and Mashrak countries also perform a useful information function, although this is not their prime task. In countries where the Commission is not represented the embassies of the member states disseminate Community information, for which purpose they receive all necessary information and materials from the Commission in Brussels.

Other Community institutions have an information policy and information departments. Although all exist separately efforts are being made to improve cooperation. At the Secretariat of the Council the press and information office is largely responsible for dealing with current events. After each Council meeting it publishes a press release which receives widespread distribution among the press in Brussels and in member states. It is also the task of this office to provide both the embassies of the ten member countries and the Commission information offices with information in the form of reports and background notes on important decisions taken by the ministers, so that press offices responsible for disseminating Community information, in both government departments and Commission information offices, can answer questions from the general public.

Since 1979 the European Parliament has acquired a new status as a result of direct elections and the increase in the number of its members. This has led the European Parliament, like the other institutions, to develop its own information policy, structures and network, the general aim of which is to provide information both inside and outside the Community on the part it plays and its contribution to the Community's long-term development. This policy is also designed to enable the directly elected Parliament to project itself more clearly in all its democratic legitimacy and thereby to increase its influence. A major handicap is that Parliament's activities are performed in three different places of work, Luxembourg, Brussels and Strasbourg. The consequence is that journalists cannot always be present for major debates when important decisions are taken, or are informed too late to have an impact on the news. To take account of these circumstances information functions have been reorganized. Responsibility for information policy rests with the Directorate-General for Information and Public Relations which organizes information activities from its base in Luxembourg, from Brussels and through information officers in the capitals of the ten member states (see Chapter 5 for more information on the work of the London Office of the European Parliament).

The Court of Justice, the Economic and Social Committee and the European Investment Bank have also developed their own information networks and established press and information services. Their objectives are similar to those pursued by all institutions.

Information inside and outside the Community

Every year, in February, the President of the Commission appears before the European Parliament to present the Commission's programme for the next twelve months. Guidelines for action are established that take account of the current economic and political situation in the Community. In his address to the European Parliament on 15 February 1984 the President, M. Gaston Thorn, defined the tasks for 1984 as being to '(i) get the Community machinery moving again; (ii) embark on revitalization of the Community; (iii) assert our presence in the world in relations with our major trading partners and with the developing countries'. Such programmes not only form a framework for Commission action during the following twelve months but also serve as guidelines for Commission information policy during the same period.

In shaping its annual information programme the Commission seeks to achieve a balance between policy as it relates to audiences within the Community and to those outside the Community. As has been noted earlier, the general aim of information policy as it relates to member countries is to associate the people of Europe with the building of a strong Community, to create a sense of European identity and to draw attention to the positive aspects of belonging to a Community Europe. In addition, specific themes relevant to current circumstances are identified in each annual programme. Recently these have included the reform of the CAP, the enlargement of the Community, action to combat inflation and unemployment and the development of the less prosperous regions of the Community. Other topics reflecting current concerns include improvements in the quality of life, of which environment and consumer policies form an integral part. Information on such topics is aimed not only at the general public as a whole but also at specific sectors or groups who are thought to have an important influence over the formation of public opinion. Priority attention is given to trade unions, teachers, political organizations, consumers and agricultural organizations among others.

Outside the Community the aim of information policy is to project the image of an organization which desires to contribute to world peace and prosperity. Special emphasis is placed on explaining those Community policies which impinge upon industrialized or developing countries as the case may be.

The means employed by the Commission to implement its information policy are various. Publications play a vitally important role as a vehicle by which information is disseminated throughout the Community. Newsletters, magazines and general publications are produced by the Directorate-General for Information. Two important series which have a wide readership are *European documentation* and *European file*, which provide readable introductions to priority themes such as employment, energy and social affairs. In addition to publications prepared centrally in Brussels, press and information offices in member states prepare material tailored to the needs of national audiences. Examples of titles issued by the London Office are mentioned later in this chapter.

Major importance is attached to television as a channel of information. All the necessary studio facilities and equipment have been provided in Brussels for the use of national television networks in the recording of interviews and for covering stories. There is also close collaboration with the television networks on the co-production of programmes and the supply of film material on Community subjects.

Another way of reaching the public is to establish a Community presence at national or international fairs and exhibitions. In most member countries travelling exhibitions have been mounted in cities and towns in order to open up a dialogue with the local people. In the United Kingdom an 'information double-decker bus' is used, modelled on exhibition lines, complete with information material and manned by a team of staff from the Commission information offices. Presented under the slogan 'Bus for Europe', it aims to take information about the Community directly to the people.

More specialized means are used to reach certain groups of people who are considered to have an important influence on the formation of public opinion. These include information visits to Brussels and Luxembourg for groups that have regular dealings with Community institutions, and the provision of computer-based information retrieval systems which enable those with the necessary facilities to obtain up-to-date information and data.

Where to obtain information on the European Community

In the United Kingdom information on Community events and the work of Community institutions is available from the Commission and European Parliament offices. Community publications and documents may also be consulted in European Documentation Centres (EDCs) and Depository Libraries (DEPs).

THE LONDON OFFICE OF THE COMMISSION

The London Office of the Commission has been in existence for more than twenty-five years. It was established as a delegation of the High Authority of the European Coal and Steel Community (ECSC) and became an information office soon after the United Kingdom joined the Community in 1973. The tasks of the information offices maintained by the Commission in member states are as follows:

a)   to represent the Commission in each member country and to act as a point of contact with the representative national authorities and institutions;

b)   to inform as wide a public as possible of the aims and nature of the European Community, its institutions and policies;

c)   to keep in close contact with the national press and media organizations;

d)   to provide information to the Commission headquarters by regularly reporting back to the appropriate departments on all internal developments in the member states relevant to European policy.

In the United Kingdom these tasks are carried out by the London and regional offices, which comprise the most comprehensive and reliable storehouses of knowledge on Community affairs in this country.

It is the job of the London Office to inform the British people about the European Community. The first and foremost task is to provide factual information and to make it available to all, friend or foe of the Community. To do this there is a team of five information officers, including the Head of the Office. Each is responsible for services as they relate to particular sectors, such as the press, employers' organizations, trade unions, consumer groups, trade organizations, women's organizations and schools and universities. In addition, each information officer is expert in one or more aspects of Community policy.

In the front line in handling enquiries from the general public is the Information Unit, a small team with responsibility for documentation, publications, research and for providing general information on all subjects. The Unit has the back-up resources of a library and a data-room.

In the library one can find a good selection of reference books and other works on European economics, history, politics, etc., as well as Commission documents, the reports of the European Parliament and such official publications as the *Official journal of the European Communities*, Eurostat statistics, monthly bulletins, reports and studies. The library also contains a vast range of information about the Community available from other sources.

The data-room contains virtually all official documents. It has about 1,500 files reflecting Community policies, covering all areas of work dealt with by Community institutions. They give as up-to-date a picture as is possible of the current position of Commission proposals as they pass through the various stages of the decision-making process. The data-room also contains a microfiche collection of the internal documentation system and copies of the speeches made by members of the Commission and important politicians on Community affairs. The data-room is also responsible for access to the Commission's internal data-bases and to those connected to the European network Euronet Diane, and for relations with EDCs and other libraries in the United Kingdom.

All material in the data-room and the library is available for reference and can be consulted in the library reading room during library opening hours (Monday to Friday, 2 p.m. to 5.30 p.m.). The Information Unit also operates a 'question and answer service' on weekdays from 9.30 a.m. to 5.30 p.m. Enquiries on both general and technical matters are dealt with directly, or, if necessary, referred elsewhere for specialist attention.

The London Office is kept informed by daily telexes on developments in Community institutions. These telexes are analyzed and used as a basis for the preparation of press releases which summarize decisions taken and provide a record of recent and future events. Weekly press briefings on general and topical issues and press conferences are given by visiting members of the Commission. Background reports are produced on major Commission proposals, summarizing their contents and considering their likely impact on United Kingdom legislation.

The London Office also produces a number of free publications, of which the most important is the magazine called *Europe*. Published ten times a year this magazine is designed to communicate, in a lively way, information about Community policies and decisions and to show their impact upon the lives of the British people. The magazine incorporates a section called 'Euroforum', which provides European news and accounts of activities in the Commission and other institutions. Other publications include *Uniting Europe*, a brochure which describes the development of the Community since 1950, and two basic introductions to the Community and its institutions entitled *Europe at a glance* and *The European Community: how, what, why*. Somewhat more specialized are *The common agricultural policy*, which explains the workings of the CAP and *Finance from Europe*, a guide to Community grants and loans which contains useful information on how firms, authorities and organizations in the United Kingdom can obtain financial help from the European Community.

The Office also provides specially written material and audio-visual aids for schools, universities, professional associations, social groups and individuals. It has its own photographic archives from which photographs may be borrowed on request.

The United Kingdom sub-offices perform a complementary informational role. Information facilities similar to those provided by the London Office are available from these offices.

THE EUROPEAN PARLIAMENT

The European Parliament is also represented in the United Kingdom. An information office in London provides Members of the European Parliament (MEPs), political organizations and individuals with information concerning the work of the Parliament, including the progress of draft legislation. Like the European Commission, the London Office of the European Parliament has a reference library which contains a comprehensive collection of material published by the Parliament since 1973. A telephone enquiry service is also maintained for those who wish to find out about current activities in Parliament. Further information on the European Parliament and its information offices appears in Chapter 5.

DEPOSITORY LIBRARIES AND EUROPEAN DOCUMENTATION CENTRES

Public access to Community publications and documents is improved by virtue of the fact that copies of official publications and public documents are sent free of charge to four major public libraries in the United Kingdom. In return for the status of Depository Library, these four libraries — the British Library Reference Division, the British Library Lending Division, the City of Westminster Libraries, and the Liverpool and District Scientific, Industrial and Research Library Advisory Council — agree to make Community documentation freely available to the public during normal hours and without prior conditions.

In addition to these collections, established to serve the needs of the general population, a further 44 collections of Community publications and documents have been established in British universities and polytechnics. These European Documentation Centres (EDCs) have been established primarily to stimulate the study of Europe in their parent academic institutions. However, they are also expected, as far as possible, to provide a service to the local community. Further information on EDCs appears in Chapter 11 and a list of both EDCs and DEPs will be found in the Appendix to this book.

Opinion polls

Another aspect of the communication process which deserves attention is the monitoring of the response of audiences or receivers. In addition to periodic reports from its information offices on public attitudes towards the Community, the Commission receives more detailed information from a survey carried out twice a year in June and December on its behalf by public research institutes in member states. The results of this survey, published under the title *Eurobaro-meter*, provide the Commission with useful information on the impact of its short-term action and on the effectiveness of its information strategy. Opinion polls are also carried out on specific topics, such as women in society and the European public's attitude towards scientific and technical development. The results of these polls can often be used as a basis for further information action.

Historical archives

Another important development in information dissemination is the opening of the historical records to the public in accordance with the thirty-year rule.

At present the General Archives of the European Commission in Brussels hold approximately 15,000 linear metres of records. This department has custody of the archives of the High Authority of the ECSC (1952–1967), the EEC Commission (1958–1967), the Commission of Euratom (1958–1967) and the records of the present European Commission.

Historical archives may briefly be defined as that portion of the total mass of records which, being no longer current, have been appraised and selected for permanent preservation.

The General Archives is a specialized service within the Directorate-General for Personnel and Administration (DG IX). Its objectives in making available the historical records, are to provide a service to the institutions on the one hand and to the research public on the other. This has led the department to establish an information unit and a search room to provide visitors with the necessary information and to answer written enquiries.

Historical analysis is a very important part of this department's work: files are processed, finding-aids to records are compiled and a small reference library is also available. In order to improve public knowledge about Community institutions and their activities, and to encourage research into the European Communities, it is at present preparing a publication of finding-aids. It is also organizing exhibitions of documents and photographs, both in Brussels and in the capitals of member states. Contacts are also being developed with research institutes and universities, the national archives and those of the ministries of foreign affairs in the member states, given that they hold a large number of complementary records relating to Community activities.

4

Disseminating the Results of European Community Research

JOHN MICHEL GIBB and EDWARD PHILLIPS

Other chapters in this book examine European Community (EC) information relevant to users whose professional lives have often been markedly affected by British membership of the Community. These users will be motivated to seek information on EC matters, and will want to become familiar with the publications of the European institutions whose activities are important to them. Scientists and researchers are undoubtedly less obviously affected as groups by EC affairs than, say, civil servants or the legal profession. Yet the European Community has become a major originator of scientific and technical information.

The following figures will give an idea of the commitment to science and technology at Community level. Since 1974, when 70 million units of account (ECU) were spent on Community research, the research budget has risen at well above the inflation rate to 590 million ECU in 1982, which is about 2.6% of the Community's overall budget. It is estimated that in 1982 the total public expenditure on research in the member states (i.e. government funding) amounted to 26,490 million ECU, so that Community research funding in 1982 was about 2.2% of the total equivalent public expenditure in the member states. Over the four years 1984–1987 it is planned to spend 3,750 million ECU at Community level, and it is expected that by the end of this period research will be accounting for 4% of the Community budget.

Research in the three Communities

To see how this involvement in science and technology arose, one should bear in mind that legally the 'European Community' is composed of three individual

Communities, each established by a separate international treaty: the European Coal and Steel Community (ECSC), the European Atomic Energy Community (the EAEC, or Euratom), and the European Economic Community (the EEC or 'Common Market'). Prior to 1968 each of the three Communities was run by its own executive body, called Commissions in the case of the EEC and the EAEC, and the High Authority in the case of the ECSC. In 1968 the three executives were replaced by a single Commission of the European Communities, which is responsible for the functioning and development of the trinity of Communities.

Both the ECSC and EAEC Treaties make specific mention of the promotion of research in their respective domains, in contrast to the EEC Treaty in which research is not mentioned apart from a reference to measures for the coordination of research in agriculture. It is not surprising, then, that there is now a long history of European Community publications on coal, steel and nuclear research, including research on safety aspects connected with these industries. Despite the fact that the EEC Treaty, which is after all the kernel of the European Community idea, makes no general provisions for a contribution from scientific and technical research towards the Treaty's objectives, it has proved possible to develop programmes in fields other than coal, steel and nuclear research. Fears in the late 1960s about the menace of pollution led to the creation of programmes on environmental protection, and the energy crisis of the early 1970s encouraged programmes on non-conventional energy sources and energy saving. Work on health and safety which began under the provisions of the ECSC Treaty has diversified into other areas where it has been deemed that cooperation between member states could be fruitful. Uncertainty about the future of some of Europe's traditional industries has encouraged programmes on 'new technologies', notably information technology and biotechnologies. Research policy at the European Community level has itself come under scrutiny, and has included an experimental programme to test whether long-term forecasting, with a view to predicting the impact of future developments in science and technology on the development of the Community, is likely to be useful and practicable.

FINANCING THE RESEARCH

At this stage, having sketched how the European Community commitment to science and technology came about, we would like to describe the different degrees to which the Community can become involved in individual research projects, since this can be relevant to the publication process. Two terms used in this context are 'Joint Research Centre activities' and 'shared cost activities'.

The term 'Joint Research Centre activities' refers to research done in the research establishments of the Commission itself, of which there are four, at Ispra in northern Italy, Karlsruhe in the Federal Republic of Germany, Petten on the coast of the Netherlands, and Geel in northern Belgium. Collectively known as the Joint Research Centre, these laboratories were originally set up under the Euratom Treaty as the Joint Nuclear Research Centre. In common with some national nuclear laboratories they have diversified into other fields during the past decade while retaining a strong commitment to nuclear problems.

The Commission also contracts research to external laboratories or organizations. Such research, covered by the term 'shared cost activities', is generally partially funded from other sources so that Community financial support covers only a proportion of the costs. The Commission's solar energy R. & D. programme, which is part of a broader R. & D. programme on alternative energy sources, is a typical example of a shared cost programme: more than 400 contracts were let during 1979–1983 with varying levels of financial support from the Commission.

The ECSC Treaty makes special provision for technical and economic research relating to coal and steel and to occupational safety in those industries, which is partly financed by levies imposed on coal and steel production and partly by the undertakings that execute the research on behalf of the ECSC. Another special case is research on nuclear fusion. Euratom has entered into contracts of association with all fusion research laboratories in Europe, under which expenditure in the associated laboratories is shared between the national governments and the Community. The Community makes both a 25% contribution to general expenditure in the running of each laboratory and a 45% contribution to the construction of specific large experiments which are recognized as having an interest in the Community as a whole. On average, the Community's participation works out at about 30% of total expenditure in the laboratories.

The JET project (the Joint European Torus for fusion research, built at Culham, Oxfordshire) is financed differently, with 80% of expenditure being borne by Euratom, 10% by the United Kingdom Atomic Energy Authority and 10% shared between all organizations having contracts of association with Euratom.

So far we have described ways in which EC funds may be directed to the support of particular research projects. The Commission also has programmes in the scientific and technical field, where its role is primarily that of a coordinator. It is natural that the European Community should provide a convenient framework within which problems of interest to all member states and susceptible to research may be discussed, research priorities set, and work allotted to individual national laboratories in order to avoid unnecessary duplication and speed up progress. Such coordination-type programmes are known as 'concerted activities'. A special case are the so-called COST programmes, which are undertaken through an inter-governmental framework proposed by the European Community to promote wider European cooperation in science and technology, and adopted by a group of nineteen European states in 1971.

In all this the immediate aim of the Community's financial support is the acquisition of scientific and technical research results. (The long-term aim of course goes beyond this, since all Community-financed research has an application in view, even though in some areas it is agreed that the benefits are not likely to be reaped until far into the future — fusion research for example.) Scientific and technical publications may however also arise in other contexts. The fundamental aim of achieving the free movement of goods within the Community means that special attention must be paid to technical barriers hindering the transfer of goods from one member state to another. Although this may seem to be an administrative rather than a scientific problem, it often happens that scientific and technical questions are also involved. As part of the process of tackling such technical barriers to trade, the Commission may organize conferences and seminars and commission studies in order to examine the scientific and technical aspects, and the resulting reports may be published as part of the Commission's scientific and technical publishing programme.

THE RESEARCH PROGRAMMES

At this stage, having examined the different routes by which the Community supports science and research, it may be useful to briefly review the various topics in science and technology which are receiving EC support. We shall do this by describing the main lines of Community research policy, and identifying those departments of the Commission which are involved in it. Of course, this can be no more than a snapshot of research activities at the time of writing. New subjects will be broached and others will be dropped as perceived needs and priorities change. Our review can also only be based on the present organizational structure of the Commission: the roles and interests of the departments of which the Commission is composed may change in the future as they have changed in the past, and new departments may be created while others are suppressed.[1]

The main lines of research activity may at present be summarized as follows (the figures in brackets are the percentages of the 1982 budgetary allocations for research, totalling 590 million EC, which were devoted to each activity):

Agriculture and fisheries (0.85%): Much of the effort is devoted to the better coordination of research in the member states, by means of a programme of meetings, exchanges of personnel, and research under contract on agricultural topics deemed to be of special importance to the Community as a whole.

Industry (15.16%): Expenditure is largely aimed at improving the industrial competitiveness of the Community, both by promoting the development of new industries such as biotechnology, information technology and micro-electronics, and by encouraging improvements and new techniques in conventional industries such as steel (ECSC research), textiles, footwear, and foodstuffs.

Transport (0.29%): Research in this sector is concentrated on safety aspects.

Raw materials (2.11%): The main accent is on primary raw materials, with particular emphasis on the extraction and use of uranium, and on the recycling of municipal and industrial wastes. Apart from the aim of making optimum use of raw materials, the programme is relevant to the energy, environmental and industrial interests of the Community.

Energy (68.28%): At present this is by far the largest sector, demonstrating the importance which the Community places on measures to improve the management of its energy resources and to reduce its dependence on outside sources of energy. Of the 403 million ECU devoted to energy research in 1982, the largest part was spent on controlled thermonuclear fusion including JET (179 million ECU) and on nuclear fission energy, especially the safety aspects (112 million ECU). Considerable effort is also devoted to the development of solar energy in its various manifestations (such as wind energy and biomass) and to geothermal energy, under the heading of 'alternative energy sources'. Other programmes concern energy saving in industry, hydrocarbons, coal (ECSC research) and energy systems analysis and strategy studies, all with the aim of making better use of conventional energy sources.

Development (0.14%): This heading refers to research intended to be of benefit to the developing countries, notably the countries linked to the Community through the Lomé Agreement.

Social (3.35%): We have mentioned that research done under the Euratom and ECSC Treaties has always included work on the health and safety aspects of the industries concerned — mine safety and radiation protection, for example. More recently the Community has developed interests in other areas of medicine and public health where there is reason to believe that cooperation on a European scale might be fruitful. The programme has recently included the following topics: congenital abnormalities, cellular aging, extra-corporeal oxygenation, thromboses, hearing problems, perinatal monitoring and electro-cardiography.

Environment (5.58%): The main headings include climatology, water pollution, air pollution and the disposal of sewage sludges, as well as the particular environmental problems associated with the steel industry covered under the provisions of the ECSC Treaty.

General activities (4.25%): Special mention should be made of an experimental programme of forecasting and assessment in the field of science and technology (FAST), designed to test the utility and practicality of long-term forecasting and assessment as a tool for the definition of objectives and priorities for Community R. & D. The FAST programme has so far concentrated on three themes under the headings 'the bio-society', 'the information society' and 'work and employment'.

ORGANIZATIONAL STRUCTURE

Returning to the organizational structure of the Commission, the smallest administrative units are known as divisions or services. Related units are grouped together in directorates, which are further grouped into directorates-general. The latter are the largest subdivisions of the Commission.

We shall begin with Directorate-General XII (Science, Research and Development), within which many of the research activities we have listed are concentrated. The fusion programme (JET and the associations with European laboratories) is managed from within DG XII, and there are directorates dealing with:

— Technological research (which includes the division concerned with ECSC technical research on steel)
— Nuclear research and development
— Alternative energy sources, energy conservation and energy R. & D. strategy
— Biology, radiation protection and medical research
— Environment, raw materials and materials recycling
— Scientific and technical coordination, cooperation with non-member countries, and Coopération Scientifique et Technique (COST) (including the FAST programme and a division concerned with the evaluation of the effectiveness of Community research[2]).

The Joint Research Centre (JRC) is part of the DG XII structure. The largest of the individual establishments making up the Centre, JRC Ispra in northern Italy, is mainly concerned with reactor safety, safety of nuclear materials, safeguarding and management of fissile materials, thermonuclear fusion technology, new energy sources, environmental protection, and remote sensing from the air and space. JRC Geel in Belgium concentrates on nuclear measurements, and reference materials and techniques; JRC Karlsruhe (Federal Republic of Germany) on the transuranium elements; and JRC Petten (The Netherlands) on high temperature materials and the operation of a high-flux reactor.

The other directorates-general of interest to us are, in numerical order, as follows:

Directorate-General III (Internal Market and Industrial Affairs): We have already mentioned how the process of dismantling technical barriers to trade may give rise to scientific and technical publications, and these activities are concentrated in DG III. Measures for the encouragement of European industry, which are covered by this DG, may also lead to publications.

Directorate-General V (Employment, Social Affairs and Education): This DG includes the 'Health and Safety' Directorate, whose reports on public health, industrial medicine and hygiene, and industrial safety, naturally fall within the scientific and technical publications programme.

Directorate-General VI (Agriculture): The relevant department is the Coordination of Agricultural Research Division which runs a coordination programme whose main lines at present include animal pathology, improvements in beef production, integrated and biological pest control, improvements in production of vegetable proteins, Mediterranean agriculture, and studies on land use and rural development.

Directorate-General XI (Environment, Consumer Protection and Nuclear Safety): The relevant divisions are concerned with the protection and management of water, the prevention and reduction of pollution (other than water pollution) and the protection and management of space, the environment and natural resources — economic aspects and public awareness.

Directorate-General XIII (Information Market and Innovation): DG XIII has a special importance for this chapter, because it is the 'Scientific and Technical Communication Service' of DG XIII which manages the Commission's scientific and technical publications programme. We shall be examining in detail the workings of this service later. For the moment it is sufficient to say that the service is part of the New Technologies Directorate of DG XIII, and this directorate is completed by two divisions dealing with technological information and patents and with exploitation of new technologies. We shall also mention their role later. The second directorate of DG XIII is called 'Information Management' and has three units entitled 'European networks' (concerned particularly with the Euronet-Diane system), 'Transfer of information between European languages' (which notably includes the problem of machine translation), and 'Tele-informatics in documentary applications' (the transmission of documents using the techniques of tele-informatics).

Directorate-General XVII (Energy): This DG is principally concerned with policy aspects. It also includes a division handling technical coal research (ECSC research) and a Directorate for Energy Saving and Alternative Energy Sources, Electricity and Heating, which is particularly involved in the promotion of demonstration projects in these areas involving innovative techniques. The Euratom Safeguards system is part of DG XVII.

Publication policy

We have examined the different methods of financing Community research and surveyed the broad range of scientific and technical topics which figure in Community programmes because the diversity which exists in both these areas has important repercussions on the way that the Commission disseminates information about the results of the programmes. Progress in research is dependent on the piecing together of items of information from many sources, so that to the researcher the origin of the funding which financed the item of apparatus or the research result in which he or she is interested is often of only secondary importance. Because of this, communication between scientists and technologists has developed through a multitude of separate channels, specific channels being restricted to particular topics or disciplines. We are thinking here of course of the spectrum of scientific journals publishing contributions with regard only to their originality, significance and quality, and not to the origin of the funds which financed the research.

It is natural, then, that the results of the wide range of EC-supported research should be spread throughout the scientific literature, each item being found alongside research from other sources in one of the communication channels appropriate to the subject concerned. This dispersion of the results of Community research means that our scientific and technical publications are treated quite distinctly from the publications relating to other topics dealt with in this book. Although it may seem untidy to treat the research publications so differently, we believe that the method adopted is the right one for scientific and technical subject matter. We have also seen how in many cases research projects are undertaken by the Community acting in partnership with other organizations and laboratories, Community funding covering only a part of the project's costs. This is a further factor tending to diversify the channels through which Community-sponsored research is published.

ROLE OF DG XIII

As already indicated, the scientific and technical publications programme of the Commission is run by Directorate-General XIII (Information Market and Innovation) by an administrative unit known as the Scientific and Technical Communication Service. This is administrative unit number two in Directorate A (New Technologies) of DG XIII; so in Commission shorthand the unit is known as DG XIII/A-2. All scientific and technical publications, in whichever directorate-general they originate, are funnelled through this unit before publication. A unit within Directorate-General IX (Personnel and Administration) plays a similar role for all other publications of the Commission (i.e. all publications which are not of a scientific or technical nature), except that both the Statistical Office, which falls within the Commission's structure although it is not referred to as a directorate-general, and the Directorate-General X (Information)[3] handle their own publications. This means that DG XIII plays a part in the Consultative Committee on Publications (CCP). Each year DG XIII produces a publications programme which is discussed within the CCP and has a publications budget allotted to it. It also administers funds which have been set aside by other directorates-general for their scientific and technical publications. DG XIII thus acts as an agent for all Commission departments producing scientific and technical information. In Commission publishing nomenclature this makes DG XIII a 'service éditeur' or 'publishing service', while each source department is an 'author service' or 'service auteur'.

The material passing through DG XIII/A-2 describing the results of EC research can be divided into three basic groups:
  (i)   papers that are to be presented orally at conferences, and which are not going to be published in a conference proceedings;
  (ii) papers which the author service wishes to publish in a particular scientific journal, or in a conference proceedings;

(iii)   reports for which the author service is asking DG XIII to arrange publication. These may be items which are too long and detailed or too specialized for the journals, or they may be the proceedings of conferences which the author service has arranged or been heavily involved in.

All three types of material, when first received by DG XIII, are submitted to the Technological Information and Patents Division of DG XIII (DG XIII/A-1) in order to vet items for possible patentable inventions. If any such inventions are revealed, special arrangements have to be made before the material is released for publication, but in the absence of any objections from the Patents Division clearance can be given to the author service for presentation of the material orally at a conference or submission to a journal or conference proceedings. A reprint of the article as published in the journal or proceedings is retained in the archives of DG XIII/A-2, as is a copy of material presented orally at conferences but not published. The latter material, however, may consist merely of the author's speaking notes or a short list of headings which he or she covered in the talk, rather than a conventional scientific paper.

SCIENTIFIC AND TECHNICAL REPORTS

The third class of material, reports for which the author service is asking DG XIII to arrange publication, obviously requires more attention. This is material for which the Commission is seen as publisher, although strictly speaking is not. The role of DG XIII here is to select a publisher appropriate for each particular item. As already explained in our remarks on publication policy, the Commission's policy is that the results of Community research should be inserted in the usual channels of scientific and technical communication. This means that the presentation of Community research at conferences and in the scientific journals is encouraged, and we have briefly described how such publications are handled by DG XIII. The same applies to the reports published through the agency of DG XIII. Where possible, then, DG XIII arranges for these reports to be published by specialist scientific and technical publishers. In this way the reports are brought to the attention of potential readers and users by means of the publishers' normal publicity methods. At the time of writing, about 75 reports per year are issued through scientific and technical publishing houses, of which about 70% are the proceedings of conferences, the remainder mostly being the reports of studies executed for the Commission by external contractors.

There are, however, a great many reports for which publication through external publishing houses would not be appropriate. These are published for DG XIII by the Office for Official Publications of the European Communities. Such reports are, for example, the detailed results of work done in the Joint Research Centre or under contract under a 'shared cost' programme. At present around 500 scientific and technical reports per year are published for DG XIII by the Office for Official Publications.

In Commission nomenclature all these scientific and technical reports, whether published by the Office for Official Publications or by another publisher, are known as 'EUR reports', because they each carry a code number allocated by DG XIII preceded by the letters 'EUR'. This 'EUR number' may also include an indication of the language of publication of the report: for example, EUR 7998 EN would indicate a report available only in English, while EUR 8246 FR would be available only in French. The system makes use of hyphens, commas and obliques to deal with more complicated situations: DA/DE/GR/EN/FR/IT/NL would mean that the text is published in each of the languages indicated[4] and in one volume; DA,DE,GR,EN,FR,IT,NL means that the text is published in each of the languages indicated and in separate volumes for each language, while DA-DE-GR-EN-FR-IT-NL means that the text is published in one or another of the languages indicated and in one volume.

Microfiche or full size

Many of the highly specialized EUR reports, particularly those reporting the results of research projects, are issued in the form of microfiches rather than as full-size printed material. In most of these cases, however, a limited number of full-size 'blow-ups', on paper, are also produced which can be made available to users who cannot use microfiche. At present about 80% of EUR reports have microfiche as their principal form of publication.

EURO ABSTRACTS

As we have seen, in order to improve their chances of reaching the desired target groups, scientific and technical publications from the Commission are issued through a wide variety of channels. The whole output is recorded, however, in the Commission's monthly journal, *Euro abstracts*, which can be used to obtain an overview of the Commission's production of scientific and technical documents.

Euro abstracts is published for DG XIII by the Office for Official Publications, and is in two sections. Section I covers all fields with the exception of coal and steel research executed under the provisions of the ECSC Treaty. ECSC research is covered in Section II. Since each section has a different approach, we shall describe them separately.

Section I aims to provide bibliographic details and abstracts of all items within its subject coverage, whether they be EUR reports published through the Office for Official Publications or by other publishers, papers published in the scientific journals or in conference proceedings, or papers presented orally at conferences without being published. For each item the title and abstract are given both in the original language and in English, and also the identity of the authors. Other information listed depends on the nature of the item: the EUR number, the form of the publication (i.e. whether it is issued as a microfiche or a 'full-size' publication) and the identity of the publisher in the case of reports issued by the Commission, the affiliation of the authors (which may be a department of the

Commission or an organization carrying out work under contract), the contract number where appropriate, the identity of the journal or conference proceedings in the case of items published through these channels, and an assessment of the contents of the item (number of pages, references, illustrations, etc.). Information is given on how to obtain copies of the items. Patents derived from the implementation of the Communities' research programmes are also included in Section I. Inventions are announced approximately eighteen months after the priority date. For each invention, an abstract is published, possibly with an illustration, in the language of the first applicant and in English.

Section II contains similar information on ECSC research. The abstracts are however given in three languages — German, English and French. The coverage also goes beyond that of Section I in that it includes summaries of research agreements concluded by the ECSC and of certain unpublished research reports.

EABS data base

The bibliographic information published in *Euro abstracts* is stored in the EABS data base managed by DG XIII. EABS is available on the Euronet-Diane network (through the ECHO (European Commission Host Organization) host).[5] EABS contains details of all EUR reports published since 1961. Information on papers published in the scientific journals and conference proceedings, and papers presented at conferences but not published, is complete back to 1968. Note however that EABS does not at present contain the texts of the abstracts themselves — it is intended to develop the data base to include these abstracts for material published after 1 January 1984.

Coverage of Euro abstracts

All publications passing through DG XIII are recorded by *Euro abstracts* and entered in the EABS data base. It must be pointed out however that *Euro abstracts* cannot provide a total coverage of all publications of scientific and technical interest. We have mentioned that DG IX (Personnel and Administration) is also a 'service éditeur' through which Commission documents are channelled for publication, and occasionally the DG IX output may include titles of interest to the scientific and technical community. Such titles will, however, concern policy or economic aspects rather than the results of research itself. We have also mentioned that much European Community research is executed on a 'shared-cost' basis. In some cases it may be agreed that the Commission's partner may assume responsibility for publishing the results. Inevitably there are occasions when the resulting publications are not communicated to DG XIII and thus do not figure in *Euro abstracts*. Finally, the problem of conference proceedings should be mentioned. The Commission's involvement in scientific and technical conferences can take many different forms — many conferences are organized by the Commission alone, in other cases it may organize conferences in cooperation with other organizations, or it may merely lend its name as a sponsor of conferences whose aims it wishes to support but which are entirely run by other organizations. In the latter cases any resulting proceedings may escape the notice of *Euro abstracts* in spite of the nominal involvement of the Commission. DG XIII makes every effort to ensure that *Euro abstracts* is as complete as possible, but publications will occasionally miss the net.

THE PUBLICATIONS THEMSELVES

So far we have concentrated on an examination of the Commission's involvement in science and technology and on the mechanisms by which DG XIII arranges the publication of the results, but we have said very little about the publications themselves. It may be helpful if we describe them in more detail, in order to give prospective users a better idea of DG XIII output.

Much of the material comprises specialized research reports emanating from projects undertaken in the establishments of the Joint Research Centre, or by outside bodies working under contract. These are normally published as microfiche, as already mentioned, although full-size blow-ups on paper can usually be supplied on request. All are microfiched directly from the typescripts submitted by the authors. Another important class of publication is known as 'studies', and often consists of a review, or a report of 'desk research', on a topic of special interest to one of the Community's programmes. These may be issued as microfiche and blow-ups in the same way as the research reports, or, if it is thought likely that they will be of general interest, the principal form of publication will be a full-size printed report. Again, they are generally printed directly from the author's original typescripts. Thirdly, conference proceedings make up a significant proportion of the output of EUR reports. Indeed, DG XIII/A-2 contains a conference publications unit which is available to help all departments of the Commission wishing to issue proceedings of conferences in which they are involved. The unit will send instructions and typing kits to speakers, look after the collection of the papers, and make the publication arrangements, all with the aim of getting copies of the proceedings to participants and to prospective purchasers within the shortest possible time.

Specialized atlases, directories on scientific and technical themes, inventories of Community-sponsored research projects, and documents relating to the management and policy-making aspects of Community research, may also appear within the EUR series from time to time.

Language of publication

The European Community has seven official languages,[6] none having priority over the others. Most of the specialized scientific and technical publications from the Community's research programmes are however available in English only. It is well known that, at least in the Western hemisphere, English is the dominant language for the communication of research results, although the degree to which it is preferred over other languages seems to depend on the branch of science and technology concerned. It is to be expected, then, that the authors of reports of Community-financed research will tend to use English. The cost of translation, bearing in mind the highly specialized nature of the material and the terminology problems that would arise, as well as the costs involved in publication, usually prevents the appearance of the reports in more than one Community language. Nevertheless, some reports directed at a wider audience are issued in several or even all official languages.

Confidentiality

All the publications referred to so far are openly available to anyone who may require them. It should be mentioned, however, that there is also a mechanism available to DG XIII to allow for restricted distribution of reports when it is deemed not to be in the interests of the Community to make them available to anyone who may care to purchase them. At present this mechanism is comparatively little used; it is however applied to ensure a controlled distribution of certain reports on nuclear science and technology emanating from Euratom work. Such reports are sent to 'correspondents' in the member states; these correspondents are responsible for forwarding the reports to an agreed list of destinations in their own country.

Related activities

Apart from its role within the Commission of overseeing the publication of scientific and technical research results, DG XIII/A-2 is authorized to examine the wider question of the dissemination of research results in general among the member states of the Community. To this end a number of conferences have been held and studies commissioned, some of which have led to further action.[7] We shall briefly examine the main products of this work.

MULTILINGUAL PUBLISHING

Although it is clear that European researchers are usually prepared to consult research reports not written in their own language, and may often themselves write reports in a language foreign to them, the same cannot be said for other groups with a professional interest in science and technology. Indeed, the researchers themselves may show a reluctance to consult foreign-language material when it is not directly connected with their chief research interests. This has led DG XIII to undertake two programmes involving the translation of scientific and technical material.

The first involves a group of general science journals and magazines in the member states which, at the instigation of DG XIII, cooperate in the commissioning of articles for publication in their pages. The role of DG XIII is to arrange translation of the articles, so that they may be published in several of the participating journals. This allows the journals to publish points of view which they might not otherwise easily have access to, while the authors of the articles concerned have the satisfaction of seeing their work read by a wider audience than would normally be the case.[8]

In the second scheme, DG XIII is experimenting with the financing of the translation of specialized technical books from one Community language into another. Again, the aim is to facilitate the flow of scientific and technical information across language barriers within the Community. Under the present pilot scheme it is hoped to test the extent to which translation costs may be recoverable from royalty receipts, and whether some sort of 'translation fund' to aid the translation of technical books may be a practical proposition.

SYNOPSIS PUBLISHING

As a result of its involvement in the publication of specialized research reports, DG XIII has been attracted to the notion of 'synopsis publishing', whereby brief accounts or synopses describing the essential points of research reports are issued in journal format for wide distribution. The full reports themselves, which would be too long for normal journal publication, are made available on demand to persons who, after reading the synopsis, feel that they need to consult the full report. Synopsis publishing might also be relevant to the language problem, in that translations of synopses would be easier to create and publish than translations of full reports.

DG XIII has therefore issued a number of synopsis publications, and is experimenting with the publication of synopses of ECSC research results, although in this particular case the experiment involves the placing of synopses in already existing journals covering subjects of ECSC interest.

SIGLE SYSTEM

A European seminar initiated by DG XIII to investigate the problem of so-called 'grey literature' has led to the establishment of a system known as SIGLE (System for Information on Grey Literature in Europe) to help deal with this category of documentation. The term 'grey literature' refers to documents issued informally in limited amounts which are not available through normal publishing channels, a definition which includes many scientific and technical research reports. One of the main characteristics of these documents is that they are often difficult to identify and obtain, since they may not be recorded in data bases. Even if one is aware of the existence of a particular 'grey literature' item of interest, the originator may be unwilling to supply a copy, or the identity of the originator may even be unknown. With the help of the Commission a consortium of documentation centres in the member states has established the SIGLE system with the intention of creating a data base specifically for grey literature items which will be made available on Euronet-Diane. Aware that knowledge of the existence of a title is not an end in itself, the consortium also intends SIGLE to be a document supply system.

NEWSLETTERS

Some of the Commission's departments responsible for managing particular research programmes, issue newsletters with varying degrees of informality, with the aim of encouraging contacts between external contractors involved in the programmes and of publicizing the programme's results. Just as the individual programmes may last for only a limited number of years, so the newsletters emanating from the programmes come and go. The department managing a particular research programme is the best source of information about the existence of newsletters relating to the programme and other ephemeral publications, which may not have been deemed sufficiently important to be considered as 'real' publications deserving an EUR number and a listing in *Euro abstracts*.

Special mention should however be made of the *New technologies newsletter*, which gives an overview of the activities of Directorate A of DG XIII, lists the most important new EUR documents, publishes details of forthcoming Commission-sponsored conferences, and reports on the Directorate's work in promoting innovation.

Future trends

At the start of this chapter we referred to plans to increase Community spending on research, its share of the Community budget rising from the present level of 2.6% to perhaps 4% by 1987. These are described in *Proposals for a European scientific and technical strategy framework programme 1984–1987.*[9] It is proposed that the research activities of the Community, which until now have developed in a piecemeal fashion, should be integrated and adjusted where necessary so as to fit into a new research strategy which is intended to be better adapted to the needs of the Community in the 1980s. As for the main lines of the strategy, it is intended to devote a larger proportion of research funds to the promotion of scientific, agricultural and industrial competitiveness, while reducing the share taken by work on improving the management of energy resources, although this latter goal will still take almost half of the research budget. There will also be significant increases in the share devoted to work intended to be of interest to the developing countries, and to work on raw materials. The improvement of living and working conditions (safety, health and environment protection) will however have a somewhat reduced share of the budget.

Such a significant development of the research programme of the Community will be wasted if adequate measures are not taken to ensure that the results of the programme are properly exploited for the benefit of the Community as a whole. This is dealt with in a recent document entitled *Promoting the utilization of the results of Community-sponsored R. & D.*[10]

The measures envisaged in this document concern all three departments of the New Technologies Directorate of DG XIII. As mentioned earlier, as well as the

Scientific and Technical Communication Service, this Directorate also includes two units dealing with technological information and patents, and with exploitation of new technologies. The role of the 'Patents' Division in protecting the results of Community-sponsored research has already been referred to. The responsibilities of the Exploitation of New Technologies Service are the assessment of the market potential for inventions resulting from Community research, the publicizing of such inventions, and licensing and follow-up to ensure effective exploitation.

The strengthening and development of all these activities is foreseen in the document. On the publishing side, this is expected to result in the extension of the EABS data base to cover not only details of publications (which of course tend to deal only with the completed research), but also information on projected and ongoing research. The system for the confidential circulation of research results, at present little used, is expected to be expanded.

The measures concerning the protection of inventions particularly relate to the protection of results arising from research done under contract as part of a Community research programme. The aim is to improve protection in member states other than those in which the work was done: in the past this has been considered to cause problems, particularly when exploitation is in the hands of small or medium-sized businesses.

Finally, it is intended to improve the exploitation of research results by means of measures encouraging the construction of prototypes and pilot projects.

The document proposes that each year about 1.5% of the whole Community research and development budget for that year should be devoted to the dissemination, protection and exploitation of the results of the programme. This should have a major impact on the dissemination of the results of Community-sponsored scientific and technical activities and their utilization in order, in the words of the proposal, to contribute to the attainment of the economic, social and other objectives of the Community and its member states.

References and notes

[1] The organizational structure is published from time to time by the Office for Official Publications under the title *Directory of the Commission of the European Communities.*

[2] See *Evaluation of research and development: methods for evaluating the results of European Community R&D programmes*, Reidel Publishing, 1982.

[3] The aim of the publications of DG X is to provide the general public with information about the European Communities, although often its publications are aimed at particular groups, such as trade unionists, environmentalists, consumer groups, etc.

[4] The meaning of the symbols is as follows: DA, Danish; DE, German; GR, Greek; EN, English; FR, French; IT, Italian; NL, Dutch.

[5] Enquiries about EABS should be sent to ECHO customer service, 15, Avenue de la Faïencerie, L-1510 Luxembourg.

[6] Danish, German, Greek, English, French, Italian and Dutch.

[7] See:

'Scientific and technical publishing in a multilingual society', in *Overcoming the language barrier*, Verlag Dokumentation, 1977. (EUR 5731 DE, EN, FR). Summary of a seminar held in Luxembourg, 11–12 November 1976.

The future of publishing by scientific and technical societies, Office for Official Publications of the European Communities, 1978. (EUR 6109 DE-EN-FR). Proceedings of the seminar held in Luxembourg, 3–4 April 1978.

J. M. Gibb and E. Phillips, 'A better fate for the grey, or non-conventional literature', *Journal of research communication studies*, vol. 1, 1978/79, pp. 225–234. Summary of a seminar on grey literature, York, 13–14 December 1978.

The impact of new technologies on publishing, K. G. Saur, 1980. (EUR 6830 DE, EN, FR). Proceedings of the symposium held in Luxembourg, 6–7 November 1979.

Future roles for synopsis publishing, Office for Official Publications of the European Communities, 1980. (EUR 6958 EN). Report of a seminar held in Luxembourg, 9–10 October 1979.

Videotex and the press, Learned Information, 1982. (EUR 7828 EN). Proceedings of a seminar held in Luxembourg, 14 January 1982.

[8] Members of the group at the end of 1983 were *Umschau in Wissenschaft und Technik* (Federal Republic of Germany), *La Recherche* (France), *Technology Ireland* (Ireland), *Scienza & Tecnica* (Italy), *Natuur en Techniek* (Netherlands), *Endeavour* (United Kingdom).

[9] COM(82) 865 final. 21 December 1982.

[10] COM(83) 18 final. 3 March 1983.

5

European Parliament Information

ANTHONY S. REID

The role of the European Parliament

Before examining the information services of the European Parliament, it might be useful to give an outline of its role and its method of working. It will be seen that it differs in many respects from a typical national parliament, and it is because of these differences that the information facilities are so unlike those, say, of the British House of Commons.

The first 'Assembly' was set up to monitor the work of the European Coal and Steel Community (ECSC). It met for the first time in Strasbourg in 1952 and since that time has developed in terms of its size and its responsibilities. Until 1979, Members of the European Parliament were nominated by their national parliaments but in June of that year the first elections by universal suffrage were held in each of the nine member states. Elections cover a five-year period.

The European Economic Community (EEC) Treaty of 25 March 1957 endowed the European Parliament with 'advisory and supervisory powers'. In practice the Parliament has the right to be consulted on draft legislation proposed by the Commission. The Council of Ministers is under no obligation to accept Parliament's opinion and rarely does so on questions of substance. The Parliament also has the right to question, orally and in writing, the Commission and the Council, to force the Commissioners to resign as a body, and to introduce 'own initiative' resolutions, which it does particularly in the field of human rights. In the field of external relations, the Parliament has initiated meetings with parliamentary delegations with which the European Community (EC) has important trade relations. Another important activity is the twice-yearly Consultative Assembly of the Lomé Convention.

It is in the control of the Community budget, however, that Parliament sometimes asserts its powers. Once the Community had acquired financial autonomy, it was only logical that the European Parliament should exercise direct control over expenditure that was no longer subject to scrutiny by the national parliaments. Parliament can reject the budget (as it did the 1980 budget) and it has the authority to modify the total volume of expenditure.

ORGANIZATION AND STRUCTURE

There are currently 434 elected Members of the European Parliament (MEPs) of which 81 represent the United Kingdom (UK). Fewer than 20% of Members are also members of national parliaments. Every MEP is entitled to an allowance for a secretary and a research assistant.

One important feature of the Parliament is the dominant role played by the political groups, of which there are currently seven. These groups, set up under Rule 36 of the Rules of Procedure, are entitled to employ a certain number of staff members according to the size of the group.

Much of the detailed work of the European Parliament is done within the 18 standing committees. Their main task is to prepare Parliament's opinions on the legislative proposals of the Commission. A rapporteur is appointed by the relevant committee to steer a particular item through the committee to produce an agreed resolution and to present it at a subsequent plenary session. As soon as the resolution has been adopted, it becomes Parliament's Opinion on the Commission's legislative proposal, and is sent to the Council to be taken into account when the final legislation is framed. Committees also prepare 'own initiative' reports. Committee meetings are normally held behind closed doors but, occasionally, a committee will decide to hold a public hearing on a given topic. Committees meet once or twice a month for two-day meetings which are usually held in the Parliament's offices in Brussels.

The Parliament normally holds a 5-day 'part-session' every month, with the exception of August. In spite of the fact that the Luxembourg government has paid for the construction of a new and fully-equipped chamber, it has now become established practice for almost all plenary sessions to be held in Strasbourg.

The Secretariat of the Parliament comprises about 2,260 officials, most of whom have their offices in Luxembourg. There are five directorates-general: Sessional & General Services (DG I), Committees and Interparliamentary Delegations (DG II), Information & Public Relations (DG III), Administration, Personnel & Finance (DG IV), Research & Documentation (DG V).

PUBLICATIONS

Responsibility for the production and distribution of documents and publications of the European Parliament and of the political groups is in the hands of the Directorate-General for Sessional and General Services.

The fact that virtually every document produced must exist in seven language versions, and that they have to be made available in several places of work, creates enormous problems for the printing and distribution services.

All the internal documents, such as those required for part-sessions, committees, sub-committees and working parties, are duplicated on offset machines on the Parliament's premises.

The major series of documents issued by, or on behalf of, the Parliament are:

(i) *Debates of the European Parliament, Report of proceedings.* This is published by the Official Publications Office as an annex to the *Official journal,* C series. It constitutes the final edition and appears in all Community languages about two months after the debate. A much earlier report, the *Verbatim report of proceedings* is normally available on the next day. This contains the text of interventions in the original language and is known universally as the 'rainbow' edition because of the practice within the Community of allocating a different colour for each language. Members have the right to correct the texts of their speeches within one day of receipt of the provisional edition.

(ii) The indexes to the debates are published annually in the *Official journal,* C series, with a delay of at least twelve months after the session. They comprise: Index of names; Index of subjects; and List of working documents. The 'Index of names' indicates the appointments and resignations to and from committees, summarizes the interventions, and lists the working documents for which the Member has been responsible. The 'Index of subjects' is based on a system of free-term keywords and includes 'see' and 'see also' entries. Every effort is made to ensure continuity of index terms from one year to another. The 'List of working documents' is in two parts, the first consisting of documents presented during the preceding session and examined during the current year, and the second comprising those drawn up during the year in question. This list indicates the dates the reports were tabled and any further action taken, such as reference back to committee, withdrawal, voting, etc.

(iii) Another important publication is the *Minutes of proceedings.* This was instituted in May 1954 and has the object of formally recording the decisions of the Parliament. It includes lists of consultations, requests for opinions, documents formally received and the committees to which they have been allocated, petitions entered on the register, a list of speakers and votes cast (when by roll-call) and the attendance list for each sitting. A provisional edition is distributed to Members on each sitting day and adopted the day after. The minutes of the last day of a part session are adopted on the first day of the next.

The amended version of the minutes is signed by the President and Secretary General of the Parliament and published within one month in the *Official journal,* C Series.

(iv) The *Bulletin of the European Parliament* was instituted in 1960 as a means
      of keeping Members currently informed of parliamentary activities. It
      indicates the activities of the President, the main decisions of the Enlarged
      Bureau and the answers to questions by Members to the Presidency. The
      Bulletin lists the appointments of rapporteurs, the titles of new *European
      Parliament working documents*, and the reports prepared by the
      Directorate-General for Research & Documentation. It also includes a
      calendar of forthcoming meetings. A special issue of the *Bulletin* contains
      the draft agenda for part-sessions, another lists the titles of all written
      questions and another shows the work in progress of committees of the
      European Parliament.
 (v) Other occasional publications of the European Parliament include the
      Rules of procedure of the European Parliament, the *List of Members*, the
      Vademecum, and the *Protocol yearbook*.
(vi) The Terminology Office publishes a range of about twenty multilingual
      terminologies covering the major subject fields of concern to the
      Parliament. These are available for purchase by direct application to the
      Terminology Office of the Parliament.

The publications of the Directorate-General for Research & Documentation and for Information and Public Relations are mentioned later in this
chapter.

The Directorate-General for Research & Documentation (DG V)

Directorate-General V is the youngest of the five DGs, having been created in
1973 at the time of Britain's accession to the European Community. Its principal
role is similar to that of the Library of the House of Commons, namely to
provide rapid, impartial and authoritative information for Members. There are,
however, some important differences resulting from the different roles of the
two bodies, the differing attitudes to 'parliamentary information services' in the
member states, and the constraints of language and of geographical separation
of MEPs from the sources of information.

Where in Westminster the needs of the Member are considered to be
paramount in terms of priority and confidentiality, in the European Parliament
the MEP, as an individual, is given much less priority than corporate bodies such
as committees or political groups. Furthermore, unless there are good reasons
for confidentiality, research studies carried out at the specific request of
Members are normally notified and made available to Parliament as a whole.

Because the proceedings of the plenary session of the Parliament are more
'ordered' than at Westminster, they inevitably lack the 'cut and thrust' of a
national chamber. One consequence of this is that only rarely do Members ask
for immediate information, for example, whilst a session is in progress. This is
fortunate because it often happens that the information required must be

communicated over long distances and, in the case of research requests, it may be that the specialist who has done the work is not able to communicate the results in the language of the Member making the request. In such cases a translation must be prepared and this of course takes time.

Directorate-General V has eight research divisions and one Library and Documentation Division, as shown in Figure 1.

Figure 1

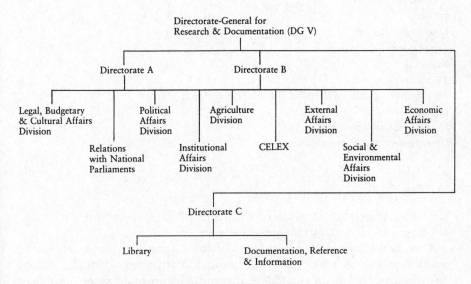

The extent to which MEPs make use of the services of Directorate-General V varies greatly according to their method of working, their nationality and even their political affiliations. All Members of course obtain information from a wide variety of sources including pressure groups, party research units, national ministries (such as the Foreign Office), universities, and European Documentation Centres (EDCs). In certain member states, MEPs have the right to use the services of their national parliamentary libraries, but this is not the case in the UK.

The current number of administrative (A grade) officials in DG V is 37, most of whom are specialists in the research divisions. The support staff include 34 administrative assistants (B grade), many of whom are professionally qualified librarians and documentalists working in the library, and 55 secretaries and clerical assistants.

Directorate-General V, in common with most of the secretariat, is located in Luxembourg. It is generally the practice for research staff to be in attendance in Strasbourg during the part-sessions and in Brussels during committee

Table 1
Breakdown of work by subject matter, 1982

	%
Political	14
Institutional	4
Legal	21
Economic and monetary	10
Community budget	6
Social	5
Education, culture	1
Agriculture	12
Regional	5
Transport	6
Environment, public health and consumer protection	2
Energy	3
External economic relations	6
Development and cooperation	5
	100

meetings relating to their special subject fields. Table 1 gives an idea of the range of enquiries dealt with by the research services.

As indicated above, a consequence of the corporate (as opposed to the individual) approach adopted by the European Parliament is that reports and analyses produced by the research workers of DG V are much more 'open' than is the case in most national parliaments. Most reports are listed in the *Bulletin of the European Parliament* and copies are available to Members on demand. They are not generally available to the public, although Members are of course at liberty to distribute them as they wish.

PUBLICATIONS OF THE DIRECTORATE-GENERAL FOR RESEARCH AND DOCUMENTATION (DG V)

Over the years Directorate-General V has published a series of occasional documents which includes volumes on a European Audit Office,[1] the future of parliaments in Europe,[2] direct elections to the European Parliament,[3] European citizens rights[4] and the position of women in the Community.[5]

Directorate-General V is also responsible for the publication of a series of *Technical fact sheets* on the Parliament and on the activities of the European Communities. This was originally intended as a set of speaking notes for candidates and others in the 1979 direct elections campaign. It had a total print run of 25,000 copies. A new series was prepared in time for the 1984 election.

Directorate-General V also published *Forging ahead: thirty years of the European Parliament*,[6] which provides comprehensive statistical and narrative information concerning the evolution of the Parliament over the first thirty years of its existence.

The major publication of Directorate-General V is *Europe today: the state of European integration*, which brings together in comprehensive form a single narrative text with references to Commission and Parliament official publications under all headings of Community policy. It is published annually, though with a few gaps in the series.

Most of the above-mentioned publications are available for purchase by the public through the normal channels.

THE LIBRARY AND DOCUMENTATION DIVISION

This is one of nine Divisions of DG V. Its main role is to provide library facilities and reference and information services to Members, the staff of the European Parliament and the political groups.

In 1972, the main library was installed on the ground floor of the Schuman Building in Luxembourg. At that time it was in an ideal position to serve the needs of MEPs meeting in the chamber on the first floor of the same building. Since that time, however, a new and much larger chamber has been constructed some distance away and, in any event, part-sessions seldom take place in Luxembourg. This has resulted in a parliamentary library which is largely inaccessible to Members. It is not surprising that there have been calls for its transfer to Brussels.

The location of the library was discussed in 1980 by the College of Quaestors whose task it is to deal with administrative matters concerning Members. Its report to the Bureau was to the effect that any removal of the library and attendant services should only take place as part of an overall decision on the siting of the secretariat as a whole. Nevertheless a small satellite library and reference service operates in the European Parliament building in the rue Belliard, Brussels. During part-sessions in Strasbourg, Members and officials have the right to use the library of the Council of Europe there, but of course this library was never designed to cater for the needs of the European Parliament.

The Library of Parliament was established in 1953 for the Common Assembly of the ECSC. Until the creation in 1972 of the Directorate-General for Research and Documentation it formed part of the Directorate-General for Information and Public Relations. There is no library committee of Members, as exists in most national parliaments.

The staffing of the Library & Documentation Division

The Library and Documentation Division has a total staff complement of 60. Of these, about 25 are involved in traditional Library activities (acquisition, cataloguing, management of periodicals, official documents, etc.), about 15 are concerned primarily with information dissemination, 11 constitute a press documentation service and 4 are located in the Brussels-based library.

The staff are in three broad grades:

— administrators (A grade), of whom there are 6;
— administrative assistants (B grade), of whom there are 25. These are normally qualified librarians, information scientists or documentalists.
— secretaries and clerical assistants (C grade), of whom there are 30.

The librarians are given a language responsibility in terms of book acquisition and cataloguing, and the reference/documentation officials are, whenever practicable, allocated a broad subject and a country responsibility.

Sources and services

The Division is called upon to provide information and documentation in any of the Community's seven languages. In this respect it differs from the documentation services of other Community institutions whose users are usually multilingual officials frequently able to read three or more languages fluently.

The library stock comprises:

(i) monographs, of which there are currently about 100,000 volumes. The main subjects covered are EEC topics, political affairs, legislation, social affairs, transport, environment and energy. A reference library contains about 7,000 titles and includes all the major reference books of the member states and a wide range of dictionaries. The 1983 budget allocation for monographs was ECU 110,000;

(ii) periodicals: about 1,000 titles are currently received. The 1983 budget for periodicals was ECU 120,000 and, as with books, an attempt is made to strike a subject, language and political balance in the titles selected. National newspapers from all the member states are received, most being stored in the form of microfilm;

(iii) international documents: in addition to a more or less complete collection of 'open' documents issued by the Community institutions, the library holds extensive stocks of publications and reports issued by other international organizations;

(iv) 'grey' literature forms a vital source of information, particularly pressure group material, university theses and departmental reports, political party manifestos and annual reports;

(v) national legislation and parliamentary documents in respect of all member states are held in the library.

Cataloguing, indexing and dissemination

An author and subject card catalogue is maintained for all monographs. The subject catalogue is based on the so-called 'Biblio' system which is of French origin and, not surprisingly, all subject headings are in the French language. The library was closed-access until 1974 when an open-access policy was adopted. The Universal Decimal Classification (UDC) is used as the basis of shelf classification and a separate UDC card catalogue is also maintained. Certain Community publications and European Parliament documents are also included in the central catalogue. A monthly accessions list is distributed within the Parliament and to a limited number of external libraries.

The library of the European Parliament cooperates with the Central Documentation Service (SCAD) of the Commission in producing the SCAD *Documentation bulletin*. A card index of periodical literature, based on the contents of this *Bulletin*, was maintained in both the Luxembourg and Brussels libraries of the Parliament until it was superseded by a computer-based system in October 1983. The SCAD *Bulletin* is widely available externally.

Press cuttings are indexed according to a list of classified subject headings adapted from the SCAD classification. Duplicate files are kept in Luxembourg and Brussels. A daily press dossier is issued and sent to European Parliament officials and political groups. Additionally, press dossiers are issued covering the specialized interests of every European Parliament committee and a range of other topics of current interest, e.g. a country to be visited by a parliamentary delegation.

The documentalists and librarians are expected to take positive steps to disseminate relevant newly published material to Members and staff as appropriate.

Use of external data bases

The 1983 budgetary allocation for the interrogation of external data bases was ECU 28,000 (about £16,000).

Bearing in mind the wide range of questions asked and the comparatively small stock of the library, it is not surprising that external data bases are being increasingly used. The fact that the European Parliament normally has more time to respond to enquiries compared with a national parliamentary library means that bibliographical data bases are frequently useful even when the articles cited have to be obtained from other libraries. Nevertheless, the most valuable type is the data bank which provides direct online information such as statistics (e.g. CRONOS), current affairs (e.g. NYT Infobank, PROMPT) or legislation (e.g. CELEX). Contracts have been signed with about 20 host suppliers; most of their data bases are accessed through Euronet-Diane.

Information to the public

When compared with national parliaments, the European Parliament is a very young organization. Furthermore, because of the lack of awareness by large sections of the electorate of the role, functions and activities of the European

Parliament, it is vitally important that a vigorous information policy be followed.

The details of the current policy are given in a *Resolution on the information policy of the European Community, of the Commission of the European Communities and of the European Parliament* (the so-called Schall Resolution), which was adopted by the European Parliament in January 1981.[7] This resolution, amongst other things:

— emphasizes that the most important task is to inform the citizens of the Community of the work of the Parliament and of its Members.

— notes that internal information for Members, journalists and groups of visitors during plenaries and other meetings is extremely inadequate, requests the publication of a daily information sheet during plenary sessions giving advance details of all parallel meetings and suggests the issuing of short, duplicated reports on the progress of debates to facilitate the work of journalists;

— calls for the further development of the *European Parliament bulletin* (see section on European Parliament publications above);

— suggests the introduction of a press review producing important articles on the Community and radio and television transcripts;

— stresses the need for a constant flow of information on the work of the committees.

DIRECTORATE-GENERAL FOR INFORMATION AND PUBLIC RELATIONS (DG III)

This Directorate-General is responsible for providing the public and the media with information concerning Parliament's work. To help it fulfil this task it maintains information offices in the capitals of each member state. The London Office, whose address is 2 Queen Anne's Gate, SW1H 9AA, has a staff of 12. It is independent of the Commission's much larger information office in the United Kingdom but of course the two services collaborate closely with each other.

The work of the Parliament's information offices comprises five elements:

— to respond to requests from the public for detailed information about Parliament's work, especially industry, voluntary organizations and the specialized press

— to educate the general public on the work of the Parliament by means of touring displays, posters, booklets, slides, etc.

— to arrange for visits of selected groups to Strasbourg and Luxembourg to see the Parliament in session and to meet officials

— to encourage improved media coverage of parliamentary activity by the issuing of press releases and by personal contacts

— to assist in the organization of European Parliament committee meetings held in their country

The major periodical publication of DG III is a monthly newspaper. The United Kingdom edition, *EP news*, has a circulation of about 30,000 copies. Other publications include *European Parliament briefing*, giving the background to the major topics to be debated by Parliament, *The week* summarizing the major events of each part-session, and a new one, *Committee roundup*. The Directorate-General also produces monographic publications which may be obtained free of charge from the London Office.[8]

European Centre for Parliamentary Research & Documentation

European Communities information is required in varying degrees in all Western European parliamentary assemblies, and it is therefore worth mentioning the existence of the European Centre for Parliamentary Research & Documentation.

This was instituted at the 1977 Vienna Conference of Presidents of European Parliamentary Assemblies, which charged the Presidents of the European Parliament and of the Council of Europe Parliamentary Assembly with setting up and running the Centre. At its May 1980 meeting in Madrid, the Conference expressed the wish that the Centre should continue to operate for the benefit, and with the cooperation of all the parliamentary assemblies, and that the appropriate national parliamentary bodies should authorize the departments concerned to take part in its various activities.

The Centre's aim is to promote the exchange of information between parliaments, to prevent duplication of often costly research, and to establish close cooperation for documentation purposes between parliamentary libraries and research departments (this includes access to the European Community's data banks and to national data banks). It collates studies centrally and issues a *Newsletter* four to six times a year, which reports on the activities of the Centre and its working parties, gives notice of various meetings of specialists (librarians, archivists and so on) and publishes their findings. The bulk of the *Newsletter*, however, consists of lists of parliamentary research and documentation studies, publications by or concerning parliaments and information on the development of computer-based documentation systems within Parliaments.

The members of the Centre are the parliamentary assemblies of the member states of the European Communities and of the Council of Europe, together with the European Parliament, the Parliamentary Assembly of the Council of Europe and the Assembly of the Western European Union. It is run jointly by the European Parliament's Directorate-General for Research and Documentation and by the Clerk of the Council of Europe. Its general strategy is established by a

Committee of 'Correspondents', these being senior officials of parliamentary libraries or research services. Working groups exist to establish policies for data processing, libraries, microform and terminologies/thesauri.

The use of information technology

In contrast to the majority of national parliamentary assemblies, the European Parliament has tended, until recently, to devote most of its data processing resources to the development of administrative rather than documentation applications. The only applications having documentation aspects which have been developed to date are PARQ and DOSE. These were both established as tools to assist the management of parliamentary procedures. PARQ relates to parliamentary questions and enables officials to follow them through the various steps from the tabling of the question to its publication in the *Official journal*. DOSE is a similar program for the management of the working documents and the passage of resolutions, etc., through the Parliament. These two programmes enable a simple system of indexing by keywords to be employed. It is possible therefore to employ PARQ and DOSE to a certain extent as documentation data bases since, in addition to the subjects, one can search by the name of the Member and by certain other criteria. These two files can be interrogated from several terminals located in the Luxembourg offices and from Brussels and Strasbourg. They will soon be accessible to the Parliament's information offices in the capitals. It should be stressed, however, that they do not permit sophisticated searching of parliamentary documentation. Furthermore, all the information available from PARQ and DOSE is in French only.

Responsibility for coordinating the development of the use of data processing, office automation and telematics rests with the Steering Committee on Data Processing (CDI). This Committee is appointed by the Secretary General and is composed of representatives of each directorate-general, the Finance Controller and observers from the Staff Committee and the political groups. No Members sit on the Steering Committee.

Cooperation between the institutions is achieved at various levels, notably by an inter-institutional data processing committee (CII) which was set up in 1981 and which has worked towards the coordination of programme developments and compatibility of hardware and software. One product of cooperation between the institutions is CELEX, a data base on Community law. CELEX is described elsewhere in this book. The European Parliament is responsible for the input to CELEX in respect of parliamentary questions and adopted resolutions. Similarly, the Parliament supplies material for inclusion in the Community terminology data base EURODICAUTOM.

The following parliamentary reports and resolutions relating to information technology within the Parliament have been issued since the first elections:

— In February 1981 the Committee on Budgets drew up for the Bureau of the

European Parliament a report on the data processing needs of the Parliament (Jackson Report, PE 67.830/rev.II).

— In July 1981 Parliament adopted a resolution on the seat of the institution (Zagari Report 1-333/81) which contains, for the first time, a decision to use the most modern means of telecommunication and the most advanced technology to overcome the problems arising from the dispersal of the different places of work. Following the adoption of the resolution the Bureau commissioned a study from a firm of consultants, Ernst and Whinney, on possible improvements to the organization and working methods of Parliament.

— In May 1982, in the resolution on the draft estimates for 1983 (Saby Report 1-185/82), Parliament indicated its intention to make any necessary adjustments to its estimates in order 'to use to the full, modern methods and the most advanced management techniques'.

In practical terms, the approval by the Bureau of the Parliament's 'five-year plan for data processing and office terminology' should now permit the introduction of:

— an integrated system, with input from text processing machines, for the production of parliamentary documents and for the tracking of parliamentary acts through their various stages within the institution.

— an information retrieval system for parliamentary documents such as debates, resolutions, reports. It is anticipated that the system will permit local data capture by the appropriate services.

— a similar information retrieval system in respect of external documentation such as periodical articles, book chapters, reports, press items, etc.

— a library housekeeping system.

— a videotex system enabling simple information, such as timetables of meetings, draft agendas, biographical details of Members and press releases, to be communicated internally and externally.

The subject indexing for the documentation systems will utilize the EUROVOC thesaurus which is being developed inter-institutionally and which is based on a thesaurus established by the documentation services of the European Parliament. Selective dissemination of information (SDI) for Members and officials will be an essential part of the documentation system.

No decision has been taken yet as to the commercial exploitation of the proposed European Parliament data bases.

The future

It is likely that within the lifetime of the second directly elected Parliament, it will be possible for the public to have access to the internal and external data bases of the institution. It may well be that information technology will have advanced to such an extent that efficient searching of videotext terminals will be possible.

The research programmes being sponsored by the Commission's Directorate-General for Information Market and Innovation (*DG XIII*) should ensure that the full texts of cited documents could be made available to the user cheaply and quickly.

All the Members themselves will eventually be provided with their own terminals, both in their Parliament office and in their home country.

In spite of all these exciting developments there will always be a need for personal contact between Members and the staff of information services.

References and notes

[1] *The case for a European Audit Office*, Office for Official Publications, 1973.

[2] *European integration and the future of parliaments in Europe*, Office for Official Publications, 1975.

[3] *Elections to the European Parliament by direct universal suffrage*, Office for Official Publications, 1977.

[4] *Special rights and a charter of the rights of the citizens of the European Community and related documents*, European Parliament, 1979.

[5] *The situation of women in the European Community*, European Parliament, 1981.

[6] *Forging ahead: thirty years of the European Parliament*, 1982.

[7] *Official journal of the European Communities*, C28, 9 February 1981.

[8] These include *The European Parliament: its powers; The European Parliament; The European Parliament and the wider world* and *Your MEP*.

6

The Library and Documentation Services of the Commission of the European Communities

ERIC GASKELL

Central Library

The Commission Library in its present form dates from 1974. It arose out of a merger that year between the Euratom and the European Economic Community (EEC) libraries (both founded in 1958). This measure was the logical if belated sequel to the creation nine years before of a single Commission of the European Communities to administer the three Communities.

Looking back from the present days of austerity one must be thankful that the Euratom and EEC libraries were able to lay the foundations of strong collections in their respective fields. The merger made them jointly more effective as well as more economical to run. In the years since, steady if recently slower growth has increased the size of the combined stock to about 300,000 volumes, including 2,524 runs of periodicals. Expansion continues, thanks in no small part to the receipt of gifts and exchange publications from various sources.

At the core of the collections lies an almost complete set of official publications issued by the Commission and its sister institutions. These are supplemented by large quantities of documents of the same provenance, and by a wealth of material received from European Community (EC) member states and other inter-governmental bodies such as the United Nations (UN), the International Labour Organization (ILO), the Organization for Economic Cooperation and Development (OECD), the United Nations Educational, Scientific, and Cultural Organization (UNESCO), etc. In addition there are relevant monographs and serials systematically chosen over the years from the various national bibliographies. Together, all these items make up a homogeneous working and research collection of some amplitude to which academics and other types of external reader are increasingly attracted, quite apart from the Commission's own officials and trainees ('stagiaires') who are of course the primary target. Indeed, it is no exaggeration to claim that the Library's stock has an unequalled coverage of literature on the subject of European integration, in all its manifold aspects (economic, political, legal, scientific, linguistic, or other).

SPECIALIZED LIBRARIES

As well as its Central Library, the Commission maintains a network of specialized library/documentation units spread thoughout its services. These function as ports of first call for officials stationed nearby, and also as relay points to the central collections. Such an arrangement is well suited to the conditions of an administration dispersed around several buildings, some of which are a distance apart. It combines the virtues of delegation and centralization insomuch as the libraries function as independent units within the hierarchy of their respective directorates-general, leaving the budget and all processing routines in the hands of the Central Library. In an environment of overlapping interests between directorates-general, in no other way could harmonious and economic acquisition policies be conducted. Nor otherwise would it have been possible to create the existing union catalogues.

AUTOMATED CATALOGUING

Until 1978 these catalogues were of the traditional kind. When automation started that year they were photographed and converted into microfiche for use in cassettes on automatic Bruning readers. This is an acceptable half-way stage to automation for older material. New catalogue entries made since the changeover have been fed into a computerized batch system named ECLAS functioning on a Siemens machine placed at the Commission Computer Centre in Luxembourg. A direct online link using GOLEM software was added in 1982.

It is of interest to note that automation developed erratically. This was no bad thing since it provided an opportunity to prepare minds and unravel technical problems. A particular handicap was that the Library had no computer team of its own, nor machine nearby, assigned to the specific task in hand: both of these facilities were in Luxembourg, which caused frequent visits between there and Brussels for consultations and tests, more on a goodwill than mandatory basis. Another snag was the existence of entrenched divergent cataloguing habits among the multinational staff, not to mention their fear of the unknown. Account also had to be taken of the disparate make-up and wide age-spread of a reader community which consists of Commission officials and trainees plus diverse visitors from outside. Quite clearly there could be no hope of coaxing such a variety of users into a uniform behaviour pattern.

All this explains why a cautious attitude was at first adopted towards automation, and why the batch package was designed first and foremost to produce elegant and easily readable catalogues. These products are today much consulted in the Library. They are also greatly appreciated by the many external libraries, notably European Documentation Centres (EDCs) to which selections are distributed. Supplemented as these catalogues now are by COM fiches and terminals, reference duties in the Library have become more productive and demanding than they were previously.

ECLAS is naturally aimed at all the Commission's services, whether situated in Brussels or Luxembourg, not just merely at visitors who call personally or telephone to the Central Library's premises. With this in view courses are being held at present to enable the directorate-general librarian/documentalists to search the data base from terminals in their immediate surrounds. The same facility will be taken up by the European Parliament, Council, Court of Justice, and the College of Europe in Bruges. There is also a scheme afoot to help services create specialized data bases of their own using ECLAS norms. In the longer term it is hoped to make the Library's data base publicly accessible via Euronet.

The worksheet used for ECLAS contains much fewer partitions and less use of blocking symbols than does the MARC format; this simplification was decided upon in order to reduce editorial control, the Library having no higher grade chief cataloguer to undertake this task. There are nineteen fields in all, one of which (12) fuses a number of main elements from other fields to form the main entry that is printed in the various catalogues. Regularly updated, these fields are grouped according to:

— author/title (fields 9, 10, 11);
— descriptor (field 7);
— broad subject group (field 8);
— country and region (parenthetic code in field 8);
— form or characteristic, such as 'dictionary', 'European Community publication', 'statistical publication', etc. (field 6);
— periodical or serial (fields 6 and 16);
— and diverse other elements.

Further products of the batch mode are occasional cumulated extracts, made from fields 6, 7 and 8, which are printed and distributed widely as supplements to the Library's *List of additions*[1] (see Figures 1 and 2). Principal among these is the *Catalogue of EC publications and documents*.[2]

As concerns the online mode, Boolean searches may be made within particular fields or by combinations of them, with the possibility of locating subjects by descriptor (field 7), subject group and country (field 8), or natural

94

Figure 1

Specimen page from the Library's *List of additions*, items arranged by main groups

burgo: Partito Popolare europeo 1982. 102 p.
N 035538
02.02.01   04.20.02
* * *

*Oeuvrer pour l'unification européenne: Politique sociale / Parti populaire européen du Parlement européen. Luxembourg: Parti populaire européen 1982. 109 p.
N 035536   cote:EU8/01332
02.02.01   04.20.02
* * *

*Op weg naar de europese integratie: Sociaal beleid / Europese Volkspartij van het Europese Parlement. Luxemburg: Europese Volkspartij 1982. 108 p.
N 035539   cote:EU8/01335
02.02.01   04.20.02
* * *

*Working towards European unification: Social policy / European People's Party of the European Parliament. Luxembourg: European People's Party 1982. 100 p.
N 035540   cote:EU8/01336
02.02.01   04.20.02
* * *

02.03   SECURITE SOCIALE

*Conservation des droits en matière de sécurité sociale / Genève: BIT 1983. 101 p.
=Conférence internationale du travail. 1983/69. Rapport 05
N 034958   ISBN 92-2-203131-8   cote:IN8/01495
02.03.01
* * *

*Maintenance of rights in social security / Geneva: ILO 1983. 101 p.
=International labour conference. 1983/69. Report 05
N 034959   ISBN 92-2-101131-4   cote:IN8/01496
02.03.01
* * *

03.01   RECHERCHE ECONOMIQUE. SCIENCE ECONOMIQUE

*The book of CHAC. Programming studies for Mexican agriculture / Ed. by Roger D. Norton and Leopoldo Solis. World Bank, Baltimore (etc.): Hopkins University Press 1983. XX, 602 p.
N 035591   ISBN 0-8018-2585-7   cote:IN8/01533
07.01.01(72)   03.01.02(72)
* * *

*Economic analysis of agricultural projects / J. Price Gittinger. World Bank. 2nd ed. rev. and exp. Baltimore (etc.): Hopkins University Press 1982. XXI, 505 p. Bibliogr. pp. 445-455
N 035593   ISBN 0-8018-2913-5   cote:IN8/01535
07.01.02(31)   03.01.02(31)
* * *

*Evaluating the reliability of macro-economic models. Papers presented at the International Symposium on Criteria for Evaluating the Reliability of Macro-economic Models, held Dec. 16-18, 1980, Pisa, Italy, org. by the IBM Scientific Center of Pisa / Ed. by Gregory C. Chow, Paolo Corsi. Chichester (etc.): Wiley 1982. VII, 315 p. Bibliogr.   ISBN 0-471-10150-8
N 035419   cote:83A/00481
03.01.02
* * *

*Indicator systems for political, economic, and social analysis / Ed. by Charles Lewis Taylor; Science Center Berlin, International Institute for Comparative Social Research. Cambridge, Mass.: Dalgeschlager, Gunn & Hain (etc.) 1980. X, 242 p.
=Publication of the Science Center Berlin. 22
N 035033   ISBN 0-89946-031-3   cote:83A/00354
03.01.02   05.01.02   04.20.00
* * *

*Is the bargaining theory still an effective framework of analysis for strike patterns in Europe? / By Alessandre Venturini. Florence: EUI 1983. 51 p. Bibliogr. pp. 49-51
=EUI Working Papers. 46
N 035573   cote:EU4/01385
13.06.00(4.10)   03.01.02(4.10)
* * *

*Mathematics for economists. An integrated approach / E. Roy Weinraub. Cambridge (etc.): Cambridge Univ. Press 1982. XXI, 130 p. Bibliogr. pp. 177-178
N 035524   ISBN 0-521-24535-4   cote:83A/00364
18.08.00   03.01.02
* * *

*Modern macroeconomic theory an overview / Jean-Paul Fitoussi. Florence: EUI 1982. 47 p. Bibliogr. pp. 39-47
=EUI working papers. 34
N 034933   cote:EU4/01300
03.01.01
* * *

*Regional development modeling: theory and practice / by Murat Aibagov (e.a.). Amsterdam (etc.): North-Holland 1982.
=Studies in regional science and urban economics. 08
N 035315   ISBN 0-444-86473-3   cote:83A/00427
03.02.03   02.01.02   03.01.02
* * *

03.02   CONDITIONS ECONOMIQUES

*Binnenland Amsterdam. Onderzoek naar ontwikkelingen in het bedrijfsleven / Kamer van Koophandel en Fabrieken voor Amsterdam, Afd. Regionaal economische beleidsadvisering. Amsterdam 1982. 84 p. Bibliogr. pp. 81-84
N 035273   cote:83B/00046

Figure 2
Specimen page from the Library's *List of additions*, items indexed by descriptors

14.06.00(410)

MOUVEMENTS POLITIQUES - BERLIN / ELITE
* * *
*New protest elites in the political system of West-Berlin: the eclipse of consensus / Dietrich Herzog. Florence: EUI 1982. 31 p. Bibliogr. pp. 28-29
=EUI working papers. 38
N 034937   cote:EU4/01297
04.20.02(430.0)   05.03.05(430.0)

MOYENS DE COMMUNIC. DE MASSE - RFA
cote:83A/00117 SL
*Handbuch der neuen Medien. Information und Kommunikation, Fernsehen und Hoerfunk, Presse und Audiovision heute und morgen / Dietrich Ratzke. Stuttgart: Deutsche Verlags-Anstalt 1982. 688 p.
=(SL 659.3)
N 035265   ISBN 3-421-02728-5
05.07.04(430.1)
* * *

MULTINATIONALES - AMER. LAT.   cote:83A/00051
*Transnational corporations in Latin America. Interactions between nation states and transnational corporations: the case of German and Swiss firms operating in Colombia Brazil and Mexico / Jean-Max Baumer, Kindrecht von Gleich (e.a.). Institut fuer Iberoamerika-Kunde, Hamburg. Diessenhofen: Ruegger 1982. X, 175 p. Bibliogr.
=Buchreihe / Institut fuer Lateinamerikaforschung St. Gallen
Entwicklungszusammenarbeit an der Hochschule St. Gallen fuer Wirtschafts- und Sozialwissenschaften. 25
N 035042   ISBN 3-7253-0157-3
12.01.00(080)
* * *

MULTINATIONALES - PAYS EN DEVEL. / COMMERCIALISATION
cote:IN4/01357
*Aspects juridiques de la création d'entreprises multinationales de commercialisation entre pays en développement / ONU CNUCED. New York: ONU 1982. VI, 81 p.
=(TD/B/C.7/28/Rev.1)
N 034976
12.01.00(31)   09.03.01(31)
* * *

cote:IN4/01358
*Juridical aspects of the establishment of multinational marketing enterprises among developing countries / UNO UNCTAD, New York: UNO 1982. V, 81 p. (TD/B/C.7/28/Rev.1)
N 034977
12.01.00(31)   09.03.01(31)
* * *

MULTINATIONALES - RFA / CODE DE CONDUITE   cote:82A/01537
*Internationale Verhaltensregeln fuer Private. Voelkerrechtliche und verfassungsrechtliche Aspekte. / Brun-Otto Bryde. Frankfurt/M.: Metzner 1981. XI, 125 p. Bibliogr. pp. 69-76
=Veroeffentlichungen aus dem Institut fuer Internatio-

nale Angelegenheiten der Univ. Hamburg. 10
N 035264   ISBN 3-7875-1910-6
05.04.01(430.1)   12.01.00(430.1)
* * *

MULTINATIONALES / INVESTISSEMENTS INTERNATIONAUX   cote:IN8/01510
*Investment incentives and disincentives and the international investment process / OECD. Paris: OECD 1983. 249 p.
=Titre de couv.supplémentaire: International investment
N 034945   ISBN 92-64-12400-4
12.01.00   11.03.03
* * *

cote:IN8/01509
*Les stimulants et obstacles à l'investissement et le processus d'l'investissement international / Paris: OCDE 1983. 287 p.
=Titre de couv. supplémentaire: Investissement international et entreprises multinationales.
N 034944   ISBN 92-64-22400-9
12.01.00   11.03.03
* * *

MUTATIONS DE PROPRIETE - RU / LEGISLATIONS   cote:83J/00357
*Ruoff & Roper on the law and practice of registered conveyancing / Theodore B.F. Ruoff, Robert B. Roper. 4th ed London: Stevens 1979. LXIX, 1101 p.
=Property and conveyancing library. 05
N 035320   ISBN 0-420-45150-1
03.03.05(410)   04.07.00(410)
* * *

NATIONALISATIONS / DROIT INTERNATIONAL   cote:RF/00070 82
*Contrats d'Etat et nationalisation: les apports de la sentence arbitrale du 24 mars 1982 / Philippe Kahn. (Journal du droit international. Année 109. No 4. Octobre-décembre 1982. pp. 844-909).
N 035663   01.02.04
03.03.05
* * *

NIVEAU DE VIE - ZAMBIE / PLANS NATIONAUX   cote:83A/00410
*National development plans and the standard of living in black Africa: the Zambian case / Emil Katona. Budapest: Institute for World Economics of the Hungarian Academy of Sciences 1982. 113 p.
=Studies on developing countries. 111
N 035328   ISBN 963-301-099-3
02.01.02(689.4)   03.02.05(689.4)
* * *

NON-PROLIFERATION / ARMES NUCLEAIRES   cote:83A/00367
*World nuclear energy. Toward a bargain of confidence / Ed by Ian Smart. Royal Institute of International Affairs Baltimore (etc.): John Hopkins Univ. Press 1982. XIV, 394 p.   ISBN 0-8018-2652-7
N 035309 p.
08.11.03   01.02.06

language, using field 6 to highlight a number of other characteristics such as whether an item emanates from or deals with the European Communities.

THESAURUS INDEXING

With the changeover to automation it was found necessary to introduce thesaurus indexing in place of the complex and cumbersome UDC. The scheme chosen for this purpose was the OECD *Macrothesaurus*. It had several advantages in the stated context. Firstly, there was the fact that it was under revision. Secondly, there was an obvious overlap between the OECD's and the Communities' main areas of interest. Another attraction was that it existed in French, English and Spanish. Fourthly, it had an inbuilt classified notational structure (nineteen groups each subdivided by facets) which were almost tailor-made for the production of subject catalogues. A further point in its favour was that the International Labour Office used it, with small variations. In the event, the Commission Library has proceeded further along the road of modification and enlargement in order to satisfy local requirements, such as new groups for the European Communities (01.05-01.11) and remodelling of group 04 (law, politics and public administration). Beyond that, the *Macrothesaurus* is naturally in continuous revision by the Library. It contains at present 8,000 French descriptors, which is three times more than the original. It exists in alphabetical, permuted and classified forms, and is in the course of being translated into Italian, German and English (copies can be supplied on demand).

On this same point we may note that the European Parliament's Library has evolved a specialized thesaurus of its own, partly from the Commission Library and OECD input. This work has been accomplished with the help of DG XIII's computer programme ASTUTE. Arising from this, the Office for Official Publications recently sponsored a related multilingual thesaurus named EUROVOC,[3] to which the Commission Library made a significant contribution. It is due to appear soon in printed form and will be used primarily for indexing the *Official journal*.

It will be realized from the above paragraph that the Commission Library has interests in common with other departments. A good instance is its friendly relationship with the service in DG X responsible for coordinating the European Documentation Centres (EDCs): this link explains the Library's presence at national meetings called between DG X and the EDC documentalists, and its responsibility for editing the *EDC/DEP bulletin*. We may also mention its advisory role as a member of the Publications Committee: apart from bringing library expertise to bear, this activity creates useful contacts and leads to the unearthing of information that smooths daily working in the Library itself.

Central Documentation Service (SCAD)

The closest of all liaisons is that maintained with the Central Documentation

Service (SCAD). Administratively separate from the Library since 1972, SCAD maintains a central file and enquiry office placed fairly close to the former's reading rooms. Annual input to the file is about 13,000 entries for periodical articles (most of them in the Library's holdings), plus COM and SEC documents, European Parliament reports, directives, regulations, etc., and items in the *Official journal*. The foregoing are announced in a weekly *Documentation bulletin* (see Figure 3), edition B of which cumulates selections of material on particular themes. Until quite recently the *Bulletin* was compiled by manual methods, but from No. 26 of 1983 onwards it is achieved by automation, though with the same appearance and format as before. A useful new feature is indexes in French using descriptors from the Library's thesaurus.

Integrated Information Systems (SII)

The Library also works closely with the above division (known by its French acronym) which has responsibility for an important family of data bases, most of them reserved for internal use. This work is done in an essentially decentralized way. That is to say, input of data is made by a network of 'information officers' (aided by 'correspondents' and a band of student 'analysts' on short-term contracts) placed in the different directorates-general. These people meet regularly with the central SII control team to coordinate ideas and working practices. They carry out online searches in their respective data-rooms, one of which is situated in the Central Library.

The SII data bases are as follows:

ECO 1

Covers internal documents of a functional and inter-institutional nature created as part of the decision-making process (e.g. working documents of the Commission, studies written under contract by outside bodies, parliamentary questions, Council decisions, minutes of Commission meetings).

PRC

Fed in by the Secretariat-General, this data base records progress of Commission proposals and communications to Council.

ACTU

Makes daily updatings on written procedures etc., and on documents issued by the Secretariat-General.

ASMODEE

Chronicles the application of directives by and within the member states.

Figure 3
Specimen page from SCAD's *Documentation bulletin*

SOZIALE ANGELEGENHEITEN / SOCIAL AFFAIRS / AFFAIRES SOCIALES

SCD-84/05-B/0040
Wad, Peter

Industrialisering og fagbevägelse i Malaysia.

(DEN NY VERDEN. København. 17. årg. Nr. 2/3. 1983. s. 113-157. Tab. Bibliogr;)

Artiklen forsøger at vise, hvordan industrialiserings- og organiseringsprocessen er integrerede størrelser i den malaysiske udviklingskamp, og forfatteren fremhäver, at en stärk og samlet fagbevägelse er en forudsäcning for at omdkanne økonomisk väkst til økonomisk udvikling.
MF-33766

SCD-84/05-B/0042
Waterman, Peter

Internationale arbejderstudier i socialdemokratiernes højborg: Ideer, indtryk og overvejelser.

(DEN NY VERDEN. København. 17. årg. Nr. 2/3. 1983. s. 193-213. Bibliogr.)

Der foregår i dag en nyudvikling inden for internationale arbejdsstudier i de skandinaviske lande.
Forfatteren beskriver den forskning og de uddannelses- og udgivelsesprogrammer, der eksisterer på dette felt i Skandinavien.
MF-33768

SCD-84/05-B/0047
Groenendijk, C.A.

Recht tegen rassendiscriminatie op de arbeidsmarkt.

(SOCIAAL MAANDBLAD ARBEID. Alphen aan den Rijn. Jaarg. 38. No. 11. November 1983. p. 660-672)

Onderzoek naar discriminatie van leden van etnische minderheidsgroepen op de arbeidsmarkt in Nederland.
MF-33875

SCD-84/05-B/0049
Haank, D.J.; Kasper, J.D.P.

Arbeidsduurverkorting in de praktijk.

(MAANDSCHRIFT ECONOMIE. Deventer. Jaarg. 47. No. 11. 1983. p. 459-472)

Werkgelegenheid. Overcapaciteit en behoud van werkgelegenheid door arbeidsduurverkorting. Kosten. Bedrijfstijd. Onderzoeksresultaten.
MF-33868

SCD-84/05-B/0041
Wangel, Arne

ILO-konventioner og eksportindustrialisering;.

(DEN NY VERDEN. København. 17. årg. Nr. 2/3. 1983. s. 158-192. Tab. Bibliogr.)

Gennem 70erne rejstes spørgsmålet om at gøre handelsliberalisering over for u-landenes industrivarer betinget af en overholdelse af de mest grundläggende ILO-konventioner. Den såkaldte "socialklausul" afvises imirdlertid kategorisk af u-landene. Artiklen diskuterer indholdet i dette politik-forslag og belyser samtidig virkemåden i systemet af "internationale arbejdsnormer", som er fastlagt gennem vedtagelsen af konventioner i Den internationale Arbejdsorganisation (ILO). Endelig påpeges det, at ekspertkredse i ILO og EF som alternativ til en socialklausul overvejer, hvorledes virkeliggørelsen af de vigtigste internationale arbejdsnormer kan fremmes som en integreret del af et udviklingssamarbejde.
MF-33767

SCD-84/05-B/0046
Bakels, H.L.

Om de grenzen van de verboden arbeidsbemiddeling (Nederland).

(SOCIAAL MAANDBLAD ARBEID. Alphen aan den Rijn. Jaarg. 38. No. 11. November 1983. p. 651-659)

De Arbeidsbemiddelingswet 1930. Legitimiteit van de arbeidsbemiddeling met winstoogmerk. Rechtspraak betreffende het begrip arbeidsbemiddeling.
MF-33874

SCD-84/05-B/0048
Van Kessel, J.G.F.M.

Cumulatie van inkomen in het Nederlands sociaal-zekerheidsrecht.

(SOCIAAL MAANDBLAD ARBEID. Alphen aan den Rijn. Jaarg. 38. No. 11. November 1983. p. 673-692)

Cumulatie van inkomen in relatie tot de herziening van het stelsel van sociale zekerheid in Nederland.
MF-33876

SCD-84/05-B/0083
Plassard, Jacques

Conjoncture internationale: Entraînements internationaux et spécificités nationales.

(CHRONIQUES D'ACTUALITE DE LA SEDEIS. Paris. T. XXIX. No.11. 15 novembre 1983. p.442-454. Graph.)

Etude de la situation et des perspectives de l'économie mondiale: la stabilisation des prix sur les marchés internationaux a permis de ralentir la hausse des prix internes; La reprise de l'expansion économique n'est ni générale ni vigoureuse; en Europe, on constate dans tous les pays, un plafonnement du chômage.
MF-33715

CELEX

A rich data base on Community law made up of the following sectors:
— the treaties setting up the European Communities and subsequent amending ones (full text in French, German and English — other languages to follow);
— derived and complementary Community law;
— case-law of the Court of Justice (full text);
— questions and answers at the European Parliament;
— Commission proposals; opinions and documents of the European Parliament; opinions of the Economic and Social Committee;
— national measures implementing EC legislation (see also ASMODEE file above);
— decisions of national courts;
— a selection of published doctrine relating to Community law.
CELEX can be searched via Euronet by subscription to the host EURIS.

Statistical Office data bases

CRONOS contains more than a million statistical time series grouped in about thirty categories such as 'foreign trade', 'national accounts', 'energy', etc. Its complex structure can be searched with reasonable ease by means of a device called 'CADOS ('Statistical document catalogue'), which employs keywords to lead the user to countries and periods.

COMEXT and SIENA give monthly data for the past eighteen months (plus the eight preceding quarters) with respect to imports and exports between member states and 200 partner countries, expressed in values and quantities for goods codified by NIMEXE.

A useful source of information on statistical data banks and prospects for them is the special issue of *Eurostat news* published in 1982.

ECHO data bases

Over the last ten years Directorate-General XIII ('Information Market and Innovation') has made signal achievements in the field of automated documentation. Its greatest success is Euronet-Diane, the communications network through which more than 300 data bases may be accessed from different points in Europe. This vast operation involves about forty host companies, one of which (ECHO) is run by the European Commission itself. The data bases managed there (accessible free of charge except for line fees) are:

EABS

This is the online version of DG XIII's periodical *Euro abstracts* where references are given to published results (EUR numbered reports)[4] of scientific and technical research programmes conducted or sponsored by the Commission (fields covered include coal and steel, nuclear and other sources of energy, the environment). Accessible also in the form of synoptic frames over national viewdata services.

ENDOC

A directory of more than 500 environmental documentation centres, input coming from the member states. A printed version, *ENDOC directory*, is updated every two years.

ENREP

A directory of environmental research projects in more than 1,500 establishments. It is indexed by a multilingual descriptor system. Contents are printed in the *ENREP directory*.

AGREP

An inventory of agricultural research projects conducted in member states. Here again data are fed in nationally and managed centrally in Luxembourg, whilst there is also an annual printed version published by the Commission.

EURODICAUTOM

This vast multiple access 'open' dictionary (compiled by the Terminology Office)[5] contains 370,000 terms and contextual phrases as well as over 90,000 abbreviations. It is invaluable to translators as a means of winning them more time to develop the stylistic aspects of their work; it also ensures the necessary concordance of vocabulary for use within the Community institutions. Printed mini-glossaries are turned out by batch mode. Online information comes in the form of:
— monoterms or multiterms filled out by definitions as fixed in illustrative contexts;
— monoterms or multiterms with their equivalents in other languages;
— equivalents of sentences or phrases in several languages.
  A related project is SYSTRAN (an automated translating system).

Other data bases

AGRIS

An international information system (akin to AGREP) for the agricultural sciences, compiled by the Commission in concert with member states, management of which is in the hands of the Food and Agriculture Organization (FAO). Hosted by DIMDI (Deutsches Institut für Medizinisches Dokumentation und Information).

SDIM

A metallurgical data base to which input is mainly by Britain, France and Germany, plus a certain amount by the Commission. Hosted by INKA (Informationssystem Karlsruhe).

SIGLE

Launched recently, this 'System for Information on Grey Literature produced in Europe' acts as an online document supply system over a range of twenty-two scientific and technical subject fields. There are plans to extend coverage to the social sciences and humanities. Input from national centres is processed into an international machine-readable format identical with that used in AGRIS. An automatic order system provides document delivery on a decentralized basis. Hosted by INKA (soon BLAISE also).

References and notes

[1] The *List* appears monthly; there have been supplements so far on theses, dictionaries, statistical publications, European Community matters and the labour market.

[2] The *Catalogue* appears in an annual updating followed in the year after by three supplements. It contains references to: official publications (i.e. those announced in the sales catalogue); a selection of non-legislative COM documents (e.g. memoranda) and reports of European Parliament committees; some documents put out by the directorates-general; some writings by Commission officials; and articles from periodicals judged substantial enough for adding to the base. From 1985 the *Catalogue* will be renamed *Recent Publications on the European Communities*.

[3] V. Lazzeri, 'Eurovoc', *Terminologie*, 44, 1983, pp. 31–36.

[4] A *Catalogue of EUR documents 1968–1979* was recently published as a volume in the series *Information management* (1983, EUR 7500). Another related newly established documentary source is the periodical *European environmental science synopses: a summary guide to the non-conventional literature on environmental science*, published for the Commission by D. Reidel Publishing Company of Dordrecht (Holland) and Boston (USA).

[5] Articles on the Commission's terminological projects may be found in the bulletin *Terminologie* (an official publication) and in the periodical *Multilingua* published under Commission auspices by Mouton Publishers of Amsterdam, Berlin and New York.

Part Two

Sources of European Communities
Information and Their Use

7

Parliament and the European Communities

DERMOT ENGLEFIELD

Introduction

The European Communities Act 1972 is a short statute running to just twelve clauses and four schedules — a mere thirty-six pages in all. Considering its significance, not least in its effect on Parliament, each word must be of quite unusual significance.

The European Communities Bill was introduced by the British Government to enable it to carry out its obligations under the treaty of accession to the European Communities, which Prime Minister Heath signed in January 1972. Treaties do not need to be ratified by Parliament but, as in the case of this one, their consequences may require legislation.

Short as the European Communities Bill was, the debate on it was a prolonged one. After its introduction on 25 January 1972, the second reading (the debate on its principle) was held over three days, 15–17 February, an exceptionally long period. Then, because it was a bill of constitutional significance it was not referred to a standing committee; the committee stage was taken in the House of Commons itself, with eight days between 29 February and 26 April being spent just on clause one and the beginning of clause two. So slowly were things going that the Government had to introduce an 'allocation of time on committee stage' motion, that is, to insist on a timed programme for the bill. Discussion of this motion took a further day, 2 May. There then followed a further twelve days of debate on the committee stage before the House of Commons gave it a third reading on 6 July. It was debated a further nine days in the House of Lords and finally received the Royal Assent on 17 October 1972. It had dominated life at Westminster throughout the year.

The effect of the Act was profound. Firstly, it altered United Kingdom (UK) law where it conflicted with European Community (EC) law. (Legislation may be necessary when international treaties are entered into.) Secondly, it empowered the Government to carry out existing and future Community directives through delegated legislation. Thirdly, it legalized the application of existing Community regulations to the United Kingdom. Fourthly, it legalized the application of future Community regulations to the United Kingdom. What was strange about this last point was the 'acceptance in advance as part of the law of the United Kingdom of provisions to be made in the future by instruments issued by the Community institutions — a situation for which there is no precedent in this country'.[1] 'No precedent in this country' — is it surprising that Parliament and its members were troubled by it all? It was not of course just the legal and constitutional implications of the bill that caused worry and hence prolonged debate. There were deep political divisions about joining the European Community but this political question is not the subject of this chapter.

As a result of the Act, the British Parliament had to accept that some of its legislative powers had been taken away and transferred to the European Communities, especially to the Council of Ministers. Naturally, therefore, Members of Parliament required the Government of the day, and especially its ministers who are responsible to Parliament, to keep it thoroughly informed concerning Community matters, and also to return to Parliament regularly in order to hear its views and to receive the advice that either House might offer. Ministers, on the other hand, were involved in legislating through private negotiation in the Council and therefore needed a reasonably free and flexible hand, especially on smaller matters, to enable them to bargain. However, on major matters, the view of Parliament might be a useful aid to ministers in their negotiations. Clearly, in connection with our joining the European Communities the compromise needed to be struck as between the power of the Government and the power of Parliament. In the course of the debates on the bill this new constitutional landscape was sketched out.

Faced, therefore, with this unprecedented situation both Houses of Parliament reacted in the traditional way. They each set up a select committee to examine the problem, take evidence and report back with recommendations as to what should be done.

House of Commons Select Committees

THE FOSTER COMMITTEE

On 21 December 1972, just ten days before Britain actually joined the European Communities, the House of Commons set up a Select Committee under Sir John Foster 'to consider procedures for scrutiny of proposals for European Community Secondary Legislation'. In February 1973 a speedy interim report[2] was made which recommended that in the case of legislative proposals sent from the Commission to the Council, the Government should furnish the House of Commons with a statement that included:

(1) The general effect of the document, and its title.

(2) The U.K. ministry which takes primary responsibility, indicating where appropriate what other ministries have substantial but subsidiary responsibility.

(3) The effect which the proposed instrument would have on U.K. law and what supplementary and/or additional legislation would be introduced if the instruments were made; Your Committee is of opinion that responsibility for this part of the statement should be placed on the Law Officers.

(4) The policy implications of the document, including the effects on existing governmental practice.

(5) Whether the proposal awaits consideration by any other Community body (in particular the European Assembly or the Economic and Social Committee), and the date on which it is likely to be considered by the Council of Ministers, to any extent that this is known.

(6) Any other information which Her Majesty's Government may wish to add.

In addition, to keep the House informed more generally and to set the proposals in context, the Committee recommended that the Government should provide additional information as follows:

(A) There should be published well in advance a monthly list giving the possible agenda of forthcoming meetings of the Council of Ministers, or if this is impossible, at least a monthly list of subjects likely to be dealt with at the next meeting of the Council. It is true that the formal agenda of the Council of Ministers is not known even to the participants themselves until a day or two before they meet, but the Committee felt that such a list each month would be, even if only provisional, of great assistance to Members.

(B) A monthly statement in the House should be made by the Chancellor of the Duchy to accompany the list in (A), on which he could then be questioned. The statement would give Members the opportunity of eliciting what the forthcoming events in the Council would entail.

(C) The Chancellor of the Duchy, or if the subject warrants it, a particular Minister, should make a regular report to the House after each month's meeting of the Council of Ministers, similar to the statements made on a regular basis during the course of the pre-accession negotiations.

(D) Ministers engaged in negotiations at Community institutions should report regularly to the House of Commons, if their negotiations are of sufficient importance.[4]

On 18 April 1973 the first Foster Committee report was debated and a number of the proposals were accepted.[5]

On 25 October 1973 the second Foster Committee report was laid before the House.[6] With greater time to reflect, the Committee tried to grasp the central issue. Having noted that Council regulations 'take effect immediately as part of the law of the U.K. and prevail over any law of the U.K. which is inconsistent with them' and that Council directives 'place upon Parliament an obligation to make or change the laws of the U.K.'[7] the Committee asserted nevertheless that 'it remains central to the United Kingdom concept and structure of Parliamentary Democracy that control of the law making processes lies with Parliament.'[8]

To meet this new situation the Committee went on to recommend that a Select Committee on European Legislation etc. ('the Scrutiny Committee') be established to sift proposals and select the more important ones for consideration by the House. The task of the Scrutiny Committee would not be 'to debate the reasons for or against a proposal but to give the House the fullest information as to why it considered the particular proposal of importance and to point out the matter of principle or policy which it affects and the changes in U.K. law involved.'[9] The Committee should have the full powers of a select committee and be able to examine ministers and civil servants; it should also be given research support staff.

The Foster Committee made a number of further recommendations designed to keep the House informed about matters relating to the European Communities. Firstly, the Committee thought that the Government should report in writing to Parliament every six months on EC matters; secondly, six days a year should be devoted to EC debates, including two days debating the six monthly reports; and, thirdly, there should be a regular Parliamentary question time period for EC matters. (In practice this is part of the Foreign Office Questions once a month.) Broadly speaking, the House of Commons and the Government accepted the proposals of the Foster Committee and the House of Commons Scrutiny Committee was set up on 7 May 1974 and held its first meeting under the chairmanship of John Davies MP a week later.

THE SCRUTINY COMMITTEE

The Scrutiny Committee faced a severe backlog of work as the United Kingdom had by this time been a member of the European Communities for nearly eighteen months. The Committee made three quick reports and at its fifth meeting it took evidence for the first time. This was from the Rt. Hon. Frederick Peart MP, the then Minister of Agriculture, and from members of the Civil Service. By the summer of 1974 twelve reports had been made. The Scrutiny Committee then made a second special report[10] in which it set down a number of comments, complaints and suggestions for improving the system. For instance, the Government agreed to the Committee's request that they should place in the Vote Office of the House of Commons, which is the organization responsible for distributing papers to Members, on about the 26th day of the month, a paper called 'Estimates of subject headings likely to come up for discussion' in the Council of Ministers during the following month. The Government also agreed to the Committee's suggestion that departmental memoranda should be lodged for a broader range of documents than just draft legislation. Table 1 covers the work of the Scrutiny Committee and indicates the special reports which it has issued on its work, the number of reports it has issued on the draft documents it has considered, and the number of occasions on which it has taken and published oral evidence during the sessions 1974 to 1978–79 inclusive.

Table 1

Reports of the House of Commons Scrutiny Committee 1974 to 1978–79

Session		Special Reports	Reports	Evidence
1974	HC 258	1st		
	HC 258ii	2nd	12	3
1974–75	HC 45	1st		
	HC 234	2nd		
	HC 613	3rd	38	11
1975–76	HC 336	1st	39	12
1976–77	HC 400	1st	32	7
1977–78	HC 642	1st	38	9
1978–79	HC 252	1st	22	4

During these early years the Scrutiny Committee in its special reports made a number of suggestions for improving its work. It requested that the departmental memoranda should include the financial implications of proposals, and from mid–1975 it started to take written evidence. In its thirty-fifth report for the session 1974–75[11] it considered the EC Draft Budget for the first time and reported that the timing was difficult as Members had to consider it during the summer recess. By the next year it was possible for the Scrutiny Committee to consider the Draft Budget and report to the House by 5 July 1976.[12] In its next special report[13] the Committee pressed the Government to update explanatory memoranda when significant amendments were made to draft proposals. It concluded that the Scrutiny Committee was keeping up with the flow of documents from Brussels and noted with satisfaction improvements in the number and timing of debates. However, some problems still remained. These were soon to be considered by the Select Committee on Procedure which was just starting work.

The report of the Select Committee on House of Commons Procedure concerning Public Business was laid before the House on 17 July 1978 and chapter four was concerned with European Communities legislation.[14] The problem for Parliament about Community legislation was set down clearly: 'The practical obstacles stem mainly from the sheer volume of EEC legislation, the complexity of the Communities' own decision-making structure, and the very limited time available for the consideration of many proposals including some of the most important'.[15] However, the Procedure Committee endorsed the way in which the Scrutiny Committee had built up a code of practice during its first few years and reported that 'the work undertaken by the Select Committee on European Legislation, etc., is of a specialised nature which could not easily be devolved on other committees'.[16] It then made two major recommendations in connection with European matters. Firstly, it recommended against any extension of the specific terms of reference of the Scrutiny Committee. Secondly, in connection with its main recommendation, the establishment of a system of departmental select committees which were set up in 1979, it recommended that if any of the new departmental select committees wished to examine draft documents as part of a European dimension to its work, then it should do so. But the Procedure Committee emphasised that the initiative for doing so should rest with the departmental select committee itself.

In the course of its report the Procedure Committee compiled a table, of the work undertaken by the Scrutiny Committee during its first few years 1974 to 1977–78 (see Table 2).

Today, the House of Commons Scrutiny Committee has a membership of 16 and the quorum is 5. The terms of reference are:

> ... to consider draft proposals by the Commission of the European Communities for legislation and other documents published for submission to the Council of Ministers or to the European Council whether or not such documents originate from the Commission, and to report its opinion as to whether such proposals or other documents raise questions of legal or political importance, to give its reasons for its opinion, to report what matters of principle or policy may be affected thereby, and to what extent they may affect the law of the United Kingdom, and to make recommendations for the further consideration of such proposals and other documents by the House.[17]

This means that the Scrutiny Committee has to make a political judgement as to which of the documents laid before it have political or legal implications which should be drawn to the attention of the House itself. It may or may not recommend them for debate but its judgement is not concerned with the merits of what is proposed, just with the implications. The Committee has the normal powers of select committees to send for persons, papers and records, adjourn from place to place and to appoint sub-committees. In practice the Committee receives written evidence regularly and takes oral evidence occasionally. It does

Table 2

Work of the House of Commons Scrutiny Committee 1974 to 1977–78

Session	1974	1974–75	1975–76	1976–77	1977–78
No. of documents deposited	442	796	649	527	313
No. of documents recommended for debate	29	47	116	110	65
No. of documents debated	5	63	82	117	67
No. of debates in House	2	28	28	42	28

not normally have its written evidence printed but when the latter has been reported to the House then a copy is placed in the House of Commons Library for Members to consult and a copy in the House of Lords Record Office, where, with the agreement of the Clerk of the Committee, the public may consult it. Its oral evidence it *does* order to be printed and this is published as a House of Commons Paper.

The Scrutiny Committee very seldom meets outside Westminster and although it has the power to appoint sub-committees, it has been seldom used. Originally, sub-committees were to hold concurrent meetings with the appropriate sub-committee of the House of Lords Select Committee on the European Communities in order that they might take oral evidence together. However, concurrent meetings have only occasionally been held, not least because of the difficulty of taking oral evidence in front of so many Members of both Houses. However, the two Scrutiny Committees keep in close touch in order to avoid duplication of work either by Members or those giving evidence, including taking lengthy oral evidence on the same documents. The Commons Scrutiny Committee takes most of its oral evidence from Government departments and, unlike the House of Lords Committee, has little contact with either the European Commission or MEPs. (Table 3 below indicates that it does not take oral evidence very frequently.)

The meetings of the Committee, which, unless they are actually taking oral evidence, are in private, are normally held weekly. In addition to the chairperson and members, the Committee is assisted by a clerk, a legal adviser, who is one of Mr Speaker's Counsel, and three clerk/advisers. The Committee clerk and the clerk/advisers are part of the Overseas Office in the Department of the Clerk, which also provides the supporting staff, documents, offices, secretaries, etc. The legal adviser is part of the staff of Mr Speaker. The whole Committee works on documentation as, unlike the House of Lords, there is no preliminary sift of proposals by the Chairperson.

The legal adviser is a new post at the House of Commons created since entry into the European Communities. The holder is required to clarify the likely impact on United Kingdom law of proposals from the European Communities. The clerk/advisers are the posts authorized in response to the Foster Committee's second report requesting research support staff for the Committee. Each has a broad Community area of responsibility and for each draft they offer the Committee advice and prepare an advisory brief. The Committee considers, therefore, not only the draft sent by the Commission to the Council, but also the Government explanatory memorandum and the advisory brief prepared by its own staff. It also has the services of its legal adviser and, of course, its clerk.

After each weekly meeting the Committee makes a report to the House of Commons which is printed as a House of Commons paper. The report covers the following points.

(1) It lists proposals raising questions of political (and legal) importance with

recommendations that they should be considered by the House. An analysis based on the evidence and other information available to the Committee is included.

(2) It lists proposals raising questions of political (and legal) importance but with no recommendations for further consideration by the House. As before, the arguments are included in the report.

(3) Sometimes the Committee has recommended that the House should consider a proposal which has subsequently been the subject of further negotiation in Brussels. The minister may then write to the chairperson of the Committee explaining that its points have been met. Then the Committee may withdraw or reiterate its recommendation and will explain its decision in the report.

(4) It lists documents and instruments which do not raise questions of legal or political importance. Just a list is given, no explanation.

(5) It lists documents and instruments which have been recommended to the House for further consideration but which have not yet received such consideration. The items on this list are grouped according to the various sponsoring Government departments.

There are usually about thirty to forty such reports every session. The work of the Commons Scrutiny Committee in recent sessions is set down in Table 3.

If the Committee recommends that any drafts should be debated by the House, it is of course so that Parliament may give its views to ministers before they go to Brussels to legislate in the Council. If a debate is recommended then it sometimes takes place in a standing committee,[20] but whether it is debated in such a committee or in the House itself it is on a motion 'that this House takes note of European Community Document Numbers ...'. The motion to debate the matter in standing committee is made by a minister and can be rejected by a minimum of twenty Members signifying their objection.

As already mentioned, the 1978 Procedure Committee recommended that the new departmental select committees being set up might on their own initiative examine draft European documents and make recommendations to the House. Few of the committees have responded to this recommendation, although there is no procedural reason why they should not do so. Pressure of time as the new system of committees settled down, and the fact that there are divided views on membership of the European Communities, in other words the pressure of politics, may partly explain a lack of enthusiasm for taking on this additional work. The experience of other national parliaments in this connection has not been particularly encouraging either. Recently, however, there have been a number of straws in the wind. In session 1981–82 the Social Services Committee included a visit to consult the Commission in Brussels when preparing a report on the age of retirement. In session 1982–83 the Committee on Welsh Affairs examined the impact of EC membership on Wales and visited Brussels before they began to take their evidence.

Table 3

Work of the House of Commons Scrutiny Committee 1979–80 to 1982–83

Consideration of instruments	1979–80[18]	1980–81	1981–82	1982–83[19]
Meetings of the Committee	46	32	30	18
Oral evidence	5	2	4	1
Instruments reported on	963	745	723	461
Instruments reported as raising questions of legal or political importance	340	208	168	161
Instruments recommended for debate	138	81	53	59
Instruments deposited during session but not yet reported on	42	78	32	31
(of which preliminary consideration given to)	15	8	9	—
Debates held				
Instruments undebated at start of session which had been recommended for further consideration by the House	67	61	49	57
Instruments added during session to list of recommendations for debate	138	81	53	60
Instruments withdrawn from list	42	20	10	7
Total of instruments accumulated for debate during session	163	122	92	110
Instruments debated in Chamber	102	66	24	33
Debates held in Chamber	27	22	9	12
Instruments debated in standing committee	—	7	12	—
Debates in standing committee	—	5	10	—
Balance of instruments still awaiting debate at end of session	61	49	57	77

House of Lords Committees

THE MAYBRAY-KING COMMITTEE

Two days before the House of Commons set up the Foster Committee, the House of Lords, on 19 December 1972, set up a Select Committee 'to consider procedures for scrutiny of proposals for European Community Instruments'. The Chairman was Lord Maybray-King who had been Speaker of the House of Commons during the period 1965–70. On 2 March 1973 the Committee issued an interim report [21] which recommended a 'joint sifting committee' consisting of Members of both Houses. No action was taken on this proposal, but the Maybray-King Committee continued to take a great deal of evidence during its twenty-seven sittings. The witnesses included the Librarian of the House of Commons and the author of this chapter, who were questioned on the facilities being prepared in the House of Commons Library with respect to the European Communities and the extent to which they might be made available to the Members of the House of Lords.

In their second report[22] to the House of Lords the Maybray-King Committee, after giving a lucid account of the institutions of the European Communities and their working relationships, recommended a Select Committee on the European Communities ('the Scrutiny Committee') with terms of reference as follows:

> to consider Community proposals, whether in draft or otherwise, to obtain all necessary information about them, and to make reports on those which in the opinion of the Committee raise important questions of policy or principle, and on other questions to which the Committee consider that the special attention of the House should be drawn[23]

The Maybray-King Committee also recommended that the Scrutiny Committee should have the power to appoint sub-committees to deal with specialist fields of Community activity and initially suggested:

Finance, Economics and Regional Policy
Agriculture
External Trade and Treaties
Environment, Social Health and Education
Energy and Transport
Law[24]

The Law Sub-Committee, normally chaired by a Law Lord, was given specific terms of reference, which have been altered to read:

To consider and report to the Committee on:
  a) any Community proposal which would lead to significant changes in

UK law, or have far-reaching implications for areas of UK law other than those to which it is immediately directed;

b) the merits of such proposals as are referred to them by the Select Committee;

c) whether any important developments have taken place in Community law; and

d) any matters which they consider should be drawn to the attention of the Committee concerning the vires of any proposal.[25]

The House of Lords debated the two Maybray-King reports on 6 December 1973, when Lord Shepherd, supporting the appointment of a scrutiny committee, suggested that Parliament had an important role to play in providing 'first of all, the opportunity to influence Ministers; secondly, the acquiring of information and knowledge; and thirdly, the securing of a full appreciation of the consequences of any decisions and proposals'.[26] He thought the Scrutiny Committee's work would help in this connection.

At the end of the debate it was agreed that a scrutiny committee should be established. However, the Government supported rather narrower terms of reference than those proposed in the Maybray-King report and the subject was referred to the Procedure Committee. Shortly after the Christmas recess, on 30 January 1974, the Procedure Committee reported,[27] supporting the terms of reference originally proposed by the Maybray-King Committee. It was these terms which were finally agreed and which are used today. The Scrutiny Committee was set up on 10 April 1974 and its membership was announced on 7 May 1974.

THE SCRUTINY COMMITTEE AND ITS SUB-COMMITTEES

The method of work agreed was that the chairperson of the Scrutiny Committee would make a first sift of proposals and divide them into two groups. List 'A' would consist of proposals which, in the opinion of the chairperson, would not require the attention of the Scrutiny Committee. List 'B' would consist of proposals which the chairperson thought should be looked at by sub-committees of the Scrutiny Committee and which they might recommend to the Scrutiny Committee for debate in the House. The Maybray-King Committee had thought that about 5% of proposals would find their way into list 'B' for further scrutiny, but in the early months it was more like 33%. In the period 1975–76, 28% appeared on list 'B' and during the session 1982–83 the figure was 31%. For the period from 1974 to 27 January 1984 there were 4,525 in the 'A' list and 2,476 in the 'B' list.

From the beginning, the sub-committees, which occasionally meet jointly, have sought witnesses not just from the Government but also from outside organizations. Oral evidence is normally taken in public and is usually published. In the early years, evidence to sub-committees was sometimes published as separate House of Lords papers, but in recent years it has usually been published with the report of the Scrutiny Committee. Sometimes, however, separate volumes of minutes of evidence are published when evidence is copious. In taking evidence the sub-committees have spread their net far wider than the House of Commons. MEPs, Commissioners, officials from the Council and the Commission, judges, advocates-general and others from the Court of Justice have all been invited to give evidence.

The House of Lords Scrutiny Committee is more sparing in its recommendations of proposals for debate in the House of Lords than is the House of Commons Committee, and it has a category of reports made to the House 'for information' only. A complete list of reports prepared by the Select Committee since 1974 is published as an annex to the *Progress of Scrutiny* report (see below) every six months.

Since the beginning of session 1976–77 the Scrutiny Committee has published a fortnightly report on its work, with proposals listed in the following groups:

List A: proposals thought not to require special attention (the 'A' list)

List B: proposals which have been remitted to sub-committees either for information or for further consideration (the 'B' list). These are listed by the sub-committees to which they have been referred.

List C: proposals which have been considered by sub-committees but are not to be reported upon.

List D: proposals reported for the information of the House.

List E: reports to the House of proposals for debate, including reports debated since ... and those awaiting debate.

At the beginning of 1979 the name of this paper was changed to *Report of progress of scrutiny*, but it continued as one of the numbered reports of the Scrutiny Committee. From the beginning of the session 1980–81, however, as an economy measure, this routine information has been prepared on a word processor and brought out as a paper which is no longer a report of the Scrutiny Committee and therefore no longer a numbered House of Lords paper. It contains the same information however. It is obtainable from Her Majesty's Stationery Office (HMSO) but only together with a complete set of the reports of the Scrutiny Committee.

Today, the membership of the Scrutiny Committee stands at 25, together with some 72 further co-opted members. Much of its work is done in one of its seven sub-committees. These are:

A Finance, Economics and Regional Policy (17 members)
B External Relations, Trade and Industry (18 members)
C Education, Employment and Social Affairs (14 members)
D Agriculture, Food and Consumer Affairs (13 members)
E Law (13 members)
F Energy, Transport, Technology and Research (15 members)
G Environment (10 members)

Sub-committees normally meet either fortnightly or weekly and the main Committee meets regularly once a fortnight.

The staff of the Scrutiny Committee consists of six clerks, about a quarter of the complement of Clerks of the House of Lords, a legal adviser, who is second counsel to the Chairman of Committees, a legal assistant and eight supporting staff. Unlike the House of Commons, the Scrutiny Committee makes considerable use of specialist advisers who are hired for specific enquiries, though some continue to advise specific sub-committees over a number of years on a variety of subjects.

Table 4 outlines the work of the Scrutiny Committee, work which includes fairly regular consideration of the European Communities' Budget.

Table 4

Work of the House of Lords Scrutiny Committee

Session	*Drafts considered*	*Reports*	*Reports for debate*	*Reports debated*
1974–75	884	37	21	21
1975–76	959	63	35	21
1976–77	620	50	30	20
1977–78	819	46	17	10
1978–79	442	13	7	6
1979–80	1101	50	24	22
1980–81	809	30	16	19
1981–82	800	21	12	15
1982–83	492	10	6	5

NB: From session 1978–79 the figures for reports on drafts is confined to substantive reports and does not include routine ones.

If we examine the more recent reports of the Scrutiny Committee in detail, it is clear that they are quite different from those of the House of Commons Scrutiny Committee. The latter, as we have seen, has specific terms of reference which result in regular reports covering, briefly, a large number of documents. When making their scrutinies, Lords sub-committees consciously group drafts if they can. Table 5, which lists the Scrutiny Committee reports for session 1981–82, together with their titles and the pagination of both the reports (in roman numbers) and of the evidence (in arabic), makes it clear that the Lords reports and evidence are more general, far longer and are themselves important additions to the literature of the subject. They are, in short, much more like traditional select committee reports. They cover about 10% of the proposals first put before the chairperson of the Scrutiny Committee.

The length of time that the House of Lords devotes to debating recommended draft legislation and consultative documents is rather more than the House of

Table 5

Reports of the House of Lords Scrutiny Committee Session 1981–82

Report No.	Title and HL Paper	No.	Report	Evidence
1	Combined transport	HL 19	xiipp.	60pp.
2	Agricultural trade policy	HL 29	xxixpp.	177pp.
3	Summer time	HL 41	vipp.	7pp.
4	Annual accounts of banks etc.	HL 42	xvipp.	121pp.
5	Beverage containers	HL 68	xvpp.	108pp.
6	Family benefits	HL 89	xipp.	50pp.
7	State aids to agriculture	HL 90	xxxiipp.	155pp.
8	Competition practice	HL 91	xxxivpp.	81pp.
9	Policies for an oil supply sub-crisis	HL 92	xiiipp.	38pp.
10	Guidelines for European agriculture and the 1982–83 farm price proposals	HL 101	xlviipp.	222pp.
11	Radiation protection	HL 108	xipp.	66pp.
12	Revision of the European Regional Development Fund	HL 126	xxiipp.	81pp.
13	Noise in the environment	HL 175	xxxipp.	76pp.
14	Tractors	HL 189	xipp.	37pp.
15	Natural gas	HL 190	xviipp.	125pp.
16	EEC environment policy: the proposed third action programme	HL 191	xiiipp.	87pp.
17	Internal market: movement of manufactured goods within the EEC	HL 204	xxxpp.	260pp.
18	Group accounts	HL 215	xvpp.	58pp.
19	Voluntary part-time work	HL 216	xxiipp.	164pp.
20	Strategic materials	HL 217	xliiipp.	328pp.
21	Borrowing and lending activities of the European Communities	HL 226	xliipp.	202pp.

Commons, and has amounted to as much as 5% of the sitting time of the House of Lords. Recently, however, it has been more like 2½% and in 1981–82 it was about 24 hours of debate during the session, covering 12 Scrutiny Committee reports. There were in addition a number of minor debates on EC matters. A new development has been the asking of 'unstarred questions' on Scrutiny Committee reports which enables a short debate to take place before the Government spokesperson replies.

Documentation services

The Vote Office of the House of Commons, which is part of the Library Department, is the organization responsible for the distribution of official documents to Members and staff. Before January 1973 small numbers of documents were received from the European Communities, usually in French. However, Parliament's needs changed as soon as the United Kingdom joined. It was decided that all the documentation of the Commission, the Court and the European Parliament should be taken in English and be held for two years. After that period, just an archive would be kept and photocopies would be made when required. Documents now distributed include the *Official journal* and the internal documentation of the European Parliament, which allows Members to keep abreast of the work of that institution. The *Working documents of the European Parliament* provide an insight into the proceedings of parliamentary committees. In order to keep Members up to date with debates in the European Parliament, the 'rainbow' edition of the report on debates, which prints speeches in the languages used in debate, is available in addition to the English language version which appears some weeks later as an *Annex* to the *Official journal*.

Proposals for legislation and consultative documents are made available by the Government through the Cabinet Office. The documents which arrive for Parliament are about 10% of those sent by the Committee of Permanent Representatives (COREPER) in Brussels to the Foreign and Cabinet Offices. They number seven to eight hundred a year out of seven to eight thousand. The Vote Office uses the Council numbers, which start at 4,000 at the beginning of each year. One hundred copies of each document arrive and are listed, together with other Community material, on a Yellow Form distributed to Members each Tuesday and Thursday. A typical Yellow Form might list individual issues of the *Official journal* 'C' and 'L' series, *European Parliament working documents, Minutes of proceedings* and *Debates of the European Parliament*, draft instruments and consultative documents from the Commission, explanatory memoranda prepared by Government departments on draft instruments, and other publications such as *The week in Europe*. Members may order copies of any items listed on the Yellow Form. The Committee Office takes twenty-five copies of draft instruments and consultative documents for the work of the Scrutiny Committee and its staff.

The Vote Office takes two hundred copies of each explanatory memorandum prepared by Government departments on the legal and political implications of Commission proposals for legislation. In order to make such memoranda publicly available arrangements have been made to deposit copies in a small number of major libraries.[28] The Vote Office also receives from the Cabinet Office on about the 26th day of each month a forecast of meetings of the Council of Ministers for the following month. It should also be noted that the list of draft instruments and consultative documents prepared for the

Yellow Form is reproduced in the *House of Commons weekly information bulletin*, prepared by the Library and published by HMSO on Saturdays.

The Printed Paper Office of the House of Lords is the chief source of documentation for that House, and it follows a similar routine, preparing its own list of documents and distributing them to interested Peers. The Printed Paper Office relies on the House of Commons Vote Office to maintain an archive of the documents of the European Communities from which copies can be made. It has recently been decided that the United Kingdom parliamentary archive, which is the responsibility of the House of Lords Record Office and which is housed in the Victoria Tower, will not include European Communities material.

Information services

When the United Kingdom joined the European Communities on 1 January 1973 the House of Commons Library introduced a number of changes in its organization and routines. Until that date Community documentation had been received in French, except for the occasional important item which had been translated into English. Now English was an official language, and a new European Community Desk, manned by two staff, was established within the International Affairs Section to supply oral advice, information and documentation to Members.

During 1972, as the European Communities Bill slowly worked its way through Parliament, a full review was made of the Library's documentation on the European Communities and decisions were taken as to the material which would be required in future. The documents which are currently taken are listed below by organization in order to illustrate that the flow of information from the European Communities institutions, the Government and from the work of Parliament itself, all come together in the resources of the Library.

European Parliament

Minutes of proceedings, Working documents, Verbatim record of proceedings (the 'rainbow' version), *Official handbook, Annex* to the *Official journal* (for debates and oral questions), *Official journal* 'C' series (for written questions, etc.); and *Press notices*.

European Commission

Draft regulations, directives and decisions, Consultative documents, *Directory of the Commission, General report on the activities of the European Communities, Report on competition policy* (annual), *The agricultural situation in the Community* (annual), *Report on social developments* (annual), *Bulletin of the European Communities*, and *Press notices*.

Council of the European Communities

Review of the Council's work (annual), *Official journal* 'L' series, and *Press notices*.

Economic and Social Committee

Bulletin, and *Official journal* 'C' series.

Court of Justice

Record of cases and brief judgements, Reports of cases before the Court, Official journal 'C' series and *Press notices*.

United Kingdom Government

Statements in Parliament (HL and HC *Hansard*), Questions in Parliament (HL and HC *Hansard*), Six-monthly reports (Command papers), and Explanatory memoranda (unpublished).

United Kingdom Parliament

House of Lords: Select Committee on the European Communities: reports and evidence (HL papers), Progress of scrutiny, and Debates on draft legislation and documents (HL *Hansard*).

House of Commons: Select Committee on European Legislation, etc.: reports and evidence (HC papers), Standing Committee on European Community documents (HC Standing Committee Debates), and Debates on draft legislation and documents (HC *Hansard*).

Each of these institutions therefore makes its contribution to what is a new information network resulting from British membership of the European Communities. This has caused the Library to study the ways in which the documents should be analyzed and indexed for Members and for staff working on their behalf.

It was decided to prepare two new visible strip indexes in order to capture this information. The first of these, the European Communities Index, covers material relating to the broad range of Community activities, but excluding draft instruments. Subject entries are given for books, journal articles and the following material prepared by the institutions of the European Communities:

(a)   Consultative documents which communicate information from the Commission to the Council, some of a routine nature and some concerning policy which may require legislation. This includes Budget documents.

(b)   *European Parliament working documents*, which are reports from parliamentary committees on Commission proposals and other subjects. Also included are the motions for resolutions tabled by Members.

(c)   European Parliament *Minutes of proceedings*, from which the actual resolutions are indexed.

(d) The *Official journal* 'C' series for written questions, the *Annex* to the *Official journal* for oral questions, and the *Hansards* of both Houses for relevant debates.

(e) House of Commons and House of Lords Select Committee reports on non-legislative matters, where the Committee recommends that the subject of the report should be debated by either House.

(f) Press releases emanating from the Commission, the Council, the Court of Justice, the European Parliament and the European Investment Bank.

(g) The *Bulletin of the European Communities*, which is a detailed monthly summary of the developments in each main policy area.

(h) A number of other miscellaneous official publications from the European Communities.

From the beginning of 1984 this European Communities Index has been entered into POLIS (the Library's Parliamentary Online Information Service), a computer-based indexing system with its own thesaurus.

The second index is the European Secondary Legislation Index, which covers the history of draft regulations, etc. from their arrival at Westminster until finally promulgated in the *Official journal* 'L' series. This index is in two main sequences. First it is under subject, with cross references to Council document numbers. Secondly, the chronology of draft regulations, etc. is to be found under the numbers, and includes the full range of documents already mentioned. An example follows:

10443/81

Amending Regulation (EEC) No. 724/75 establishing European Development Fund: Council Reg:

26.10.81. EP Doc 735/81	Referred to European Parliament.
3.11.81. 10443/81	Commission to Council 29.10.81.
27.1.81 HC 21-IX	9th report of House of Commons Committee recommending further consideration by the House and
HC 114-ii	Minutes of evidence.
5.4.82. EP Doc 61/82/A&B	Report of European Parliament Regional ... Committee.
6.4.82 HL 126	12th report of House of Lords Committee recommending for 'information only' and minutes of evidence.
22.4.82 EP Mins	Resolution of European Parliament.

30.6.82. HL Deb 432 c.262	Motion on 12th report of House of Lords Committee.
14.9.82 9401/82	Amendment sent from Commission to the Council — 9.9.82.
26.10.82. HC 21-xxx	30th report of House of Commons Committee recommending further consideration by the House.

This entry, which tells the story over a year, shows that on 26 October 1982 the House of Commons had not yet considered the draft amending regulation, which had itself been amended on 14 September 1982. When it is finally agreed and promulgated, then the chronology will conclude with a reference to the *Official journal* 'L' series. From the beginning of 1983 this kind of information on Community legislation has been entered into POLIS. Already the chronology of several hundred draft regulations and other instruments is available as part of this growing data base. Both the European Communities Index and the European Secondary Legislation Index have been merged in the POLIS data base.

While POLIS gathers together and displays much material on the European Communities the Government continues to publish a summary of events, because one of the important recommendations of the Foster Committee was that the Government should report regularly to Parliament concerning the major developments in the Communities. Table 6 sets out the way this has been done since 1974 through Command papers in the European Communities Treaties Series.

The form of the report has not changed greatly over the years, although the House of Lords has pressed the Government for more information under the section 'Parliament'. However, the number of annexes to these reports *has* increased and these also can be helpful. The paper includes a summary of facts under ten main headings, such as Agriculture and Fisheries, Environment and Transport, Energy and Enlargement, External Relations, Trade and Aid. This is followed by annexes listing meetings of the European Council and the Council of Ministers during the period, including the names of UK ministers attending and the date and place; major proposals adopted by the Council, arranged by broad subject; major treaties and agreements made; the dates and occasion of major ministerial speeches made outside the House of Commons and sometimes the texts of speeches made by senior British ministers to the European Parliament. These Command papers are a very handy way of keeping abreast of matters, especially as they are published reasonably promptly following the six-month period.

In this chapter I have outlined the development of a new feature of work at Westminster resulting from the entry of the United Kingdom into the European Communities over a decade ago. But the importance of this new work is not

Table 6

Developments in the European Communities: European Communities Treaty
Series

Period	Treaty No.	Command Paper No.
March–October 1974	No. 40 (1974)	Cmnd. 5790
November 1974–March 1975	Membership of the European Community	Cmnd. 6003
April–October 1975	No. 155 (1975)	Cmnd. 6349
November 1975–April 1976	No. 14 (1976)	Cmnd. 6497
May–November 1976	No. 29 (1976)	Cmnd. 6695
December 1976–June 1977	No. 17 (1977)	Cmnd. 6887
July–December 1977	No. 8 (1978)	Cmnd. 7100
January–June 1978	No. 36 (1978)	Cmnd. 7361
July–December 1978	No. 5 (1979)	Cmnd. 7489
January–December 1979	No. 5 (1980)	Cmnd. 7780
January–June 1980	No. 42 (1980)	Cmnd. 8042
July–December 1980	No. 19 (1981)	Cmnd. 8195
January–June 1981	No. 53 (1981)	Cmnd. 8365
July–December 1981	No. 13 (1982)	Cmnd. 8525
January–June 1982	No. 40 (1982)	Cmnd. 8669
July–December 1982	No. 18 (1983)	Cmnd. 8838
January–June 1983	No. 56 (1983)	Cmnd. 9043
July–December 1983	No. 4 (1984)	Cmnd. 9214

confined to Members in the Palace of Westminster, nor indeed to the triangle of
Westminster, Whitehall and Brussels. It is clear that as a result of this new
dimension to Parliament's work we can all be better informed, not only about
the policies which the Commision and the Council consider appropriate but also
the mechanics by which they are introduced. Parliament has many roles,
including the important one in a democracy of distributing information to the
electorate, either through select committee work, proceedings in the House or
through insisting on the Government laying papers before it 'for information'. It
is right that we should all make use of this work.

References and notes

[1] *Legal and constitutional implications of UK membership of the European Communities*, Cmnd. 3301, para 22, 1967.

[2] *First report from the Select Committee on European Community Secondary Legislation*, 1972–73, HC 143.

[3] Ibid, para 7.

[4] Ibid, para 9.

[5] HC Deb, vol. 855, col. 550–619.

[6] *Second report from the Select Committee on European Community Secondary Legislation*, 1972–73, HC 463 (I–II).

[7] Ibid, para 33.

[8] Ibid, para 36.

[9] Ibid, para 69.

[10] *Second special report from the European Secondary Legislation, etc. Committee*, 1974, HC 258–II.

[11] *Thirty-fifth report from the Select Committee on European Secondary Legislation, etc.*, 1974–75, HC 45–xxxv.

[12] *Twenty-seventh report from the Select Committee on European Secondary Legislation, etc.*, 1975–76, HC 8–xxvii.

[13] *First special report from the Select Committee on European Secondary Legislation, etc.*, 1976–77, HC 400.

[14] *First report from the Select Committee on Procedure*, 1977–78, HC 588 (I–III).

[15] Ibid, para 4.1.

[16] Ibid, para 4.3.

[17] *Standing orders of the House of Commons: public business*, 1982–83, HC 307, Standing Order No. 105.

[18] This session ran from May 1979 to October 1980.

[19] This session ran from November 1982 to May 1983.

[20] The use of standing committees was a proposal in the *First report from the Select Committee on Procedure*, 1974–75, HC 294, paras 36–43. See also *Standing orders of the House of Commons: public business*, 1982–83, HC 307, Standing Order No. 80.

[21] *First report by the Select Committee on Procedures for Scrutiny of Proposals for European Instruments*, 1972–73, HL 67.

[22] *Second report by the Select Committee on Procedures for Scrutiny of Proposals for European Instruments*, 1972–73, HL 194.

[23] Quoted at the beginning of each report.

[24] *Second report by the Select Committee on Procedures for Scrutiny of Proposals for European Instruments*, 1972–73, HL 194, para 113.

[25] *Progress of scrutiny*, D.8-i, 28 June 1983, p. 5.

[26] HL Deb, vol. 347, col. 772.

[27] *First report from the Select Committee of the House of Lords on Procedure of the House*, 1973–74, HL 58.

[28] From May 1982 explanatory memoranda have been sent to the four European Communities Depository Libraries (DEPs) in the United Kingdom, namely, the British Library Reference Division, the British Library Lending Division, the Liverpool and District Scientific, Industrial and Research Library, and the City of Westminster Libraries. Memoranda are also sent to Queen's University, Belfast, the National Library of Wales and the National Library of Scotland.

8

The European Community
and Local Government Information

PAUL BONGERS and ANTHONY CROMBIE

Whatever the impact of British membership of the European Community (EC) on commerce, industry and society in general, the years since 1973 have been marked by a steady growth in the number of sectors of local authority interest in which the European Community has become involved. Increased activity in, and expenditure on, new common policy areas has, in turn, led local authorities to pay greater attention to the European dimension and in many cases to reassess and upgrade their response to it. This chapter begins with a brief description of local government structure in the United Kingdom (UK) and of the ways in which Community membership has impinged upon local government activities and functions. Attention is then focussed on the arrangements that have been made and services that have been provided to satisfy the many information needs that arise from this relationship.

Local government structure and functions

Local government occupies an unusual position in relation to the European Community because of the diversity of its services and the complexity of its structure. In England and Wales there are two major levels of local government, county and district, separated into metropolitan and non-metropolitan areas, with each level and type of area being responsible for different functions. The system in London is different again, with the thirty-two boroughs forming the basic units of local government and the Greater London Council (GLC) being responsible only for those services which, by their nature, require unified administration and control over the whole area. In Scotland the mainland government is also two-level, consisting of nine regions divided into fifty-three districts. The Scottish Islands — the Orkneys, Shetlands and Western Isles — because of their isolation from the mainland, have single, virtually all-purpose authorities. In Northern Ireland local government has had a much reduced role since 1973, taking the form of a single-level structure of twenty-six district authorities with limited functions, with many of the other services being provided by state boards.

The interests of these authorities are represented at the national level by five local authority associations, which, as will be shown, play an important role in the handling of European Community information. The interests of the non-metropolitan county and district authorities in England and Wales are looked after by the Association of County Councils and the Association of District Councils respectively, while the Association of Metropolitan Author-ities is comprised of the metropolitan county and district councils and the London authorities. There are also various groupings of authorities at the regional level, with a restricted range of functions. In Scotland the single association for both regional and district councils is the Convention of Scottish Local Authorities; the representative body for the Northern Ireland district councils is the Association of Local Authorities of Northern Ireland. In turn, these five major local authority associations constitute the British Sections of two international local authority associations, the International Union of Local Authorities (IULA) and the Council of European Municipalities (CEM)[1]. The British Sections, operating through a joint secretariat in London, act as a service unit to the associations on European and international matters.

The individual authorities vary in size, from major metropolitan areas like Greater Manchester and Merseyside to predominantly rural districts. They carry out functions conferred on them by Acts of Parliament, some of which are mandatory and some discretionary. These range from town planning, transport, education, environmental health, the police, the fire service, trading standards, housing, and personal social services, to the provision of public amenities such as libraries, museums, swimming pools and car parks, waste collection and disposal, and the promotion of tourism. The allocation of functions between the different levels of local government is a major determining factor in the impact of the Community on an authority, as the nature and degree of Community involvement varies from service to service. If one also includes the way in which Community legislation affects the internal administration of the local author-ities themselves as complex organizations and major employers of staff in their own right, it is possible to identify, in broad terms, five different ways in which local government is influenced by the Community, although there is inevitably some degree of overlap between the categories.

Local government — the Community dimension

The first area of Community involvement concerns Community legislation governing policy areas for which, in the UK, local government has direct responsibilities. In this instance the local authority is in the front line, whether the Community legislation involved is directly applicable in the UK or whether it has to be incorporated into UK national legislation. To date, Community action of this kind in policy areas regulated by local authorities has been concentrated mainly in the environmental and consumer protection fields. On the environment policy front, the Community has adopted, or is currently considering, legislation on water and air pollution, waste disposal, noise pollution, dangerous substances, and the vexing question of environmental impact assessment. In the consumer protection field, Community action programmes were agreed in 1975 and 1981 and legislation has been adopted within this framework. Attention has focussed on the labelling of foodstuffs, the testing and approval of food additives, the marketing of dangerous substances, safety standards for the slaughter of meat and poultry, and control of dangerous cosmetics. Because of their ultimate involvement in the application of the law, local authorities need to receive early warning of such initiatives, so that they can make the appropriate Community institutions and UK central government aware of any defects in the draft legislation which would lead to problems in its enforcement.

Secondly, Community legislation can actually affect the conditions and manner in which a local authority provides a service for its area. Into this category would come the regulations covering social provisions in respect of road transport, such as drivers' hours and the use of tachographs, which have an impact on the provision of public transport. The requirement that public sector works and supply contracts above a certain value have to be advertised in the *Official journal*, in order to allow companies in other member states the opportunity of tendering for the contracts, is another example, as local authorities which, in the course of operating their services or carrying out infrastructure works, put out contracts to tender, have to abide by these regulations. Community rules may also affect the provision of grants or loans by local authorities to industry in their area, for, as with state aids to industry, this assistance must comply with the Treaty of Rome's requirements on public aid. If it fails to do so, the authority could be obliged to withdraw it.

A third area of Community involvement relates to the way legislation impinges on local authorities as organizations. Overall, local government is one of the largest employers in the UK, and individual authorities are big, complex organizations sharing many of the problems facing any large business. Recent moves in Community legislation towards action in the employment field and on working conditions have meant that this area has now assumed a greater prominence in local authority thinking. The general question of working time has recently been a dominant theme; temporary work, part-time work, flexible retirement and the reduction and reorganization of working time are all policy areas in which the Community is involved. Local authorities would be affected by measures concerned with ensuring the application of the principle of equal opportunities in terms of pensions and superannuation, and it appeared for a time that they could be caught by the 'Vredeling' proposal on informing and consulting employees, which is essentially aimed at multinational companies. Local authorities, like other public bodies, are not allowed to express a national preference in their purchasing policies. Some local authorities are currently under investigation for their alleged contravention of the Rome Treaty by their imposition of a 'buy British' requirement when allocating loans to officials to help them buy cars to be used for official business or when selecting their own vehicles and other major purchases.

The fourth, and from the local authorities' point of view, the most positive, impact of Community membership is the finance that can be obtained from the various Community funds. It is undoubtedly this factor that has been instrumental in stimulating local government interest in the Community and encouraging the development of information-handling processes. However, the initial level of UK local government interest in this dimension of the Community at the time of the UK's entry was not high, because the opportunities were so limited. The European Social Fund (ESF) was much smaller in size and the UK Government retained any aid awarded from the Fund. The European Regional Development Fund (ERDF) was not yet in existence and in general the amount of money available for non-agricultural spending was restricted.

The first boost came with the establishment in 1975 of the Regional Fund, with the aim of reducing regional imbalances. A large proportion of the Fund was allocated to infrastructure projects, and this proportion has grown with the decline of industrial activity, until in 1983 it represented 89% of the quota section of the Fund. The benefits to be gained from using Fund assistance to help with local authority capital projects on roads, drainage, industrial sites, etc., were obvious. Its relevance was increased by an amendment to the Fund rules in 1979 setting up a 'non-quota' section which was not restricted to the Assisted Areas. A change in the UK Government's handling of the finance flowing from the Social Fund in 1978 to allow the successful applicant to retain the money, although accompanied by a rider that it should not be used to increase local authority expenditure, kindled further interest, as did the adoption of amending legislation allowing grants to be made for recruitment premiums and wage subsidies.

These changes coincided with a growing conviction amongst local authorities that positive action to improve local employment conditions could usefully include: training provisions for entrepreneurs and workers at all levels; assistance in cooperative and other small business development agencies; and wage subsidies to encourage existing and new enterprises to take on the unemployed. The 1982 Local Government (Miscellaneous Provisions) Act ensured that local authorities could spend up to a 2p rate, which, under Section 137 of the 1972 Local Government Act they had been allowed to use for the benefit of their areas, to assist industry and commerce. Thus the legal basis for such measures was secured. Local authority applications to the Social Fund rocketed almost overnight.

In addition to the Regional and Social Funds, the European Investment Bank has served as a major source of finance for local authorities, which have also benefited under some of the European Coal and Steel Community (ECSC) schemes and from other, often very small, pockets of money in the cultural and educational fields. Funding has also come under specific programmes to help the disabled and combat poverty. The prospect of assistance for transport infrastructure and the environment appears to be a closer one, and opportunities are opening up in sectors like energy (where local authorities have received support under the energy demonstration programme), research and information technologies. The successful conclusion of current efforts to reform the Community, with their emphasis on the need to develop new common policies, holds out the prospect that an increasingly wide range of local government projects and programmes will look to the Community for financial support.

The Community has one final, more tangential impact on the functioning of local authorities. This is the general effect which legislation and policies have on the economic health of a locality. Thus, the imposition of steel quotas will have a significant bearing on the industry of any area largely dependent on steel production. With the passage of time, this concern with economic development and prosperity is becoming a more significant feature of the work of the larger authorities in particular. Similarly, general changes in the structure of the budget, budgetary discipline, member states' contributions and related matters will obviously impinge, for good or ill, on the development of individual regions.

Thus, any examination of the provision to local authorities of information about the Community, and their use of it, should be seen against this backdrop. Obviously it cannot embrace every aspect of the Community's impact, but it does serve as a general guide. In some respects the local government position *vis-à-vis* the Community parallels that of central government, although in the case of any treaty infringements it is the national government of the member state which has to answer before the Court of Justice any case against a local authority's actions. Both central and local government are involved in the implementation of Community legislation, while they, in turn, must respect legislation governing the operation of their services and the administration of their organizations. They are also both eager to tap any funds for which they may be eligible. But, lacking the institutional involvement of central government in Community policy-making, local authorities are particularly concerned that they should be in the best position to lobby all the key organizations so that their viewpoint can be taken into account when legislation is being drafted and discussed. An early warning system on prospective new measures is essential to allow the authorities to make a thorough examination of any proposals and to formulate a considered response which can then be presented to the appropriate bodies.

We have so far examined the Community's role in relation to local authorities in terms of its impact and the local government response. However, there is a further dimension to the relationship which is no less important, and which is particularly relevant in the UK at this time. For the local authorities themselves have a vital role to play in building a democratic Community, as they represent that part of the European Community's governmental apparatus that is closest to the general public and its aspirations and is best able to reflect the prevailing situation and its problems. To fail to provide local authorities with the information they need to make their voice heard on any given subject is to prevent the Community, which is already one step more remote from the British people than Whitehall, from getting the most up-to-date and well-informed feedback on the position at the local level. Conversely, given the still limited powers of the elected European Parliament and the predominance of the civil service machines of the member states because of their role in the Council, the involvement of local government provides a positive means of bringing direct practical experience to bear upon this 'distant' legislative machinery. Moreover, the perpetuation in certain quarters in the UK of the image of the Community as a remote interfering irrelevance is assisted by the general level of ignorance on Community matters. Increased dissemination of information at the local level is one way of redressing the situation.

Community information — provision and dissemination

The dissemination of information to, and gathering of information by, local government is a multi-layered, complex operation. The official Community bodies, and in some cases the British Government, often serve as both information providers and disseminators, while organizations like the British Sections IULA/CEM function as disseminators in terms of official information, while also providing informed comment. Community information can reach the individual local authority by circuitous routes involving a whole series of intermediary disseminators. We do not propose to look at the process from the point of view of the originating provider or disseminator, like the Commission, but to approach it from the angle of the recipient in local government, whether it be at the centre — the local authority associations or IULA/CEM, who would further disseminate the information — or the individual local authority, which in turn has to pass it on to particular departments and/or the general public.

ACTION BY UK CENTRAL GOVERNMENT AT THE NATIONAL LEVEL

We intend to look first at the relationship of the local authority associations with UK central government: this is vital in the Community context in view of the predominant position of the Council of Ministers in the Community's legislative procedure. National civil servants play a significant role in the preliminary stages of policy formulation and it is the Council of Ministers which ultimately decides on the adoption of most major proposals. Given this UK

Government–Community relationship, the local authority associations clearly need to be kept informed of the UK Government's stance on relevant draft legislation and of the trend of discussions within the Council's Working Group, so that they can make the UK local government viewpoint known to central government in order that this can be taken into consideration when any national position is being formulated.

At this point, it is worth recalling briefly the UK Government's method of handling Community matters, in order best to highlight the ways that local government can benefit from a close association with it. In principle, UK government departments treat Community subjects as part of 'normal business' and no special arrangements are made for handling them, except to the extent that the Cabinet Office carries out a coordinating function in relation to constitutional and procedural requirements. Thus, when a proposal is still in the process of being drafted by the Commission, it is left to the individual policy divisions responsible within departments to decide whether to consult interested organizations, and if they do, which ones they should approach. Naturally, departments are wary of launching consultations at an early stage on draft proposals which may in due course take a very different shape, and the Government has underlined that, until the proposal is under consideration in the Council machinery, a member state has no real power to secure changes in it. Therefore, in the preliminary phase in the formulation of a proposal the main concern of the UK Government is to make clear the basic facts and fundamental issues that will guide its attitude to any formal proposals. In many cases, this attitude is directly related to existing policy and legislation on which the views of local government are already known. In others, prior knowledge of upcoming Commission proposals may affect the development of national measures which are already the subject of consultation with local government through existing channels.

The situation changes once the Commission has finalized its proposal. The governments of member states are then notified formally of its contents and the sponsor divisions in departments consult outside bodies with an interest in the proposal, normally through an existing recognized system of consultation. A study carried out by the local authority associations before the entry of the UK into the European Community in 1973, of the likely impact of Community legislation on local government, identified a number of ways in which the Community would affect local communities and local government services. This prompted the associations to seek a regular forum for discussing Community matters in general with the Government and led to the establishment of the European Joint Group to oversee the conduct of such consultations.

The Group, the chairman and secretariat of which are now provided by the Department of the Environment (DoE), involves twice-yearly meetings between the associations and representatives of departments concerned with local government questions. At regular intervals, the DoE produces a background paper which aims to set out the position on all the Community topics of potential interest to local government at the time, together with a list of contact points within departments on these subjects and, in some cases, a summary of the UK Government's attitude. Using this paper, the associations identify issues on which they would like further information and discussion, and these are included on the meeting's agenda. The background paper is designed as a progress report and early warning system, not as a primary source of information, and the Group is intended to complement, not supplant, the information/consultation process which should be taking place between central and local government. It enables local government to develop a closer relationship with the key officials on particular subjects of interest; to keep a regular check on the state of Council of Ministers' negotiations; and to convey its feelings on the relevant issues.

From Group meetings have flowed a series of *ad hoc* meetings with individual departments which have looked in depth at major policy areas. In recent years, subjects considered in this manner have included: the review of the European Regional Development Fund; the proposed extension under the existing regulation of quota financing to the designated inner city areas; the Regional Development Programme, in the preparation of which local authorities are now closely involved; the review of the European Social Fund; a whole range of employment initiatives covering part-time work, temporary work, early retirement and employees' information and consultation rights; and proposals for transport infrastructure funding. The information gleaned in these sessions is passed on, as appropriate, to the relevant association sub-committees, officer groups and individual authorities, and detailed reports of what takes place are carried in the *European information service* (EIS) bulletin (see below).

ACTION BY UK LOCAL GOVERNMENT AT THE COMMUNITY LEVEL

Having examined the central government/local government link and information flow, it would seem appropriate to examine UK local government links with the Community institutions and consultative bodies. At the international level, IULA and CEM have established a formal consultative arrangement on regional policy through the Consultative Committee of Local and Regional Authorities of the Member Countries of the European Community. Delegations are appointed to the Committee through the National Sections of the two organizations and periodic meetings have been held since 1976 with the Commissioner responsible for regional policy and with his officials. The Committee has issued a number of major statements on regional policy, with many of its ideas being incorporated in the Commission's proposals for the review of the European Regional Development Fund and Social Fund. Other policy statements have been made on transport infrastructure and on the Social Fund review, and the scope of the Committee's activities will be progressively extended into other areas of Community policy. The advantage of such an international grouping is that the Commission prefers dealing with bodies representing interests transcending national frontiers. The differences in the structures and powers of local and regional authorities in each state and their divergence of approach can, however, cause fragmentation at the international level and make the process of articulating a European-level local government view a rather slow one.

With regard to the European Parliament, a liaison group — the Intergroup of Local and Regional Representatives of the Political Groups — has been set up. This is comprised of nineteen MEPs who are, or have recently been, involved in local government, and who are drawn from the various parties in proportion to strength in Parliament. The Intergroup is seen as a means of bringing issues of particular local government concern, going through the Parliament's committees, to a wider group of potentially interested Members and of providing a focus for effective lobbying on behalf of local government. In addition, public hearings have been held under the auspices of the Group on the problems of the inner cities, ports and youth unemployment. However, the Intergroup is not an official part of the Parliament's machinery and its effectiveness is therefore limited. Efforts have been made also to establish a dialogue with the relevant standing committees of the Parliament on the local government-related policy issues being considered by them, but such contacts have been somewhat sporadic. Steps are now being taken to improve these links after the second European elections.

Turning to the Economic and Social Committee (ECOSOC), from 1978 to 1982 UK local government had one nominee on the Committee and whilst no nominee of the local authority associations was included amongst the UK members appointed in September 1982 for a four-year term, three of the new members have been asked by ministers to take a general UK local government interest in matters before the Committee. These members keep in touch with the British Sections IULA/CEM for briefing on local government views, and arrangements have been made for several UK local authority officers to serve as technical experts in helping the Committee draw up its opinions. These connections provide local government with an important additional source of intelligence about Commission thinking and a further channel through which their views may be aired at the Community level.

ACTION BY THE UK LOCAL AUTHORITY ASSOCIATIONS
AND THE BRITISH SECTIONS IULA/CEM AT THE
NATIONAL LEVEL

Moving from the international to the national theatre, the local authority associations have their own arrangements for dealing with Community matters. The Association of District Councils and the Association of Metropolitan Authorities have elected member-level European and international sub-committees respectively, which consider Community proposals and issues which are referred to their policy committees. The Convention of Scottish Local Authorities has recently adopted a similar approach. The Association of County Councils has a multi-disciplinary international sub-group of officer advisers which prepares guidance for its committees on particular Community proposals. In addition to these structures at the national level, the associations keep their member authorities informed of progress on major proposals and also usually supplement any UK Government measures stemming from Community legislation by their own commentary. The Association of District Councils now produces on an annual basis a publication entitled *EEC policies: issues of concern to districts*, which sets out its views on Community activity in the fields for which district councils are responsible. The associations make their individual representations to central government when required, and have submitted both oral and written evidence to the House of Lords Select Committee on the European Communities on issues such as the Social Fund review and the transfrontier shipment of hazardous wastes.

Much of the material on which the work of the associations is based reaches them through the British Sections IULA/CEM. Following the entry of the UK into the European Communities, and faced with the growing number of local authority-related Community initiatives, the associations felt the need to improve the flow of information both to themselves and to their member authorities. To this end, they decided to expand the joint secretariat of the British Sections IULA/CEM with effect from 1 April 1978, so that *inter alia* it could introduce an information service on European Community developments and provide the associations with information at as early a juncture as possible, so as to allow them to take action at the policy level.

The main product of the monitoring process, to which every local authority has access, is the *European information service*, a current awareness bulletin first produced in 1978. Initially this was issued at irregular intervals, but since 1981 it has appeared ten times a year (i.e. monthly except for September and January). Its coverage includes: summaries of European Commission reports and proposals for legislation which may impinge on local authority interests and services; details of relevant Community legislation adopted by the Council of Ministers; reports of relevant debates, resolutions and opinions of the European Parliament and of the Economic and Social Committee; reports on the anticipated impact of Community legislation assembled from UK government sources; statements of views on Community policy issues by groupings representing local and regional authorities and other related interests; more generally, information about possible future developments and thinking at Community level; and notice of coming events and publications relevant to these themes.

Great reliance is placed in the production of the bulletin on primary source documents, as the complexity of much of the material, technical legislation in particular, is such that even most well-informed and painstaking reports or summaries can, for reasons of length, translation, sub-editing etc., sometimes contain errors of detail or give a misleading impression of a document. Moreover, reports on legislation which has a general application and only partly affects local authorities, often fail to cover the clauses or articles of interest to local government; it is important to have the original document so that the relevant sections can be extracted. However, the complex language of some of the Community's documentation does in itself pose problems. The inevitable difficulties that come with the need to translate material into seven different languages are often compounded by the attempt to find the '*mot juste*' to embrace a variety of situations or systems which may vary from state to state, or indeed within states. As the interpretation and impact of a proposal may turn on a single, key definition, the importance of the terminology used cannot be underestimated. It is therefore often hard to escape the grip of the official phraseology for fear that, in doing so, the meaning of the material will be altered or lost.

The primary sources used, like COM documents, the *Official journal* and European Parliament reports, resolutions and minutes, are, in most cases, self-selecting. In addition, the press releases on Community grants and loans, produced by the Commission's London Office, are particularly useful, as they can provide local authorities with ideas for future projects or indicate which other authorities are working on the same lines so that contact can be made and experience and ideas shared. A further highly-rated source of information is the series of reports produced by the House of Lords Select Committee on the European Communities. This Committee takes evidence from all quarters, including the European institutions and UK central government, as well as from interested groupings like local authorities. The level of knowledge of the Committee members and its support staff means that its questioning is often keen, and the quality of its reports is underlined by the degree of attention paid to them by the Commission.

One aspect of EIS coverage which is worthy of explanation is the amount of space devoted to ECOSOC activities. The role of ECOSOC in the legislative process has sometimes been questioned, as has the extent to which its opinions ultimately influence Community legislation. However, its composition of representatives of employers, employees and other interest groups make it a valuable forum which can often accurately reflect the likely reaction to proposals of a broad spectrum of groups and organizations. This suggests that its views should receive greater attention, and IULA/CEM try to play their part in ensuring that this occurs.

In addition to using the primary printed matter, IULA/CEM keep in close contact with Commission officials both in the UK and in Brussels, and with the relevant UK departments. The Commission's 'open-door' approach is well-known and the official responsible for an area of policy is often the best point of contact on general as well as detailed queries on proposals and legislation. This sort of contact can help overcome delays in the production and transmission of documentation, like Commission proposals, by enabling information on draft legislation to be obtained from the desk officer long before the official printed version has appeared. The same officer can also assist in unravelling some of the more obscure 'Eurojargon' of complex legislation. In the same vein, the relevant Government department should normally be in the best position to analyze the domestic effect of any Community document. For the impact on local authorities, IULA/CEM often go to association officers or advisers in local authorities who have specialized knowledge of the particular area. Whilst some of the information from the UK Government and from Brussels is inevitably provided off the record — and in the case of central government one sometimes runs up against the Whitehall wall of secrecy — these informal contacts help to give more substance and detail to the primary material itself.

However, to help track down the primary sources, the production of which can often be delayed because of the time taken in resolving the legal and linguistic niceties, it is necessary to resort to secondary sources. For the purposes of the *European information service*, the best of these is *Agence Europe*, a newspaper produced in Brussels on a more or less daily basis. This covers the majority of the major new proposals of local authority interest and goes wider than the Community to cover international agreements/meetings/conventions on related themes. Its particular strength is its ability to penetrate some of the more secretive parts of the Community's institutional machinery. It often reports on the current state of working group discussions within the Council and the stances adopted by the member states on any given subject. Such information considerably amplifies the bland and laconic synopses which characterise Council press releases. *Agence Europe*'s Commission connections also appear to be impeccable, and the likely contents of any proposal are often carried well before it has been agreed by the Commission. Detailed industrial, economic and commercial statistics are frequently given, and another regular feature is an analysis of the economic and political situation in each member state in turn. Especially important Community documents are also reproduced in full. One note of warning that should be sounded, however, is that, because of the speed of preparation, mistakes are not infrequent. The clarity of the language also leaves something to be desired, especially in an economic context where the whole meaning of an article can depend on the translation of a few key words. One other, possibly prohibitive, factor is the high cost of the annual subscription.

A further important secondary source comes from the stable of the Europe Information Service Group. This is also based in Brussels and its publications include the twice-weekly newsletter *European report*, which covers much the same ground as *Agence Europe*. The Group also produces specialized fortnightly publications, of which *Europe environment* and *Europe energy* have most relevance to local government. *Europe environment* carries useful reports on the activities of the lobby groups and related employer and trade union associations in the environmental, consumer protection and research fields and appears to have good leads into the relevant Commission directorates. It, like

Agence Europe, adopts the helpful practice of publishing important documents, notably new Commission proposals, in full.

In addition to these secondary sources, a wealth of other specialized periodicals which are produced less frequently, are scanned. These cover areas such as regional policy, education, culture, environment, research, consumer protection, informatics and science and technology. They help to flesh out the bare bones of official documents. But for once one runs up against the time factor. The ponderous nature of Community procedures usually helps the information disseminator. Today's news tends to be tomorrow's news. However, in producing a bulletin on even a monthly basis, one is often torn between including the scanty, undigested and possibly inaccurate details of a new proposal, which inevitably leaves a series of unanswered questions, and holding fire until fuller information is available, and thereby missing a publication deadline.

So, the information drawn from the scrutiny of this wide-ranging and authoritative series of sources is summarized in self-contained articles in the *European information service*. These are designed to include the main points of interest on any issue to the general reader who wishes to keep abreast of current events without having to refer to any further documentation. However, full source references are given and for the specialist the summary should serve as the starting point of his investigations. We provide a follow-up enquiry service to help the interested reader to find additional material and documentation. Obviously, because of the range of sectors covered by local government and the small size of the secretariat, IULA/CEM cannot give expert advice in detail on all areas affecting local authorities. What it can do is try to ensure that the inquirer is made aware of the most suitable contacts in the UK Government, the Commission or elsewhere who hold the specialist knowledge being sought. For various reasons, also, an authority might not want it made known that it had an interest in a particular subject; in that case IULA/CEM can serve as an intermediary in supplying the information. We often have spare copies of Community literature and our close proximity to the London Offices of the Commission and Parliament enables us to save local authorities time and effort in getting the relevant documents. The publications and documentation sections of these Offices are unfailingly helpful in spite of the pressure under which they are placed.

In terms of the enquiries that we receive, those generated by the *EIS* bulletin tend to be for original documentation and further background information, which can generally be obtained from the Commission or UK central government. Enquiries not stimulated by the bulletin are predominantly concerned with funding opportunities. Initially we normally refer interested parties to two publications — *Finance from Europe*, which is produced by the Commission's London Office, and *Guide to European grants and loans*, which is produced by Eurofi (UK) Ltd. For more detailed information, the relevant sections of the Departments of Employment and the Environment can give authoritative advice on the major funds and are always ready to help the potential applicant. (See also Chapter 10 of this book for further information on grants and loans.)

With local authorities, the major problem is to get the information onto the desk of the official to whom it will be of the greatest use. There are 521 local authorities in Britain, each divided into a series of self-contained departments. Although there are regional groupings of local authorities, the opportunity for officials from different councils to meet or even to talk together on a regular basis is limited. Even within authorities, information held in one department does not automatically get transferred to others. The sheer number of officers involved means that staff at one level might not be aware of information held further up or further down the line. Although the number of such individuals who actually require Community information represents a minority of officials, this still constitutes an obstacle for IULA/CEM and other central bodies.

Under our current operation, one copy of the *European information service* bulletin is circulated free of charge to the chief executive of every principal local authority as well as to organizations in associate membership of the British Sections IULA/CEM. However, from this point on its distribution is beyond the control of IULA/CEM. Many authorities photocopy the bulletin or relevant extracts from it and distribute them to the appropriate departments. Alternatively, the information supplied is carried in in-house journals or current awareness bulletins. Obviously, however, because of local circumstances and perceptions, not all chief executives are persuaded of the need to circulate the information provided, or indeed of its relevance to their activities. Thus, sometimes the information does not reach those officers who would benefit most from access to it. IULA/CEM therefore run a direct subscription service to bring *EIS* to a wider audience. To make officers aware of its existence, they periodically conduct mail shots directed at individual local authority departments, and are currently examining ways in which *EIS* can be publicized more extensively. It also numbers amongst subscribers government departments, MEPs, financial consultancies, banks, Commission officials and interested voluntary and commercial organizations in a variety of sectors.

The *European information service* is thus the main vehicle through which IULA/CEM keep local authorities up to date with developments at the Community level, but they are also involved in other methods of information dissemination at the local level. One of the most important and successful of these is the British Sections' collaboration with the School for Advanced Urban Studies (SAUS), located in the University of Bristol. Between 1978 and 1983 the School, which was set up jointly by the University of Bristol and central government in 1973 as a post-experience teaching and research centre in the field of urban policy, has co-sponsored with IULA/CEM nineteen seminars and workshops on various aspects of European Community policies. These seminars are mainly aimed at local government officers and councillors, although representatives of voluntary organizations, industry, etc., may also attend. Speakers include MEPs, civil servants from a variety of central government departments (in particular Environment, Employment and Transport) and Commission officials. One regular annual feature is the participatory workshop for officers with particular responsibility for European affairs, with whom we shall deal in more detail later, whilst another annual fixture is a general seminar directed specifically at elected members. Much of the success of these meetings stems from the presence of the civil servants who are involved in the Council working groups and are thus in the best position to comment on progress on any proposals. The informal relaxed atmosphere is also conducive to a greater expansiveness on the part of even the most reticent of speakers.

A second forum for increasing knowledge of Community affairs is provided by the European information seminars organized by IULA/CEM with European Commission financial support. In October 1981, the Greater London Council played host to a seminar on Community transport policy, whilst a similar event on environmental policy was held in December 1981 in Chester. This was followed by a meeting on employment matters held under the auspices of Leicestershire County Council in Leicester in December 1982. These occasions attract eminent Commission and local authority speakers and the papers presented at the meeting and the ensuing discussions are usually published. Participants come from a wide variety of local authorities and other interest groups, and this is reflected in the debates.

So far, in dealing with the problem of ensuring the dissemination of information to local authorities, we have focussed primarily on the officer structure. Getting information to elected members poses even greater problems because they are one step further removed and do not have the daily opportunity of scanning relevant material passing through their offices. Certainly, some authorities circulate to their members Community information drawn from a variety of sources, including the *European information service*, and elected members can attend various conferences and seminars such as those held at SAUS. But, to supplement these efforts, IULA/CEM also produce a quarterly broadsheet *IULA/CEM news*. This is devoted mainly to the activities of international local authority groupings and provides information on interesting local government developments and innovations throughout the world. It carries accounts of meetings of the Consultative Committee of Local and Regional Authorities of the Member Countries of the European Community and of the European Parliament's Intergroup, and also contains a regular feature based on *EIS* summarizing major developments in the Community. As well as going to all local authorities, it is distributed through the European Movement to the individual members of CEM, who are elected members and officers with a special interest in Europe. This obviously is only a starting point, but, given the intractability of the problem, it does represent one sure channel of information for councillors who wish to take advantage of it.

ACTION BY INDIVIDUAL UK LOCAL AUTHORITIES
ON COMMUNITY AFFAIRS

The activities we have considered constitute the main thrust of the dissemination of information by IULA/CEM on the Community. However, as we have indicated, this is only one side of the coin, as local authorities individually have become increasingly more sophisticated in pursuing their objectives in this field. The initiatives taken and approaches adopted are many and varied, and IULA/CEM do not hold comprehensive information at the centre about the action taken by each individual authority, although advice is provided in many cases. Obviously, the reaction to the Community of a large metropolitan authority in an Assisted Area with declining traditional industries is going to be different to that of a district council in south-east England, although general Community legislation would be equally applicable to either area, and the south east, as local authorities there constantly remind the Commission, has its unemployment blackspots. But in general terms, the use made by an authority of the information it receives and the degree to which it acts on its own initiative to gather information or to help influence Community policy, is broadly determined by the factors of size and eligibility for Community aid.

The incentive of financial returns transcends political boundaries and objectives and, as we have shown, has been the main stimulus for increased Community involvement. With the majority of the Community's funding flowing to the UK Assisted Areas, the councils situated within those areas have naturally been the most active in the field. Often the majority group in these councils is of the left, but the approach to obtaining finance has been bi-partisan and pragmatic, with groups of every political persuasion avidly pursuing Community money. The success of Scottish local authorities, many of which are eligible for a wide range of funds, perhaps best illustrates how the maximum can be extracted from the Community purse, and they have utilized the experience gained in making applications to increase their expertise. The publicizing of their success has had a multiplier effect for other local authorities and led to a demand for increased information. Size is also a major factor in determining the way an authority deals with Community information. The greater financial resources and manpower of larger councils means that they can afford to devote more time and money to developing more sophisticated methods of handling Community affairs.

So, in practical terms, what form does involvement take? Perhaps the largest commitment has been made by two councils, Strathclyde and Greater Manchester, which have each appointed a liaison officer based in Brussels to serve as a link with Community institutions. These officers, by being on the spot, are able to gain early warning of impending developments; smooth the path of grant and loan applications; and lobby the Commission on behalf of their authority on relevant subjects. Reports suggest that both authorities are happy with the operation of this system and some other areas or councils are investigating the possibilities of following suit.

Secondly, many authorities have designated an officer, or a number of officers, to take special responsibility for European matters. These individuals are often located in research or economic intelligence units, planning or finance departments, or the chief executive's office itself. They may work full time on European matters, or deal with them side-by-side with other activities. Some sixty of the larger councils now have 'Mr/Ms Europes' (as they are unofficially known) deployed in this manner. Their existence enables local authorities to cope with the more detailed, primary source material and to explore more fully possible funding opportunities. Their sources of information would include many of those which we have already covered, including UK Commission officials, government departments, IULA/CEM and other authorities. As already mentioned, a special seminar is held annually for these officers at SAUS, which brings them together with Commission and government officials to discuss common problems. The network is fairly well developed and lobbying initiatives on policies affecting all or a group of local authorities have stemmed from this source.

A further element in the information/lobbying activities of local authorities is the visit to the Community institutions. The success that this has enjoyed in recent years means that a growing number of local authorities are beating the path to Brussels. The Commission's 'open door' policy has encouraged this trend, which serves a number of different functions. It enables local authorities to establish contact with relevant officials handling the areas in which they are interested and to put to them particular projects which they would like to see funded. This means that, if a scheme is clearly not eligible, unnecessary work can be avoided by an early indication that it would not be acceptable. As ERDF and ESF projects have to be submitted to the Commission through the UK Government, which only passes on projects eligible for funding, an indication that the Commission would be prepared to accept a borderline project would provide a useful lever when the application is passed to the UK Government. The visit also allows authorities to float plans for schemes, such as integrated operations, in order to make the Commission aware of an area's problems and to implant the germ of the idea in the officials' minds.

One demonstration of the successful results of such lobbying is West Yorkshire's Scheme for Textile Area Regeneration which was designed to create new jobs in the areas where the textile industry had declined and which was pressed home by Council leaders on four successive visits. The inclusion of much of West Yorkshire in the ERDF non-quota textile programme is claimed to be at least partly attributable to this persistence. Furthermore, such visits allow valuable information unobtainable through official channels to be gleaned on an informal basis. The Commission welcomes such visits as it recognizes that local people can often provide a better picture of their own region and better describe their problems than the documentation that emanates from central government. But the time of the officials is limited and it should be stressed that a visit should be specifically targetted to ensure that it is not a waste of time for both sides.

Some local authorities have taken major initiatives on issues affecting their areas which have proved extremely fruitful. This type of activity is exemplified by the seminar on coal and the environment which was organized by the Yorkshire and Humberside County Councils, in conjunction with the Commission, in September 1982. The subsequent draft programme on solid fuels, which was produced by the Commission at the beginning of 1983, contained provisions on the environmental dimension of the subject which bore testimony to the effect of the conference on the Commission's thinking.

Visits in the opposite direction are another feature of local authority/Community links, with local authorities inviting Commissioners or senior Commission officials to visit their area to see the extent of the problems on the ground and discuss possible Community approaches. This can yield substantial benefits, but again it is important that the maximum use is made of the time available.

Yet another source of information, and a powerful lobbying ally for individual local authorities, is the MEP. The degree of involvement obviously varies from area to area, depending upon MEPs' particular interests and upon political factors. In a few cases MEPs have been encouraged to set-up their offices in local authority headquarters buildings. This enables the council to have easy access to the specialized information which the MEPs may possess; to persuade them to represent the authority's interest when legislation comes before the Parliament; and to use their good offices and contacts to influence the Commission and national government on projects which are important for the area. MEPs have also been instrumental in persuading Commission officials to visit particular regions, as described above. Many authorities keep their MEPs closely informed of local developments and place them on their mailing lists so that, despite their frequent absences abroad, they are always well briefed on the situation at the local level.

The heightened level of Community awareness has led some local authorities to take the initiative and to become information disseminators in their own right. This dissemination normally takes the form of current awareness and information bulletins, primarily of an abstractive nature aimed at local industry, voluntary organizations, MEPs and other interested individuals, and dealing with matters of particular local relevance. The most substantial of these is the Greater London Council's *European digest*, which commenced publication in July 1977 and is produced monthly. This provides brief (i.e. up to about six-line) summaries of Community developments or documents, using mainly secondary sources, under the following headings: Community institutions and procedures; education, training and culture; environment; finance and economics; fuel and energy; health, safety and consumer protection; industry and trade; information; regional policy; planning and development; research, science and technology; social affairs and employment; and transport. It is intended primarily as an extracting service backed up by the GLC's substantial research library facilities, and is circulated widely within the GLC. There are also approximately seventy external subscribers and new subscribers are welcomed.

Most of the other local authority information outlets involve bulletins or news-sheets distributed free of charge. Tyne and Wear County Council produces a periodic news-sheet, *CRIU European Community news*, which contains paragraphs on Community developments drawn from the national and local press and also includes relevant information published in the *Official journal*. This goes to local higher education establishments, some chief officers of other councils, MEPs and local chambers of commerce. Mid-Glamorgan County Council issues a regular current awareness service, *European briefing* which provides short summaries of developments of general interest taken from both primary and secondary sources. This is supplied to local MPs, MEPs, academics, the press, the Commission Office in Cardiff and anyone else who expresses an interest in it. Also in Wales, Dyfed County Council has recently started up a quarterly, bilingual *Information bulletin*. This is a strongly Welsh-oriented publication, although containing pieces of more general interest and has wide distribution to community councils, local libraries, schools, MPs, MEPs and the press. Dyfed has recently established a computerized information service linked to Dundee, London and Rome, as an extension to the services which it provides to local business and industry.

In the dissemination of information both within the authority and to the general public, the local library service can play a vital role. In some authorities, the supply of Euro-information is seen as the logical extension of existing information services, and in the case of the GLC, the *European digest* is produced in the research library. Most libraries possess online systems, and if they so wish can gain access to CELEX, the Community's legal data base and to CRONOS, its statistical data bank. The GLC has its own online data base, ACOMPLINE, which may be accessed through Euronet or through the 'Packet Switching Service'. This data base contains *inter alia* information relating to the European Community. The library is often the first port of call for officers and councillors seeking further information, and some libraries have built up a network of contacts in the European Documentation Centres, Commission, IULA/CEM, etc., from which they can obtain further material.

Another dimension of authorities' Community activities is the service provided to local commerce and industry on the availability of Community grants and loans. This service is often centred on the public library, though it may also be found in the research and information unit, staffed by the Mr/Ms Europes. It may be run in conjunction with the local advisory service on the dissemination of UK national grants and loans, and normally the main aim is to point the particular company in the right direction and provide it with the appropriate Government contacts for further discussion of the project envisaged. The development agencies which have been set up to stimulate local industry may also perform this function as part of their activities. Thus, for example, the Tyne and Wear Enterprise Trust, aided by a European Social Fund grant in 1982, makes available a management team to assist the setting up or expansion of small businesses through counselling on training, management skills, new technologies, financing, etc.

Conclusion

This chapter has sought to show how British local authorities have an interest in a wide range of Community policy areas and how they obtain and act upon information relevant to their needs. As experience of Community practices and policies has developed within both central and local government, the way in which they are handled has also evolved considerably. While Community business has always been officially treated by departments as an extension of 'normal' business, rather than as a separate policy area, the process of marrying Community-level negotiations with national-level information and consultation procedures has not been an easy one. There are also grounds for believing that this segmented approach to Community affairs, combined with almost perpetual re-negotiations of the terms of British membership, has led the UK Government to take an unnecessarily narrow view of many Community initiatives, to the detriment of broader UK interests.

We have shown that local authorities — because of their executive and law enforcement responsibilities, their advocacy role in respect of the needs of their areas, and their public information function as the level of government closest to the public — have an important role to play in defining the British response to Community membership. One of the major problems to be overcome in this unique form of supranational government is that of remoteness. The institutions of national government are already fairly remote from the local scene, but at least people have grown up with them and they — and the personalities principally involved — are always in the news. By contrast, the Community institutions are themselves unfamiliar bodies, whose activities only become news in the event of major rows or minor scandals, and many of the political figures in key positions at any time will be little known in countries other than their own. The complex and protracted legislative procedures and the ponderous linguistic style of most Community documentation provide additional handicaps.

There is a real need to make the Community process more accessible and more comprehensible in all fields where it has an impact. In our opinion, both the Community institutions themselves and the British Government could do more towards this end: the *European information service* sets out to fill this gap so far as the local authority interests are concerned. Contrary to claims still heard from time to time, there is no shortage of information about the progress of Community affairs and the activities of the institutions. The problem is one of packaging and interpreting this information and targeting the relevant items to persons in key positions who have the means and the knowledge to respond effectively. With very limited resources EIS seeks to serve a multiplicity of departments in the 521 diverse local authorities of Britain. Clearly, no such bulletin can be tailored to all the individual needs of even one local authority — but at least it can provide a core of information relevant to all or most, plus a ready means of access to sources of additional help.

Being, as they are, both important beneficiaries of the Regional and Social Funds, and the main agencies responsible for implementing much of the detailed legislation in respect of trading standards, environmental controls etc., emanating from the Community, British local authorities have stronger reasons for needing to know about, and be involved in, Community affairs than many of their counterparts in other member states. The various initiatives taken by the British Sections IULA/CEM, in terms of *EIS* and other publications, conferences, seminars and training workshops, reflect this situation and should make a progressive contribution to overcoming the apparent remoteness of the Community. They will also help to achieve a proper local government input into the Community's institutional and policy processes.

References and notes

[1] Since this chapter went to press, CEM has changed its name to the Council of European Municipalities and Regions in order to demonstrate more clearly that its membership comprises all levels of local authorities and regions. The British sections implemented this change of name in November 1984 and are now known as IULA/CEMR.

9

Europe and the Business Community

JIM HOGAN

The impact of membership on British business

All business people share a common goal which is to make profit. No matter how much they may, as individuals, respect the wider political, economic and social benefits of European Community (EC) membership their overriding concern as members on the business community is with the impact of membership on the efficiency and profitability of their enterprise. The business person who is prepared to accept a setback to his enterprise as an inescapable consequence of economic change does not exist. Thus, while the debate as to whether it was right for the United Kingdom (UK) to join the Community gathered momentum, culminating in a confrontation between the political parties when the question of membership became an electoral issue in 1983, the business sector never lost sight of one vital and, fortunately, mundane factor. Whatever the circumstances, membership of the Community was meant to pay dividends. Consequently, the business community remained overwhelmingly in favour of membership while others showed their discontent.

The attitudes of the business community towards membership of the European Community have been commented on in a report from the House of Lords Select Committee on the European Communities.[1] The report, published in October 1983, gives a down-to-earth account of the way in which membership of the European Community has materially affected major British industries, whose evidence is incorporated in the report. The Select Committee observed that the main consequence of British membership was the marked shift in the direction of British trade towards the Community, which in 1983 was taking 42% of all UK exports. However, the figures were boosted by oil exports which disguised a worrying decline in the balance of trade between Britain and the rest of the Community in manufactured goods. It is worth noting that, at this time, 60% of all British exports were going to Western Europe as a whole, an area which included applicant Community countries (Spain and Portugal), and the countries which had free trade agreements with the Community, the European Free Trade Association (EFTA). At the end of 1983 all customs duties between EFTA and EC countries were phased out.

The Select Committee's report is frank about the degree of comfort which British industry could draw from EC membership:

> It is clear that the rise in sterling from 1979 on, coming on top of rapid cost and price inflation, was such as to wipe out almost all actual and potential benefits from membership of the Community.[2]

This also explains to some extent the lingering doubts about membership of the Community which had affected business morale, at least until the election of 1983, when continued membership was made secure. The major advantage, however, is that Britain has become a part of the biggest single trading area in the world, with all the attractions of tariff free access to a market covering the whole of Western Europe. Britain is also in a position to benefit from the collective strength of the Community in its dealings with non-EC trading partners and, internally, from the generous financial support for industry, the regions and the unemployed. Membership also encourages foreign investors to invest here. What is missing is the dramatic change in Britain's fortunes that the public and industry had led themselves to expect. Accession to the Community coincided almost exactly with the oil price shocks of the early seventies and the onset of the world recession; some would say that Britain managed to get into the Community in the nick of time, before the recession set in.

The Select Committee's report shows that industry as a whole thought that the first ten years of membership of the Community was generally beneficial, though it was rarely considered a major influence on exports or imports. Witnesses at the Select Committee's inquiry were reported to be almost unanimous in their feeling that withdrawal from the Community would be damaging to the future of British industry. The obvious inference to be drawn is that industry representatives believe that membership of the Community is certainly better for industry, if only because non-membership would be worse. But there has been no eldorado.

The Select Committee report also pointed out that the firms that had done well in Europe were those which were better informed about the Community's ways. The report recommends that the government 'should in particular work for the removal of non-tariff barriers to trade within the Community (constantly mentioned during the enquiry as a cause of difficulty) and should provide information and assistance to industry in developing markets there'.[3] With these two recommendations the Committee underlines the need for business to discover more about the European Community; and it openly states what many business people assumed for years, that the government should bear responsibility for improving the business sector's knowledge of the Community. Unfortunately, the report offers no recommendation as to how either of these two objectives could be achieved.

Two principal areas of Community policy which affect the business community most are free movement of goods and harmonization, both of which are described below. Of other areas of concern, finance is covered in Chapter 10 while fair competition is dealt with later in this chapter.

FREE MOVEMENT OF GOODS AND SERVICES

The free movement of goods and services is a broad objective which speaks for itself. The phrase, in a European context, relates to an ideal state of affairs in the Community's internal market which, after ten years of UK membership, was by no means fulfilled; and, not intending to place an overly pessimistic construction on the development of the Community's internal market so far, many enquiries from the business sector concern matters which actually fragment, rather than unite, the Community member states on the subject of trade. Even the Community's own regulations and procedures may be deployed to hinder the free movement of goods.

Surveillance licensing is a clear case in point. Under the Treaty of Rome member states are not permitted to obstruct imports from Community partners. But permission is sometimes granted by the European Commission to introduce a system of surveillance licensing for the purpose of monitoring imports of low-priced goods, such as clothing and footwear originating in non-EC countries, if these goods pose a threat to national industries. Unfortunately, goods of Community origin can also be held up by the surveillance system, often for several weeks. Worse still, some EC countries, under pressure from national industries, particularly in a period of world economic recession, become adept at bending the Community's rules to suit their own purposes.

At certain times, dubious interpretations of the rules have even been used as leverage in gaining ground on matters of dispute between Community partners. And on a more mundane level, a mere typing error in documentation can cause quite some delay in customs clearance. This is one reason, at least, why businesses should try to complete EC formalities with care and find out just where they should go for advice. Surveillance licensing is one question which falls squarely into the 'free movement of goods' category and does not involve the harmonization of the laws of member states.

HARMONIZATION

Harmonization of Community legislation in general is one of the most heavily debated aspects of the Common Market. It is not a question of loss of sovereignty, or the so-called British 'insularity' much vaunted in Community circles. This is far too glib a way of discussing the problem. The French are as determined as anyone can be when it comes down to protecting national interests. And they are no less French for having been in the Community for twenty-five years. What really matters to the business community, once again, is whether proposed Community legislation improves the practical working environment for business. Many in the business sector still have their doubts. The government, on a broader front, also has clear priorities in the development of Community policies, including the harmonization programme which is central to the concept of a complete common market in goods and services.

Towards the end of the first decade of British membership the British government began to grumble openly about the way in which the Community was being run. The rows over Britain's contributions to the Community budget and runaway spending on the Common Agricultural Policy (CAP), which took up two thirds of the budget, were documented blow by blow in the press. But the government also made plain its firm belief that the Community should give priority to clearing away the many legislative, administrative and procedural obstacles to the free flow of goods and services between member states. Harmonization, quaintly described in EC documents as 'the approximation of the laws of member states', includes the harmonization laws affecting free movement of goods, such as the innumerable different legally imposed technical standards applying throughout the Community — overall, one of the more onerous hindrances to the free movement of goods from one EC country to another. Harmonization also covers the harmonization of the laws of member states on matters as diverse as hairdressing certificates and the shorter working week, which have little direct influence on the free movement of goods. But progress towards harmonization does, of course, assist free and fair competition in the Community by providing that no EC business has to operate in a more restrictive climate than another.

THE COMMON MARKET

A common market, free of all obstacles, has by no means been achieved. And most of the effort, so far, has concerned intra-community trade in goods. The common market in insurance, on air travel and other services is even less complete than the common market in goods, a matter which was seen by the British government as a serious weakness in the Community's development during the first ten years of membership. As for the business sector, the prevailing opinion is that the Community has spent too much time on social engineering and too little on industrial and economic matters at a time when the world has been struggling to emerge from the recession. Harmonization of all trade and industry legislation of member states within the bounds of the Community's internal market policy, however, is central to the concept of the common market — the common market being that aspect of the Community on which the British case for membership has greatly depended.

The British business community, quite naturally, thinks of the Community mainly in terms of a common market and not, for example, as a means of political cooperation. It has a straightforward way of looking at Europe. But, as everyone working in the information network knows, confusion sets in early.

Even the term 'common market' is frequently misused as just another name for the European Community. Of the three conterminous Communities — the European Coal and Steel Community (ECSC), the European Atomic Energy Community (EAEC) and the European Economic Community (EEC) — it is the last which establishes the common market in principle and in the mind of business.

In practice, the completion of the common market — a Europe in which goods and services may be traded throughout all member states as though they were one territory — is a distant goal. The high expectations of some industries have not materialized; and in the first decade of UK membership, slow progress towards a genuine common market has been a major cause of dissatisfaction in British industry. But it would be difficult to prove that the existence, and indeed proliferation, of barriers to trade in the Community had undermined the impact of membership on British business. After all, membership of the Community is a relatively new initiative in the history of British industry and trade, and British exporters have been up against tariff and non-tariff barriers all over the world for a very long time. But lack of progress, to say nothing of the laborious negotiations to free the common market of obstacles to trade during the first ten years of UK membership, has taken its toll on business morale.

The Community image

When Britain joined the Community in 1973 it was an act of historic significance. Overnight it changed the style of Britain's relations with other European countries, with some of which it had been at war in recent history. But even today, people recall the 1951 Festival of Britain more vividly than they remember the day of accession to the Community. And when the New Year celebrations were in full swing at the moment Britain entered the Community, how many people remember raising their glasses to Europe?

At the time of entry the UK business community found itself working in a Community which had been shaped fifteen years earlier by the original six members — Belgium, France, West Germany, Italy, Luxembourg and the Netherlands. The business community entered the field at a time when the world economy was shaken by the oil price rises of the seventies. Strong economic forces, inflation and an over-strong pound, wiped out any noticeable benefits of membership to industry. The business sector was faced with an ever increasing body of legislation, some of it a source of considerable discontent, and some of it thought to be just plain silly. The business community began to see the institutions of the Community as meddlesome or, as in the case of the European Parliament, superfluous. It found itself obliged to hunt for and study eliptically worded proposals, decisions, directives and regulations, and the press siezed upon what it thought was Community folly whenever it could. It is true that the newspapers sensationalized some of the Community's absurdities and gave prominence to the unpopular practice of disposing of surplus food at taxpayers' expense. Yet, in its own way, the press was taking the lead in putting pressure on the Community to adopt a more practical outlook, and by so doing kept the subject alive in the minds of the public.

In this unsettled atmosphere, it is not surprising that enthusiasm for membership of the Community should tail off. Indeed, it tailed off sufficiently to allow membership to become an election issue. This, in turn, discouraged people from being objective about Community 'disputes'. It was easy to forget that in negotiations in Brussels, ministers of the member states usually do begin talking from different standpoints as a matter of course. They represent different countries with different traditions. The time-consuming business of reaching a consensus is part and parcel of Community life. But once the Community becomes an object of ridicule in the minds of the public, truth falls victim to ignorance and prejudice. Thus, the wrong impression was gained, for instance, when the olive oil subsidies were being 'fiddled' in Italy. This was seen as an EEC scandal when in reality it was a local matter. Admittedly, the costs of the fraud fell on the EC as a whole, but the authorities in each member state are initially responsible for the proper management of Community policies in their own countries. The Community itself perpetrated no scandal.

The stock response of those who seek to defend the Community image is to constantly reiterate the general case for UK membership. A good illustration of this is the two-page advertisement placed in the *Financial Times* on 15 May 1984 by the European Democratic Group (EDG) during the run up to the 1984 European Parliament election. The advertisement underlined many of the basic principles on which the Community had been founded over a quarter of a century earlier, points which the Euro-MPs clearly felt that the British people, twelve years after UK accession to the Community, had not yet recognized. It might be unfair to dwell on the wording of a strident piece of propaganda designed only to catch the eye of potential voters, but the wording of the advertisement nicely reflects the attitude of the British to their role in Europe — not just the attitude of people in general, but specifically the mild form of cynicism among politicians themselves as well as officials in Brussels and Whitehall. Top of the list of benefits in the advertisement was the foreign investment in Britain which could be attributed to Community membership. Overseas companies had brought jobs to Britain's towns and cities, it was said. A fair point but an old one. Next came the good news that war between member states had been rendered inconceivable, even though the prospect of war was on nobody's mind at the time. And some way down the list of benefits was a rash promise to 'slash the red tape that hinders our trade with Europe — and thereby safeguard the 2½ million jobs involved'. The European Parliament has no powers to slash red tape; it can only persuade others to do so. But more to the point, the claim that 2½ million jobs depend on slashing red tape is a misrepresentation of a CBI survey carried out in advance of the UK general election of 1983 which revealed that companies doing business in Europe employed 2½ million people. These companies would, no doubt, have been seriously worried if Britain was to have been taken out of Europe by the Labour Party. But withdrawal from the Community was a settled question when the Euro-MPs placed their advertisement. There was no longer any question of Britain leaving the Community to go it alone and the 2½ million jobs were not in danger. If indeed they ever really were.

Putting aside the question of accuracy, the main weakness in the advertisement was that, in essence, it was still campaigning for membership of the Community even though the question of membership had long been settled. It was part of a publicity campaign which was based on a presentation of Europe so outworn as to be almost meaningless. Public and politicians together seem to see the Community as a set of fine ideas in the making, or a set of promises bound to come to fruition because enshrined in the word or in the spirit of the Treaty of Rome. Fewer people speak of the Community as a living institution, one which is working inexorably towards the full economic integration and political compatibility of member states with a strong collective voice in world affairs. For the business community, however incomplete the common market may be, Europe is still the destination of almost half of Britain's exports. Western Europe as a whole — all part of the free trade area — takes 60%. One would have thought that the *Financial Times* was precisely the place to focus business attention on the subject that interests them most — how to benefit from the increased market opportunities in Europe. The European Democratic Group advertisement, on the other hand, missed the mark because it was no longer part of any live discussion by the time it reached its audience.

The communication gap

Information about the European Community, as far as UK businesses are concerned, has always been channelled through intermediaries in Whitehall, trade organizations, libraries and even some newspapers and magazines. Intermediaries are often the first line of contact with the European Community for the business community. Consequently, intermediaries have a special responsibility to convey the facts to the business community in Britain and not their own or other people's prejudices. Some organizations have recognized this and have taken steps to set up efficient information services. Unfortunately, in most sources of information to business, staff are not required to understand how the Community works and many of them can devote only a small part of their time to Community questions. Although there are many individuals in Whitehall, trade organizations and libraries who are well versed in Community affairs and very helpful, the quality of advice and information available to the business sector is not consistent throughout the country. Enthusiastic civil servants and officials often get promoted or transferred away from the subject after two or three years with no guarantee that a person of similar qualities will replace them. Most officials tend to be well versed only in a single aspect of Community membership dealt with by the branch or organization which they serve and their reactions are bound to be coloured by the policy of that organization. The unfortunate result is that not only has there never been sufficient European Community experts within the information network to close the communication gap but that we have a largely non-European minded body of officials dealing with European questions and forming part of the front line of contact with the business community.

Almost completely absent from the information network in the United Kingdom is a sense of enthusiasm for every day Community matters. It is difficult to get excited about a European Commission decision under the competition rules (Articles 85 to 90 in the Treaty of Rome) on non-competition clauses contained in agreements for the transfer of ownership of a business. But it matters to somebody. Getting to grips with the European Community using a network of sources — none of which are officially obliged to educate and enthuse the business sector about the Community — is not going to get any easier until decisions are taken at a high level to encourage training in European Community affairs. A start could be made in schools, where European studies are not automatically included in the curriculum, if at all, and where many teachers are prepared to ignore the Community on the grounds that no one has instructed them to prepare pupils for a life as Europeans. Some of those pupils will undoubtedly enter one kind of business or another which has links with Europe. By the same token, civil servants and other officials dealing with the business community could learn the workings of, if not actually work in, Brussels itself. In France, where everyone does well out of Community membership, civil servants aspiring to reach senior posts are obliged to spend several years working in a Community institution. There is no such obligation in Britain. Those civil servants who do take an interest in the Community and leave the United Kingdom to work in a Community institution automatically sever their ties with their own government service.

The business community itself must also share some of the responsibility for its own ignorance of the European Community. Widely dispersed and understaffed though the information services are, businesses often fail to grasp even the most elementary facts. Staff in the Department of Trade's European Community Information Unit, now virtually wound up, were still being asked to list the member states of the Community ten years after accession. And many enquirers still fail to distinguish between the European Regional Development Fund, which provides cash for regional economic development and recovery in the worst off regions in the Community, and the European Development Fund, which finances projects in overseas countries for which European-based firms can supply equipment and know-how.

The challenge for the information services as a whole is to meet the business sector's need for guidance and information designed to increase profits with an operation designed to clarify developments of particular interest to business and to save the business community's precious time. Sadly, the information network has not so far been able to respond adequately to the special needs of business.

The business community has become increasingly confused and information services have expected it to make do with the present fragmented system of dealing with enquirers, who are sent from pillar to post in search of answers which could, under an efficient system, be easily obtained. Short of creating a European Community information organization with a counselling capability, the most immediate improvements would result from increased coordination between existing information services. It is no good relying on conscientious individuals scattered throughout the information network; there must be an established and integrated information system whose coordination is such that when an enquirer contacts any one source he is guaranteed access to other relevant sources straight away.

To conclude this discussion on the communication gap between the Community and Britain, it is not a case of politicians and officials being 'in the know' while business and the general public are left in the dark. Responsibility for the communication gap is shared by all. It is in view of the apathy of the business sector and the shortcomings of the information network that the suggestions in the rest of this chapter are made. It is hoped that a broad summary of EC-related business information sources will help to focus attention on the key aspects of membership which the business community must eventually comprehend.

The UK government and its information services

THE GOVERNMENT'S ROLE

Not all businesses have been clear about the British government's role in the European Community. Obviously, the government represents British interests in the conduct of EC policy and in the drafting of new legislation. But it must also negotiate with an eye to wider European interests in accordance with the spirit of the Treaty of Rome. That is the principle. In practice meetings of the Council of Ministers — the Community's main legislative body — have in recent years become a forum for acrimonious dispute.

At the heart of the debate on Community budget and agricultural reforms has been the UK's insistence on a fairer budget contribution and the introduction of measures which will put the breaks on runaway spending on agriculture. Food surpluses have increased because under the Treaty of Rome the Community is obliged to meet the difference in price between produce sold within the Community and produce sold elsewhere at lower world prices. Unlike the British government, other Community governments have found it politically unacceptable to come away from Council meetings with a cut in income for their farmers.

On detailed legislation, the government's role is easier to understand. The interests of all British parties affected by any new Community law must be taken into account. If a proposal for a new regulation or directive raises important questions about the national interest then it can be sent back to the drawing board or vetoed outright. In most cases redrafting after further consultations with government and industry is required. But the process can take several years to complete while the views of the European Parliament, the European Commission and the Economic and Social Committee are being taken into account.

There are many examples of EC legislation that governments have rejected or delayed. In the UK, the so-called 'Vredeling' proposals on the disclosure of information to employees in large companies met with outspoken objections from government and industry alike. The European Commission's draft directive on product liability was also 'blocked' for several years because in its various forms it has proved unworkable in the Community as a whole.

Another aspect of the government's role is the introduction of UK legislation to meet broad EC requirements. If the Community passes a new directive it is usually implemented throughout member states by means of national legislation. In some cases the national legislation carries greater weight than the EC's directive which may only lay down minimum requirements acceptable throughout the Community. And there is a growing tendency for governments to subscribe to the broad thrust of EC ideas while reserving the right to take the kind of action they think is best suited to conditions in their own countries.

THE GOVERNMENT INFORMATION SERVICE

It is natural to suppose that the government's own information service should bear the brunt of enquiries from the business sector about the European Community. After all, what happens in the Community is more likely to have immediate bearing on the business community than on anyone else. Regulations, directives and decisions are being enacted in Brussels or Westminster almost by the hour. Most of them concern commerce and industry to some extent as the Community continues to concentrate on harmonizing legislation on technical standards, health and safety, company legislation, employee legislation and a host of other questions involving the business sector. In truth, however, the government information service is neither geared to providing such a service for the business sector nor is it large enough to do more than publish material on the Community, as required, and brief the press on current aspects of British membership. The government information service is concerned with more or less everything in life that involves government, and the European Community is just part of this huge repertoire.

The government information service, covering a wide range of expertise including press office duties, speech writing, publicity and journalism, can only focus on those aspects of membership which happen to be new and topical. But there is one exception. In order to meet the specific need for information on the European Community, the government set up in 1973 a European Community Information Unit in the Department of Trade and Industry (DTI), complete with a staff of twelve answering a barrage of enquiries from the business community, the general public and school children alike. Five years later the number of staff answering queries was down to three because the number of telephone calls had dropped to as little as twenty a day with a corresponding number of written enquiries coming in. By 1983, when Britain coolly marked, if not celebrated, the tenth anniversary of membership, the number of telephone calls had fallen to an average of ten, while the number of written enquiries totalled no more than twenty a week. Naturally enough, the question of maintaining the Unit was discussed, particularly as this was a period of public spending cuts. Some of the staff of the Unit were, with good reason, transferred to other duties and the responsibility for manning the one telephone left at the disposal of a residue of callers fell to a single officer who had other duties to carry out to justify his keep.

Clearly it was no longer reasonable to pay the costs of running the Unit on its previous scale when the demand for information had virtually ceased. But it would be wrong to imagine that the disintegration of the Information Unit signalled a general rise in consciousness about the European Community. If anything, it revealed a growing resistance to the subject and a general realization that the Unit did not know all the answers. Most of the enquirers were referred to experts in Whitehall departments as a matter of course. And, no doubt, repeat calls were directed at those Whitehall executive staff whom business callers gradually came to know.

This steady decline in demand for information from the Unit is not as curious as it may at first seem. Just as there is a hard core of companies which export regularly, so there is a nucleus of business people who have become conversant with European Community ways. The problem lies with the uninitiated who have never asked a question about the Community in their lives and whose interest in the Community, or some small aspect of it, is provoked at random by the emergence of some new piece of Community legislation. This is demonst-rated by the Lords report on trade with member states which concludes that those companies which have done best in European markets are those which have been best informed about European Community matters. It may not be a startling revelation but its undoubted value is that the plain fact has gone on record. Thus it shows that the link between exporting to Europe and knowledge of European Community developments is a conclusive one. In other words, the business community's interest in the Community increases in proportion to likely material gains.

With this new assertion in mind, it is easy to understand that a small government information service, comprised of press officers, writers, journal-ists, photographers, designers and members of other professions engaged in a wide range of duties could not be the focal point for all queries about the European Community. A much less ephemeral involvement with Community matters is required to do justice to this problem. But it is an open question at the time of writing whether the Department of Trade and Industry's European Community Information Unit should be retained, possibly strengthened in some form, to continue acting as a signposting service for business enquirers weary of negotiating a passage through the Whitehall labyrinth.

There is, of course, another limitation on the information services in Whitehall. Apart from the DTI Information Unit, information staff are employed principally to liaise with the press, not the public, and to prepare written and spoken material for dissemination through the media and by means of publications made generally available. In other words, the information service acts as the government's own voice on current aspects of membership, not as the voice of the European Community. The Community has its own information service with offices in London and in other UK cities as described in Chapter 3.

Dealing with Whitehall

In the preceding pages the European Community has been described largely as it is seen by members of the business community who have experienced difficulty in coming to grips with the European Community and in obtaining information. After all, the purpose of this book is to inform those people who do not know how to keep in touch with developments in Europe, not those who do. Whitehall's overall position has been briefly outlined, with particular emphasis upon the fact that there is no central source of information on Community questions, only the remnants of an EC Information Unit in the Department of Trade and Industry. The purpose of this last section is to draw attention in much more detail to some of the sources of expert advice available from the executive side of government departments in Whitehall. Clearly, in a chapter of this length it would be too weighty a task to describe the entire Whitehall involvement with the Community as well as the role of the banks, trade organizations and other intermediaries. The picture changes daily. So do people's addresses and telephone numbers. Almost all of Whitehall's work affects the business community in some way, however small, whether in matters of employment, consumer safety, companies legislation, customs and excise, agricultural subsidies, road haulage permits in Europe, grants and loans of one sort or another, or even passport and travel matters. In the case of trade associations European Community questions are often dealt with only as a secondary aspect of their work in monitoring the law or promoting the interests of a multitude of different trades, industries and professions. For these reasons the following guide for intermediaries helping the business sector is selective, concentrating on those matters of general interest to the business community as a whole. Naturally, the Department of Trade and Industry is the focal point for many questions about the European Community raised by the members of the business community and their advisers.[4]

However, before proceeding to the directory of official sources, a few tips on how to deal with Whitehall departments may be useful. The essential point is that the actual source of information is a particular officer in a particular division within a Whitehall department, not a general enquiry point. Enquiry points to which callers are almost always at first directed exist to sift calls and refer them to an appropriate division or branch. This is why it helps to phrase questions about the Community with care. It is no longer reasonable to expect that the question 'I wonder if you can help me — I want to speak to someone about the European Community' will yield satisfactory results. That approach is far too vague. The European Community covers too wide a range of topics for a telephone operator to guess whom the caller should be referred to. As a rule, it is much quicker and easier to ask for enquiries first (since there may sometimes be an EC enquiry point), then to ask for a contact about the precise matter in question. Needless to say, it also helps to contact the correct government department in the first place; health and safety at work, for instance, is a matter for the Health and Safety Executive not the Department of Employment. All this may sound rather basic to the initiated and to the many well-versed intermediaries in business organizations, libraries and other bodies up and down the country. But if the number of wasted telephone calls made by business personnel could be counted and the costs in overheads and time assessed, it could easily be shown that improvements are needed.

THE DEPARTMENT OF TRADE AND INDUSTRY

The Department of Trade and Industry has undergone many changes over the years. It has been split into two separate departments and welded together again. There have even been rumours of plans to scrap most of the industrial side of its work and disperse key elements, such as the work on regional and industrial aid, to the provinces. When the two departments were once more united at the beginning of 1984 the three basic aims of the DTI were said to be: to promote a climate for British industry and commerce as conducive to enterprise and competition as that in any other industrialized country; to promote the international competitiveness of British firms through increased efficiency and adaptability; and to encourage innovation to improve the products, processes and services that British industry and commerce can offer to the world.

In an eight-page booklet marking the reversion to a single trade and industry department, EC membership was touched on in three short references covering the DTI's many responsibilities. Anyone expecting a promise to help the business sector make its mark in Europe more strongly would have been disappointed. The Lords' report had not been taken to heart, despite the call for government action to 'provide information and assistance to industry in developing markets in Europe'.

Interestingly enough, the Lords' report went on to say that: 'In industry itself, firms and sectors that have fared badly in European trade have much to learn from those which have been successful' — confirmation, perhaps, that businesses will be left to help themselves. In so doing, they may want to be conversant with the work of the following aspects of the DTI's work.

Barriers to trade

Non tariff barriers (NTBs) have often been the cause of difficulty in doing business in the European Community, although there is a feeling in Whitehall that complaints by UK manufacturers about barriers such as national standards, regulations and test procedures, discriminatory public purchasing policies, subsidies and price controls, and the non-observance of international agreements or practices, are sometimes due to their lack of competitiveness in foreign markets. But many NTBs are intended to hinder imports into the countries which operate them. Generally, they contravene Article 30 of the Treaty of Rome. The whole question of NTBs is complex, and NTBs are themselves difficult to prove as deliberate attempts to obstruct trade. However, membership of the European Community means that UK businesses are increasingly vulnerable to NTBs, deliberate or unintended, which are determined on a Community basis. Experience has shown, despite the fact that some NTBs are operated quite openly by member states, that it is difficult to prove that NTBs are frustrating UK access to Community markets and to find a remedy. Proceedings initiated by the European Commission in the European Court of Justice are lengthy and carry no penalty.

Complaints about NTBs, preferably accompanied with evidence of injury to trade, can be raised with the relevant trade association, which might in turn present a case for the trade or industry affected as a whole, or they can be dealt with individually, again with evidence if any exists, by:

Department of Trade and Industry
European Commercial and Industrial Policy Division
1 Victoria Street
London SW1H 0ET
Tel. 01-215 7877 ext. 5047

However, the division prefers to receive complaints via other divisions in the DTI concerned with overseas trade or the trade or industry affected. Overall, this division of the DTI deals with European Community commercial and industrial policy, procedural and general matters — as they affect British interests — as well as the bilateral commercial relations with other Western European governments including Scandinavia. The division is mainly involved in issues of government responsibility, but it also takes complaints from industry about state aids and import practices which are referred to it by other divisions in the department. In the case of complaints from companies about NTBs affecting exports to the Community, the first point of contact should be with the Exports to Europe Branch (EEB) of the British Overseas Trade Board (BOTB). The division may then decide to help formulate a complaint to the European Commission in Brussels.

Exports to Europe

The Exports to Europe Branch of the British Overseas Trade Board consists of a series of 'country desks' grouped on a geographical basis to focus, coordinate and disseminate information about the whole of Western Europe to help companies export their goods. As yet, there is no common market in services such as insurance or travel. The general idea is that EEB should help British firms to break into European markets or expand their operations there. The whole of the European Community lies within Western Europe. Most businesses are aware that the Community of ten countries provides a market of 270 million consumers and takes over 40% of total UK exports a year. Western Europe as a whole takes 60%.

The importance of the completion of a common market in goods and services cannot be overstated for British exporters. As mentioned earlier, the case for membership of the Community rests heavily on tariff-free access to Community markets and the eventual removal of all legislative and procedural barriers to trade. Another important factor is that the Community provides a strong base from which UK companies can export to the rest of the world. That is the theory, and it works a lot of the time. But many companies still find that the common market is more fragmented than they expected. Even when Community-wide regulations do apply, for example in matters of safety at work, the stringency of laws may vary from country to country. This is because the Community sometimes resorts to laying down the minimum standards it can persuade the member states to accept *en bloc*. But some member states may decide that the Community's standards, as in the case of the permitted level of asbestos fibres in the air at places of work, are not stringent enough. In the case of asbestos, British laws are tougher than those imposed by the Community. UK exporters must ascertain what the precise regulations are for many aspects of their trade in Community countries and this is where the EEB provides valuable help. The Branch employs sixty staff, grouped in four sections with a fifth in the West European Coordination Section of the Branch to deal with multi-country enquiries.

The overall task of EEB is to coordinate trade promotion in Western Europe, using its links with the commercial staff in British embassies and consulates. The Branch provides a very wide range of specific information and counselling on each of the Western European markets to help exporters with such matters as taxes, standards, regulations, distribution, the appointment of agents, value added tax (VAT), transportation and general market prospects.

EEB works in close cooperation with the BOTB's European Trade Committee which organizes export promotion initiatives, including the use of special 'task forces' to explore the potential UK penetration of specific markets with specific products. Much of the information collected by EEB is published in a series of market profiles, obtainable free of charge. These profiles often highlight prospects for exports of particular commodities, and fuller market reports covering broad product areas, such as hospital equipment and clothing, are prepared by the commercial sections of the embassies and consulates for use by exporters.

EEB country desks pass all these market pointers to UK firms, along with specific enquiries from overseas buyers and notices of tenders from EC public authorities, via the BOTB's regional offices. A full range of services to exporters is available including the Export Intelligence Service, support for participation in overseas trade fairs and exhibitions, the Market Advisory Service and the Market Entry Guarantee Scheme. The Export Intelligence Service sends out around 20,000 notices to its 7,500 subscribers every year. Half of them concern calls for tender and the rest convey useful facts about overseas markets worldwide. A high proportion of them relate to European opportunities and market conditions.

Exports to Europe Branch of BOTB

Exports to Europe Branch
British Overseas Trade Board
1 Victoria Street
London SW1H 0ET

Belgium
tel. 01-215 5486

Denmark
tel. 01-215 5341

France
tel. 01-215 3015

Germany
tel. 01-215 5333

Greece
tel. 01-215 3984

Ireland
tel. 01-215 5336

Italy
tel. 01-215 3981

Luxembourg
tel. 01-215 5486

Netherlands
tel. 01-215 3957

Portugal
tel. 01-215 3984 (applicant member)

Spain
tel. 01-215 5510 (applicant member)

BOTB Regional Offices

SOUTH EASTERN
Ebury Bridge House
Ebury Bridge Road
London SW1W 8QD
tel. 01-730 9678

Norfolk, Suffolk, Cambridgeshire, Buckinghamshire, Hertfordshire, Essex, Oxfordshire, Greater London, Berkshire, Surrey, Hampshire, Kent, East Sussex, West Sussex, Isle of Wight, Bedfordshire, Middlesex.

NORTH EASTERN
Stanegate House
2 Groat Market
Newcastle upon Tyne NE1 1YN
tel. (0632) 324722

Northumberland, Tyne and Wear, Durham, Cleveland

YORKSHIRE AND HUMBERSIDE
Priestley House
Park Row
Leeds LS1 5LF
tel. (0532) 443171

North Yorkshire, West Yorkshire, South Yorkshire, Humberside

WEST MIDLANDS
Ladywood House
Stephenson Street
Birmingham B2 4DT
tel. (021) 632 4111

Staffordshire, Shropshire, West Midlands, Warwickshire, Hereford and Worcester

NORTH WESTERN
Sunley Buildings
Piccadilly Plaza
Manchester M1 4BA
tel. (061) 236 2171

Cumbria, Lancashire, Merseyside, Greater Manchester, Cheshire, Derbyshire (High Peak District)

EAST MIDLANDS
Severns House
20 Middle Pavement
Nottingham NG1 7DW
tel. (0602) 506181

Derbyshire (except High Peak District), Nottinghamshire, Lincolnshire, Leicestershire, Northamptonshire

SOUTH WESTERN
The Pithay
Bristol BS1 2PB
tel. (0272) 291071

Gloucestershire, Avon, Wiltshire, Somerset, Dorset, Devon, Cornwall (including Isles of Scilly)

The following also act as BOTB Regional Offices

Welsh Office
New Crown Building
Cathays Park
Cardiff CF1 3NQ
tel. (0222) 824171

Scottish Export Office
Alhambra House
45 Waterloo Street
Glasgow G2 6AT
tel. (041) 248 2855

Industrial Development Board for Northern Ireland
IDB House
64 Chichester Street
Belfast BT1 4JX
tel. (0232) 233233

Library services

The DTI Library Services maintains a Statistics and Market Intelligence Library (SMIL) which is open to the public from Monday to Friday, 9.30 a.m. to 5.30 p.m. Last admission is at 5.00 p.m. and the library is closed on public holidays.

By using SMIL, visitors can save themselves time and money by consulting a vast range of foreign statistics and market information. The library does not provide this information to telephone callers, although general EC enquiries are sometimes routed to experts in the DTI by library staff. Statistical and market information must be researched by readers themselves.

UK statistics are also available and the library houses a very wide range of publications including foreign directories, overseas business reports, market share reports and development plans. Since 1974 the library has been designated the library of the Government Statistical Service, acting as an enquiry point and advising readers wishing to make contact with all UK government departments concerning statistical enquiries.

There is also a product data store in the DTI run by the BOTB, containing product and industry based market information.

Statistics and Market Intelligence Library
Department of Trade and Industry
1–19 Victoria Street
London SW1 0ET
tel. 01-215 5444/5445

Product Data Store
British Overseas Trade Board
1 Victoria Street
London SW1H 0ET
tel. 01-215 3520

Competition policy

Articles 85 and 86 of the Treaty of Rome prohibit as incompatible with the common market certain agreements and certain concerted practices and abuses of dominant positions which may affect trade between member states of the Community. The rules do not apply to purely national competition which has no bearing on trade between member states. Articles 85 and 86, however broadly worded, are the foundation of the Community's competition policy and most people with a grievance or wishing to get clearance for their own operations in Europe need to seek clarification of the rules first of all.

In this respect the DTI acts as an advisory body and helps to formulate complaints being made to the European Commission in Brussels.

The overall intention of the competition rules is to deter private firms from setting up barriers to trade that impede the development of a single market within the Community. And competition policy is one area of activity where the European Commission does have the power to impose legislation which is binding in all member states.

Council Regulation 17/62 is the Commission's main instrument for implementing the competition rules.[5] The regulation sets out the requirement for compulsory notification of agreements to the Commission and gives the Commission powers to grant exemption to the rules. This is called negative clearance. The Commission also has powers to investigate any infringement of the rules and to levy fines in cases where a breach of the rules has been established. Complainants may take a case to the Commission directly if they wish, and they are not bound to prove that there has been an infringement. That is the Commission's job.

Apart from exercising its general power to implement the competition rules generally, the Commission has recently imposed legislation concerning restrictive purchasing agreements and restrictive distribution agreements.

It is, however, not possible to do full justice to this complex subject in a few paragraphs. Further information and advice is available from:

Department of Trade and Industry
General Policy Division
Room 2820
Millbank Tower
Millbank
London SW1P 4QU
tel. 01-215 4207

Commission of the European Communities
Directorate-General for Competition
rue de la Loi 200
B-1049 Brussels
tel. (010) 322 235 1111

EC Company law

The DTI's Companies Legislation Division is very active in the field of EC company law and is in constant touch with the business sector over the many EC company law measures either already enacted or under consideration. The division normally issues consultative documents free of charge concerning new EC instruments under consideration.

Officials from Companies Legislation Division, the Insolvency Division and Solicitors Division attend meetings of the EC Council and Commission working parties which are usually held in Brussels. There can be up to sixty such meetings in a year.

The division is willing to help callers with questions concerning EC company law directives already adopted and any other measures still under discussion. Details of the measures are contained in a booklet, published twice yearly, called *Harmonisation of Company law in Europe — timetable and progress of draft directives and other proposals.* It is available free of charge from:

Companies Legislation Division
Department of Trade and Industry
Room 511
Sanctuary Buildings
20 Great Smith Street
London SW1P 3DB

Tel. 01-215 4141
   Sixth Directive: Division of public limited liability companies (Scissions).
   Draft regulation for a European company Statute.
   Draft convention on international mergers.
   Convention on the mutual recognition of companies, firms and legal persons.
   Draft regulation for a European economic interest grouping.

Pennington report: proposal for a directive on takeovers.

Proposal for a Council directive to approximate the laws relating to guarantees and indemnities.

Proposal for a Council directive on the legal consequences of agreements creating simple reservation of title to goods.

Tel. 01-215 4249

Seventh Directive: group accounts.

Draft directive on annual accounts of credit institutions.

Proposal for a draft directive on the annual accounts of branches of credit institutions.

Tel. 01-215 5817

Draft directive on the coordination of laws relating to undertakings for collective investment in transferable securities.

Tel. 01-606 4071 ext 120

Draft bankruptcy convention.

Tel. 01-215 5359

Draft directive on procedures for informing and consulting employees.

Proposals for a fifth directive on company structure.

Draft ninth directive on conduct of groups of companies.

Tel. 01-215 5980

Directive on prospectuses issued when shares are listed on the stock exchange.

Directive on admission of securities to official stock exchange listing.

Directive on the continuing disclosure of information concerning securities admitted to listing on the stock exchange.

Draft eighth directive: qualification of auditors.

Draft directive on right of establishment for accountants.

Draft directive on prospectuses to be published when securities are offered for subscription or sale to the public.

Draft directive on canvassing securities.

Proposal for a directive on insider dealing.

Proposal for a directive on the coordination of laws covering the taking up of the activity of stockbroker.

Anti-Dumping

The DTI's Anti-Dumping Unit helps industry to obtain protection against industry from outside the European Community. Dumping is usually defined as selling at prices below those charged in a producer's own market. If a company has reasonable evidence that an imported product is being dumped or unfairly subsidized and is causing material injury to EC industry, a formal application for anti-dumping or countervailing action may be made to the European Commission. The Unit will advise and assist complainants to prepare and present their case.

Department of Trade and Industry
Anti-Dumping Unit
1 Victoria Street
London SW1H 0ET
tel. 01-215 3990

Notices of anti-dumping investigations or action taken by the European Commission appear regularly in the European Community News pages of *British business* magazine, published weekly by the DTI.

British business magazine
11th Floor
Millbank Tower
Millbank
London SW1 4QU
tel. 01-211 6088

Subscriptions:
HMSO
PO Box 276
London SW8 5DT
tel. 01-211 8667

Insurance

DTI's Insurance Division is involved in UK policy towards existing Community directives on insurance and the negotiation of draft directives including the draft directives on non-life insurance, credit, sickness and legal expense insurance, motorists' assistance schemes and insurance company accounts.

As with other divisions covering EC matters, Insurance Division represents UK interests at EC Commission Working Party meetings where most of the discussion on draft directives between member states takes place at official, rather than ministerial, level. Naturally the division maintains close contact with the insurance industry through the British Insurers European Committee.

Insurance Division
Branch 3b
Department of Trade and Industry
Sanctuary Buildings
16/20 Great Smith Street
London SW1P 3DB
tel. 01-215 5931

The Secretary
The British Insurers' European Committee
Aldermary House
Queen Street
London EC4N 1TT
tel. 01-248 4477 ext. 2632

Consumer affairs

The Consumer Affairs Division of the DTI deals with all questions dealing with EC consumer protection and safety and consumer credit. The division is responsible for negotiating for the UK on proposed EC directives in this field and implementing directives and regulations already adopted.

Views on EC proposals are sought from the business sector from time to time — usually, but not exclusively, through trade associations. Businesses can bring themselves up to date by getting in touch with their trade association although officials in the Consumer Affairs Division are prepared to advise businesses of their obligations under EC directives and regulations in force or of the implications of those still under consideration, such as the draft directive on product liability. Other matters covered by the division include doorstep selling, misleading advertising, and weights and measures legislation. Well over twenty directives concern weights and measures, though not all of them have yet been implemented or even agreed. A list of them is published twice yearly in *British business* magazine (see above).

Consumer Affairs Division
Department of Trade and Industry
Millbank Tower
Millbank
London SW1P 4QU
tel. 01-211 3337

Weights and measures: tel. 01-211 7605

Aid-funded Third World contracts

In 1984 construction, mining, agricultural and many other types of contract in the third world were worth around £10 billion to suppliers of equipment and expertise. The European Community, under the Lomé Conventions, funds a large proportion of such contracts in the sixty-one African, Caribbean and Pacific States (ACP). Details of the contracts are published in the *Official journal of the European Communities*, available from Her Majesty's Stationery Office (HMSO). Unfortunately, by the time businesses manage to get a copy of the appropriate *OJ* it is often too late to submit a tender. But the Commission does operate a computerized service, Tenders Electronic Daily (TED), which is located in Luxembourg.

The British business community is generally thought to be behind those of other European countries in getting a share of aid-funded contracts. In 1983 the EC funded contracts which entailed the procurement of goods and services amounting to £400 million. But the Lomé Conventions concern a much larger figure spread over a period of years.

As the government department responsible for the aid programme, the Overseas Development Administration has the primary interest, but the DTI becomes involved in all procurement matters and its World Aid Section goes to considerable lengths to inform and assist businesses in Britain to get aid-funded contracts, even holding weekly walk-in briefing meetings at the DTI headquarters. There is a six-man Aid-Funded Advisory Panel run by the London Chamber of Commerce and Industry, but, since a DTI expert sits on the panel, business representatives may just as well go to the DTI direct.

World Aid Section
Projects and Export Policy Division
Department of Trade and Industry
1 Victoria Street
London SW1 0ET
tel. 01-215 3997

Import licensing

International Trade Policy Division, Branch 3, Section C is responsible for UK import licensing policy. The policy section at 1 Victoria Street implements, by means of amendments to the Open General Import Licence (OGIL), EEC regulations on import licensing, prohibitions and restrictions, and announces any changes to the licensing arrangements by publishing in *British business* details in the form of notices to importers. It also oversees the Import Licensing Branch based at Charles House in Kensington High Street.

The Import Licensing Branch is responsible for the day to day administration of the UK's import licensing arrangements and for the issuing of import licenses. Any enquiries about import licensing and quantitative restrictions should be directed there in the first instance. Import Licensing Branch enquiries: tel. 01-603 4644 ext. 264/265.

Technical standards

Harmonization of technical standards is one of the Community's principal goals in creating a common market devoid of obstructions to the free movement of goods. Unfortunately, progress is slow and many countries in the Community, if not all, operate national standards across many industries, and business representatives wanting to penetrate Community markets must find out what technical and safety standards are in force.

Most of this information is housed by the Technical Help to Exporters (THE) arm of the British Standards Institution. There are 6,000 translations of foreign standards available from THE and THE engineers will even visit a company to give advice on how to meet the standards laid down in the markets at which the company is aiming. THE advises every exporter to check any relevant national laws and regulations, and national standards like insurance requirements and certification procedures before taking steps to sell products overseas.

Technical Help to Exporters
British Standards Institution
Linford Wood

Milton Keynes MK14 6LE
tel. (0908) 32003

Standards and Quality Policy Unit
Department of Trade and Industry
Ashdown House
123 Victoria Street
London SW1E 6RB
tel. 01-212 5508

References and notes

[1] *Trade patterns: the United Kingdom's changing trade patterns subsequent to membership of the European Community*. 7th report of the House of Lords Select Committee on the European Communities, HMSO, 1983–84, HL 41.

[2] Ibid, para 102.

[3] Ibid, para 103.

[4] Much more detailed information is available in *EEC contacts 1984/85*, Eurofi (UK) Ltd. (25 London Road, Newbury, Berks. RG13 1JL), 1984, prepared by the author of this chapter.

[5] *Journal officiel des Communautés européennes* 13, 21 February 1962, pp. 204–211.

10

Grants and Loans from the European Communities

GAY SCOTT

Introduction

One of the opportunities which membership of the European Community (EC) affords the United Kingdom (UK) is access to a wide variety of grants and soft loans. It would be difficult to ignore the fact that the lion's share of funding goes towards the Common Agricultural Policy. The total Community budget for 1983 provided for expenditure of about £12,000 million, 98% of which is expenditure by the Commission in its implementation of Community policies. Agriculture accounted for some two-thirds of the total. Whereas this proportion is dwindling as a percentage of the total budget, agricultural spending continues to rise in real terms.

There is evidence, however, that the Community will in future years concentrate more and more upon new industrial policies, and expenditure on these and related research and development will become more significant. The Guarantee Section of the European Agricultural Guidance and Guarantee Fund (EAGGF), which aims to provide a secure income for Community farmers (and reasonably priced agricultural products for consumers) and seeks to alleviate the problems of agriculture within the Community, is not covered within this chapter in any detail. It is sufficient to say that financial assistance is provided in the form of export restitutions and reimbursements for intervention storage via national ministries of agriculture. The main beneficiaries are of course individual farmers.

But what of other sources of Community funding that may be of interest to companies, local authorities, universities, research institutions, etc.? In this chapter the main sources of funds will be examined, and guidance will be given on how interested organizations may secure funding for suitable projects. First, to help the reader understand how finance is organized, a brief description of the Community's budgetary process follows. Some important differences exist between it and the budgetary process of most member states.

The Community's budgetary process

The Community budget is financed from a system of 'own resources', which means that the Community has a certain independence because it has its own fiscal revenue — albeit revenue collected by national governments and passed on to Brussels. These 'own resources' comprise agricultural and sugar levies, customs duties and a percentage of value added tax (VAT). Agricultural levies and customs duties are taxes on trade between the Community and the rest of the world. Sugar levies are taxes on the production and storage of sugar. VAT contributions are set at 1% of a harmonized VAT base.

The Community presents its expenditure plans in annual budget proposals, the financial year running from January to December. It is authorized in advance for one financial year. However, the budget distinguishes between appropriations for commitments and appropriations for payments, a point which is of significance to those seeking Community funding. Commitment appropriations are the total cost of legal obligations which can be entered into in the current financial year for activities which will lead to payments in the current and future financial years. Payment appropriations are the amounts of money available for spending in that year arising from commitments made in the current or preceding years. Unused appropriations may be carried forward to the following year and appropriations not used in one part of the budget may be transferred to another part.

The budget is denominated in European Currency Units (ECUs). The ECU is a weighted average of the national currencies of each member state and its value is determined day by day by the Commission according to daily exchange rates.

When the Commission formulates new policy proposals it can enter these as headings in the budget even when no agreement has been given by the Council of Ministers. Later on, if agreement is reached and if financial resources are made available, these policies can then be implemented promptly, possibly by a transfer of appropriations from another heading. Each year the drawing up of the Community's budget for the following year commences in early spring and goes through to late December. This preliminary draft budget (PDB) is issued as a COM document in about eight volumes. Eventually, once agreed, it is published in the *Official journal* 'L' series towards the end of January in the year of its implementation.

The PDB represents an assessment by each of the Community institutions — the Commission, the Parliament, etc. — of the cost, in the next financial year, of Community activities.

The budget reflects the financial consequences of Community policies already agreed or being discussed rather than new spending policies. However, decisions are taken on the amounts to be allocated to general areas of policy where the annual level is not predetermined, as in the case of food aid for example. As mentioned earlier there is a device for providing appropriations where it is expected that a new policy will be agreed, either during the course of that financial year or in the course of the financial year to which the PDB relates. This is known as Chapter 100 and each section of the budget contains Chapter 100. Later on, provisions entered under Chapter 100 can be transferred (with the necessary agreement of the Council, or the Parliament) to the relevant operational chapter in which the new policy falls. Supplementary budgets to achieve the same result can also be arranged.

Grants and loans

Expenditure by the Commission in order to implement Community policy includes the cost of Commission staff, translation, secretarial and publication facilities — all the usual items of administrative expenditure of an international organization. About 90% of the principal expenditure of the Communities consists of finance designed to contribute to implementing Community policies in the member states. The bulk of this finance is in the form of grants. In addition, the three European Communities have the ability to finance some activities by loans and can raise money on the markets for this purpose. The main sources of both grants and loans are described in the rest of this chapter. As it would be impossible to reproduce here all the details of the various regulations and directives governing individual funds, an outline of each is given, including the main objectives, criteria, etc., together with references for more detailed examination.

The European Social Fund

(A) PURPOSE
The European Social Fund is an employment, job creation and training fund. Non-repayable grants are available for vocational training and guidance, recruitment and wage subsidies, resettlement and technical advice concerned with job creation.

(B) ELIGIBLE PROJECTS
Under recently proposed changes, about three quarters of the Fund's resources will be allocated for training and employment measures for young people under the age of twenty-five. The emphasis will be upon those young people whose chances of employment are poor because they lack training and those who are among the long-term unemployed.

Fund assistance may also be given to those over twenty-five years of age in the following categories:

(i) unemployed people, those who are threatened with unemployment and in particular the long-term unemployed;

(ii) women who wish to return to work;

(iii) handicapped people capable of working in the open labour market;

(iv) migrant workers who move or have moved within the Community or become resident in the Community to take up work, together with the members of their families;

(v) people who are employed particularly in small or medium-sized undertakings and who require retraining with a view to the introduction of new technology or the improvement of management techniques in those undertakings;

(vi) Fund assistance may also be granted for people to be engaged as instructors, vocational-guidance or placement experts or development agents.

(C) FORMS OF FINANCIAL AID AND ELIGIBLE EXPENDITURE

Individuals cannot benefit from Fund support (only organizations) and all applications must be guaranteed by a recognized public authority. To be eligible for funding a private organization must be in receipt of a grant from such a body. As a general rule the level of support from the Fund for a scheme cannot exceed the amount of finance provided by a public authority nor can it exceed 50% of total eligible costs. In the case of 'super-priority' regions this can be increased by 10%. (This applies in the UK only to Northern Ireland).

Eligible expenditure includes:

(i) incomes of individuals undergoing vocational training;

(ii) the costs of:
   — the preparation, operation and administration of vocational training measures;
   — board and lodging, and travelling expenses for the recipients of vocational training;
   — in the case of vocational integration of the handicapped, the adaptation of workplaces;

(iii) the granting, for a period not exceeding twelve months per person, of aid for recruitment to additional jobs or for employment in projects for the creation of additional jobs which fulfil a public need, for young people under twenty-five who are seeking employment and are long-term unemployed;

(iv) benefits designed to facilitate the transfer and integration of migrant workers and members of their families.

(v) carrying out preparatory studies.

(D) HOW TO APPLY

Applications are made on official forms obtainable from the Department of

Employment through whom all applications must be submitted. Each year guidelines are published by 1 May for application in the following year. The deadline for applications is October of the year preceding that to which the application applies. The point of contact is as follows:

Department of Employment
Overseas Division (OB2)
Caxton House
Tothill Street
London, SW1 H9NA.[1]

The Commission has proposed guidelines for the development of training policies in the Community suggesting that an increased effort is required by member states to improve the quality and scope of training for workers of all ages. The Community dimension of this proposal, which has subsequently been agreed in a resolution, includes demonstration projects, reviews and studies which will be funded by the Community and will probably be administered by Social Fund officials.

The European Regional Development Fund

(A) PURPOSE
The European Regional Development Fund (ERDF) is designed to provide grants to correct regional imbalances within the Community, particularly those resulting from the preponderance of agriculture and from industrial change and structural underemployment.

(B) ELIGIBLE PROJECTS
There are two sections of the Fund, the 'quota' and the 'non-quota'. Ninety per cent of aid is provided under the 'quota' system, each member state being allocated a fixed quota in proportion to the seriousness of its regional problems. Five per cent is allocated to the 'non-quota' section designed to provide finance for some specific measures.

(i) The 'quota' section
Under this section the following categories are eligible for financial assistance.
Industrial investment: The Fund provides grant aid for industrial, handicraft or tourism investment projects whose total cost is over 50,000 ECU (£28,000) and which fall within the criteria established by the regional development programme in the member state concerned. Investments must be economically viable, must be assisted by national regional aids and must either create or preserve at least ten jobs.

Infrastructure investment: The Fund provides grant aid to infrastructure projects which are already being financed, in whole or in part, by public authorities in the country concerned.

Studies: Feasibility studies relating to a potential ERDF project may be funded to a maximum of 50% of the cost.

(ii) The 'non-quota' section

This section is used to finance specific regional development programmes which help to overcome problems caused by the Community's own policies. Five measures announced to date include improvement of the situation in the border areas between Ireland and Northern Ireland by promoting tourism, communications, etc.; aid for small and medium enterprises in steel closure areas (e.g. Strathclyde, Clwyd); similar measures in shipbuilding areas (e.g. Tyne and Wear, Cleveland, Merseyside).

A series of six new specific measures is currently being prepared and this is likely to include regions affected by the restructuring of the textile and clothing industry.

(C) FORM OF FINANCIAL AID AND ELIGIBLE EXPENDITURE

Assistance is not available to private individuals in the case of the 'quota system', and projects must be in receipt of a regional grant from the Government. They must therefore fall within Assisted Areas and must fit into the framework of the country's regional development programme. The creation of jobs is another important factor.

The Fund grants 20% of the cost of investment in an industrial, tourist or service project, and aid may in exceptional circumstances exceed 20%. It may not, however, exceed 50% of the total amount of regional aid granted by the national public authorities. (It should be noted that the UK Government does not pass on ERDF aid to companies in addition to their national grants.)

The Fund provides grants of 30% of the expenditure incurred by public authorities for infrastructure investments of less than 10m ECU (£5.6m) and 10%–30% maximum of the expenditure for investment of 10m ECU and above. In exceptional circumstances this aid may be as high as 40% for projects of special value to the developing region in which they are situated. Aid from the Fund may be taken in whole or in part in the form of interest rebates for 3 percentage points on loans granted by the EIB under its regional programme.

(D) HOW TO APPLY

Private sector applications are submitted through the Department of Industry Regional Offices. Public authorities submit proposals for infrastructure projects, through the Department of the Environment Regional Offices. Special forms are provided.[2]

In October 1981 a fairly radical review of the ERDF was proposed including an enlargement of the 'non-quota' section and an adjustment of the quotas for each member state. These proposals have proved to be controversial and no agreement has been reached at the time of writing.

Community lending

The Community has two 'banks', the European Investment Bank and the European Coal and Steel Community. In addition, the European Atomic Energy Community (Euratom) can raise loans to finance the construction of nuclear power stations, but this is such a specialized field that it is not dealt with here.

THE EUROPEAN INVESTMENT BANK

(A) PURPOSE
The European Investment Bank raises money on the international capital markets and then on-lends it for industrial, energy and infrastructure projects. The EIB is able to borrow money at the best possible rates, and as it is non-profit making it is able to offer loans at advantageous terms.

(B) ELIGIBLE PROJECTS
Broadly the Bank may grant loans for the financing of:
  (i) Projects for stimulating development in the less favoured regions (in the UK, the Assisted Areas).
 (ii) Projects for modernising or converting industries, or creating new activities, to offset structural difficulties affecting certain sectors.
(iii) Projects of common interest to several member states or to the Community as a whole, either because they contribute towards European economic integration (such as communications infrastructure, motorways, railways, inland waterways, telecommunications) or are projects arising from close technical and economic cooperation between undertakings in different member countries, or because they contribute towards the attainment of Community objectives such as environmental protection, the introduction of advanced technologies and more diversified and secure energy supplies.

(C) FORMS OF FINANCIAL AID AND ELIGIBLE EXPENDITURE
  (i) Direct loans
For larger loans negotiations are made directly between the Bank and the prospective borrower. There is no upper limit in absolute terms for a direct loan but a lower limit is set at about £1.5 million.
Those eligible include nationalized industries, local authorities, companies or any sound borrower (regardless of nationality). The eligible projects include infrastructural works, industry, tourism and some services. The limits are not more than half the capital expenditure on the project; the borrowers must

provide the remaining half and any working capital from other sources. The term is five to twelve years for industrial projects, and up to twenty years for infrastructure.

Rates vary from time to time but are fixed for the duration of the loan at the date of borrowing. Under the public sector Exchange Risk Guarantee (ERG) scheme, the borrower receives sterling at ½% less than the rate at which it would borrow from the National Loans Fund or Public Works Loan Board. If approved under the private sector ERG scheme (see section on Exchange Risk Guarantees) the borrower receives sterling at a cost below the borrowing rates ruling within the UK commercial banking sector. The interest rate at 1st June 1983 inclusive of the charge for ERG was 9½%.

Repayment is normally by equal half-yearly payments of capital and interest after a moratorium on capital repayments of up to five years, depending on project completion date. When its resources allow, the EIB may grant loans on which capital is repaid in full at term (bullet loans).

If ERG is approved, the borrower's liability is in sterling; if ERG is not available, 100% sterling may still be possible at rates near to EIB's borrowing costs. Loans may be made in a mixture of currencies according to the borrower's preferences (subject to availability). Security is usually a guarantee by government, a bank or a parent company with first-class credit rating. Exceptionally a loan may be secured on a company's assets or on throughput agreements. There are no arrangement fees and there is no formal commitment until contract signature, which is normally shortly before the date of each disbursement.

(ii) Loans via agents and intermediaries

The Government acts as an EIB agent for loans up to about £4.5m (agency loans) and there are credit lines (referred to as 'global loans') to various intermediaries for smaller loans. Those eligible normally include only companies located in the Assisted Areas of the UK with less than £45 million of net fixed assets and fewer than 500 employees but projects from bigger companies may be considered exceptionally. For companies outside the Assisted Areas loans are now available under the New Community Instrument (NCI). Eligible projects include mining, quarrying, manufacturing, processing, packaging, hotels, tourist facilities and services which can benefit industry or tourism. Limits are not more than half the cost of fixed assets needed for the project, to various other maxima (see below); and to not less than £15,000. The term is normally eight years (ten year agency loans for tourist projects).

Rates are those fixed for the duration of the loan at the time of borrowing. The currency of the borrower's liability is in sterling, and security is negotiated with an agent/intermediary.

(D) HOW TO APPLY

Enquiries regarding direct loans should be addressed to:

European Investment Bank
23 Queen Anne's Gate
Westminster
London, SW1H 9BU.

or

European Investment Bank
100 Bvd. Konrad Adenauer
L-2950 Luxembourg
Luxembourg G.D.

Applications for agency loans from £15,000 to £4.5m should be made to the English regional offices of the Department of Industry (DoI), the Scottish Economic Planning Department (SEPD), the Welsh Office Industry Department (WOID), the Northern Ireland Industrial Development Board and Local Enterprise Development Unit.

Applications for agency loans for tourist projects should be made to the regional tourist board.

Loans from £15,000 to £250,000 (normal max.) should be made to the Scottish Development Agency, the Welsh Development Agency, the Clydesdale Bank, the Midland Bank, the National Westminster Bank, and the Industrial and Commercial Finance Corporation (up to £2 million).

The EIB produces a number of documents explaining its services and organization, together with a comprehensive annual report. Those can be obtained free of charge from the EIB London Office at the address given above.

THE NEW COMMUNITY INSTRUMENT (ORTOLI FACILITY)
(NCI)

(A) PURPOSE
The objective of the NCI is to promote greater economic convergence amongst the member states by raising loans on international capital markets and using them to encourage investment within the EEC in under-invested sectors and in areas of substantial unemployment.

(B) ELIGIBLE PROJECTS
Priority sectors are in energy, industry and infrastructure.

(C) FORM OF FINANCIAL AID AND ELIGIBLE EXPENDITURE
Again there are both direct and agency loans.

(i) Direct loans
These are over £250,000 for investment projects in energy and infrastructure projects. Loans are under the same kind of terms and conditions as EIB loans.

(ii) Agency loans

The scope of Community lending has been considerably enlarged during 1983 by the extension of the application of the NCI facility to small and medium-sized companies. The most significant feature is that such loans are not restricted to Assisted Areas but available throughout the UK. These loans are being made available as a global facility to a number of agencies who on-lend to companies for manufacturing or tourism projects in the UK. Amounts of between £15,000 and £250,000 can be made available for up to 50% of the cost of capital expenditure on a project. Repayment is over a period of eight years, with the possibility of repayment holiday of up to two years. The rate of interest is fixed.

(D) HOW TO APPLY

The NCI is administered by the European Investment Bank and direct loan applications should be made to the EIB. Agency loans are available from the National Westminster Bank, the Midland Bank, Barclays and the Industrial and Commercial Finance Corporation. Application should be made to local offices.[3]

On 5 July 1983 the Commission put forward a proposal that the Community should provide finance for innovative projects in small and medium-sized businesses which would supplement finance from bodies such as venture capital organizations. The Commission have asked for a sum of money of about 100 million ECUs of principal. The money would be lent to projects in sectors which introduce new products, devise new processes or apply innovatory technologies, for the benefit of small and medium-sized companies, via appropriate financial intermediaries.

EUROPEAN COAL AND STEEL COMMUNITY LOANS

(A) PURPOSE

European Coal and Steel Community (ECSC) Loans are very similar to EIB loans but have some important differences. There are three main objectives: to improve the production, manufacture and marketing of indigenous coal and steel; to improve occupational conditions and living standards of those working in these industries; and to provide facilities for re-training redundant coal and steel workers in other industries.

(B) ELIGIBLE PROJECTS

Three kinds of project are eligible for financial support.

(i) Industrial projects. Funds are lent to assist in the rationalization and regeneration of the coal and steel industries. Finance is not restricted to these industries. Any project which assists the use of coal and steel would be eligible. Funds are also available for converting industrial boilers from oil or gas to coal.

(ii) Conversion. Conversion loans are granted for economically sound invest-ment projects, in any industrial or service sector, which create new jobs suitable for former ECSC workers, if need be after appropriate vocational training. These loans are available in specially designated coal and steel closure areas.

(iii) Special payment or readaptation grants. The Commission may make grants to help workers affected by fundamental changes in market conditions in the steel and coal industries. These payments cover the following: tide-over allowances for workers, including redundancy payments; resettlement allowances; vocational training for those having to change their employment. Loans are also available for construction and modernization of housing for employees of the ECSC indus-tries.

(C) FORMS OF FINANCIAL AID AND ELIGIBLE EXPENDITURE

All forms of loan are for fixed capital only and not for working capital. The maximum amount of loan is 50 per cent of the costs of fixed assets.

(i) Industrial projects. Decisions on loans are made by the Commission on an individual basis. Interest rates relate to the market rates for the currency in which the loan is raised and all such loans are granted at rates intended only to cover costs. The maximum amount of loans is 50% of the agreed project cost. Loans are made at fixed interest rates with flexible repayment terms. Some categories of investment can receive loans at a reduced rate of interest. Such assisted loans are given at the normal interest rate, and the Commission grants an additional interest rebate which is paid directly to the beneficiary. The amount of rebate is three percentage points per year for the first five years of the loan. Such rebates are made at the discretion of the Commission and are on a case-by-case basis, according to certain criteria. Currently the Commission gives preference to conversion loans as opposed to investment loans.

(ii) Conversion loans. These are, like EIB loans, both direct and via an agency. The lower limit for a direct loan is currently 15 million ECUs. Below that figure a sub-loan can be made. ECSC can provide loans of up to 50% of the fixed investment costs of the project. Interest relief of three percentage points for the first five years may be granted depending on the number of jobs created i.e. 20,000 ECU per new job. In the case of sub-loans the interest subsidy may be increased to five percentage points.

(D) HOW TO APPLY

(i) Industrial projects. Applications are sent to the Directorate-General for Credit and Investments (DG XVIII) in Luxembourg.

(ii) Conversion loans. Applications are submitted for direct loans via the Department of Industry to DG XVIII. Applications for sub-loans should be made to the relevant agency — the Industrial and Commercial Finance Corporation; the Scottish Development Agency; the Welsh Development Agency; Barclays Bank; Cooperative Bank; Clydesdale Bank; National Westminster Bank; and the Royal Bank of Scotland.

(iii) Housing loans. The Department of the Environment is responsible for local authorities' and housing associations' participation in the scheme, and first contact should be made with the Department of the Environment, Room M11/17, 2 Marsham Street, London, SW1P 3EB.[4]

European Agricultural Guidance Guarantee Fund

GUIDANCE SECTION

The Guidance Section has as its objectives the improvement and increase of agricultural production, the improvement of the quality of agricultural products and of their distribution, and the development of outlets for agricultural produce. The scheme which offers direct aid from the Commission to support projects in the agri-food industry is described here.

Processing and marketing of agricultural products

(A) PURPOSE
The scheme's aim is to assist the primary producer (e.g. farmer, grower, fisherman) by improving the processing and marketing of agricultural products, particularly in terms of quality and presentation.

(B) ELIGIBLE PROJECTS
  (i) Projects must fall within the framework of an investment programme drawn up by each member state. Up to the time of writing, seven programmes have been introduced in the UK. These cover redmeat slaughterhouses, ware potatoes, liquid milk processing, horticulture, cereals, fisheries, and pigmeat slaughtering and processing. There is also a livestock marketing and processing programme for Wales. Programmes covering seeds and the processing of hops may also be submitted.
 (ii) Projects must benefit the primary producer and guarantee him an 'adequate and lasting share in the benefits arising from projects' (the beneficiary must furnish sufficient proof in this matter).
(iii) Projects must offer adequate guarantees of profitability.
(iv) Projects must contribute to the lasting economic effect of the aims pursued by the programme.
 (v) The granting of assistance must not infringe Community competition policy.
(vi) Projects must involve investment of at least £25,000. In addition projects

must attract a UK grant of 5% or more in order to qualify for an EAGGF grant.

(vii) Applications for an EAGGF grant are processed by the Ministry of Agriculture, Fisheries and Food and applications for aid must be accompanied by written confirmation of the availability of a UK grant of 5% or more. Any UK grant scheme may serve to provide qualifying grants. Examples are Regional Development grants and the Agricultural and Horticultural Cooperation Scheme. However, a grant under the Farm and Horticulture Development Scheme is not a qualifying grant.

(viii) A UK grant of 5% is available under the terms of the Agricultural Products, Processing and Marketing (Improvement Grants) Regulations 1977 (SI 1977 No 2112) provided that the project is eligible for EAGGF assistance under EEC Regulation 355/77. If a project is unable to attract a qualifying grant under a UK scheme the Ministry of Agriculture make it clear that grants under this scheme can only be paid if the project is successful under EAGGF.

(ix) It is a further condition that the financial contribution of the recipient of an EAGGF grant under this scheme must not be less than 50% of the cost of the project.

(x) In addition to the general criteria and conditions of eligibility set out above, the Commission publishes each year specific criteria for selection of projects. These selection criteria are intended to indicate the types of investment which, if all other conditions are satisfied, may qualify for priority in the granting of assistance. Criteria used to be published on an annual basis for a fixed period. The Commission last published its criteria for the choice of projects on 10 June 1983.[5]

(C) FORMS OF FINANCIAL AID AND ELIGIBLE EXPENDITURE

The maximum rate of EAGGF grant is normally 25% of eligible project costs, except for milk projects where it is 20%. Only certain costs are eligible for aid. These are for material investment (buildings, plant machinery and equipment). Aid is not available for land purchase, second-hand equipment, working capital or for leasing machinery.

(D) HOW TO APPLY

All projects must be submitted to the appropriate Agricultural Department on an EEC form. Forms are available from the following offices:
  For applicants in England:

Ministry of Agriculture, Fisheries and Food
Marketing Policy Division
Great Westminster House
Horseferry Road
London, SW1P 2EA.

For applicants in Scotland:

Department of Agriculture & Fisheries for Scotland
Chesser House
500 Gorgie Road
Edinburgh, EH11 3AW.

For applicants in Wales:

Welsh Office Agriculture Department
Floor 2, Crown Offices
Cathays Park
Cardiff, CF1 3NQ.

For applicants in Northern Ireland:

Department of Agriculture for Northern Ireland
EC Division Room 452A
Dundonald House
Upper Newtownards Road
Belfast, BT4 3SB.

Applications are received twice a year between 1 January and 28 February for announcement of funding in December, and between 1 May and 31 October for announcement of funding in June of the following year.[6]

Energy funds

Currently the Community has a number of schemes aimed at achieving the Community's energy policies. These policies consist of attempts to reduce UK dependency on oil by developing energy saving objectives and by developing alternative supplies such as nuclear power, coal, natural gas and various forms of renewable energy. Energy research and development falls within the scope of the *Framework programme for research and development* (see below).
There are a number of specific demonstration programmes in exploitation of alternative energy schemes, energy saving and the substitution of hydrocarbons, and in liquefaction and gasification of solid fuels.

(A) PURPOSE
Aid is given to demonstrate the viability of new techniques and technologies which have been through an R. & D. phase, but whose commercial application is held back by technical and financial risks.

(B) ELIGIBLE PROJECTS
Projects in the following fields are eligible for support in alternative energy sources (geothermal energy, solar energy, biomass, wind and ocean energy and hydro-electric power); energy saving (buildings, process heat and electricity in

industry and agriculture, energy industry transport); substitution of hydrocarbons (solid fuels, electric power, heat transmission, distribution and storage); and in the gasification and liquefaction of solid fuels. In the selection of projects for funding various criteria apply which are listed in detail in the relevant regulations.

(C) FORM OF FINANCIAL AID AND ELIGIBLE EXPENDITURE

Support for a project or feasibility study takes the form of a contribution of up to 49% of the eligible costs of the project, half of which are repayable in the case of demonstration projects, if the project is exploited commercially. This half constitutes a 'success loan' on which no interest is charged until the project has been shown to be successful in meeting its objectives and commercial exploitation. When only partial success in contracted terms is achieved, the repayment due may be reduced or waived. In the case of pilot industrial projects, financial support is not repayable.

(D) HOW TO APPLY

Calls for projects to be submitted are published in the 'C' series of the *Official journal*, from time to time, together with application forms.[7]

COMMUNITY PROJECTS IN THE HYDROCARBONS SECTOR

(A) PURPOSE

To promote new technology in exploration, production and transport and storage of oil and gas.

(B) ELIGIBLE PROJECTS

Priority is awarded to projects with the following aims: ensuring the continuity of supplies by developing new improved techniques and equipment in the fields of geophysics, oil and gas recovery, drilling, optimum use of natural gas and associated gas, and the improvement of inspection and maintenance techniques; maximising the yield, by the use of enhanced recovery techniques from the known fields and particularly from reservoirs where the natural drive is weak, so as to increase their flow rate and total production and make marginal fields viable, developing techniques for exploiting reservoirs located in difficult areas (e.g. fields in 500 metres of water and deeper); and cutting down the lead time for exploiting newly discovered fields.

(C) FORM OF FINANCIAL AID AND ELIGIBLE EXPENDITURE

The Community provides success loans for projects at 30, 35 or 40% of the estimated cost of the development work.

(D) HOW TO APPLY

The Commission normally advertises invitations for projects in the *Official journal.* Nine rounds have been invited up until November 1982. Applications are made direct to the Commission but the Department of Energy will advise UK applicants on both technical and presentational aspects of the scheme.[8]

The Department of Energy points of contact are as follows:

Marine Technology Support Unit
Building 10.69
AERE
Harwell
Oxfordshire, OX11 0RA

or

Offshore Supplies Office
Department of Energy
Thames House South
Millbank
London, SW1P 4QJ

The Commission point of contact is:

Commission of the European Communities
Directorate-General for Energy
rue de la Loi 200
B-1049 Brussels.

Research and development funds

There are three ways in which the Community implements its research and development programme:

(A) DIRECT ACTION
Projects are funded and managed by the Commission and carried out in the establishments of the Joint Research Centre (JRC) at Ispra, Geel, Karlsruhe and Petten.

(B) INDIRECT ACTION
Projects are centrally managed by the Commission but contracted out to research organizations in the member states usually with costs shared between the Commission and the contractors. The Community share, which is funded from the Community budget, varies from programme to programme, and even within programmes. The normal share is 50% but figures as high as 100% in exceptional cases or as low as 25% are not unknown.

(C) CONCERTED ACTION
Projects are coordinated by the Commission but the work is carried out and financed by organizations in the participating member states. The chief

opportunities for organizations to participate in Community R. & D. are through shared-cost contracts in indirect action research programmes. In the past the organization and implementation of Community R. & D. has been fragmented but in July 1983 the Council adopted a resolution approving the principle of an overall framework programme and the scientific and technical objectives behind it.

FRAMEWORK PROGRAMME FOR COMMUNITY
SCIENTIFIC AND TECHNICAL ACTIVITIES

(A) PURPOSE

The Framework Programme is planned to have a lifespan of four years with a review after two years.[9] On present timing the Programme will run from 1984 to 1987 with a review in the second half of 1985. An annual report will be prepared in addition reviewing the implementation of the Programme. Seventy-five per cent of the Programme's resources are planned to be devoted towards shared-costs contracts with private companies, education or research bodies or other institutions in the member states. Twenty-three per cent is to be expended on the Community's direct action and 2% on concerted action. Some of the individual programmes are now being drawn up and in one case at least the Commission has already published a notice calling for interested organizations to come forward.

The following are the objectives to be achieved under the Programme: promoting agricultural competitiveness (developing agricultural productivity and improving products in agriculture and fisheries); promoting industrial competitiveness (removing and reducing impediments, promoting new techniques and products for the conventional industries, and promoting new technologies); improving the management of raw materials; improving the management of energy resources (developing nuclear fission energy and controlled thermonuclear fusion and developing renewable energy sources and the rational use of energy); reinforcing development aid; improving living and working conditions (improving safety and protecting health and the environment); and improving the efficacy of the Community's scientific and technical potential.

(B) ELIGIBLE PROJECTS

Industrial research action programmes are being drawn up in order to implement each of the above objectives. These will list eligible sectors and projects. Some residual programmes from earlier R. & D. exist in the meantime.

(C) FORM OF FINANCIAL AID AND ELIGIBLE EXPENDITURE

The programme will be implemented mainly on the basis of shared-cost contracts with organizations in the member states. A maximum of 50% will be funded by the Community.

(D) HOW TO APPLY

Calls for projects will be advertised in the 'C' series of the *Official journal*, from time to time.

References and notes

[1] For further information on ESF see Department of Employment, *Guide to the new Social Fund*, 1983; Council Decision 83/516/EEC *Official journal* L289, 22 October 1983; Council Regulation (EEC) No 2950/83 *Official journal* L289, 22 October 1983; Commission Decision 83/673/EEC *Official journal* L377, 31 December 1983.

[2] For further information on ERDF see Regulation (EEC) 724/75 *Official journal* L73, 21 March 1975; Amending Regulation (EEC) 214/79 *Official journal* L35, 9 February 1979.

[3] For further information on NCI see Council Decision 78/870 EEC *Official journal* L298, 25 October 1978; Council Decision 79/486 EEC *Official journal* L125, 22 May 1979; Council Decision 80/739 EEC *Official journal* L205, 17 August 1980; Council Decision 80/1103/EEC *Official journal* L326, 2 December 1980; Council Decision 83/200/EEC *Official journal* L112, 28 April 1983; Council Decision 83/308/EEC *Official journal* L164, 23 June 1983.

[4] For further information on ECSC loans see Industrial loans *Official journal* C73, 18 June 1970; Industrial loans *Official journal* C146, 25 November 1974; Industrial loans *Official journal* C79, 29 March 1980; Reconversion loans *Official journal* C191, 16 July 1983.

[5] *Official journal* C152, 10 June 1983.

[6] Council Regulation (EEC) 355/77 *Official journal* L51, 23 February 1977; Council Regulation (EEC) 3073/82 *Official journal* L325, 20 November 1982.

[7] For further information on energy funds see Council Regulations (EEC) No 1972/83 *Official Journal* L195, 19 July 1983; Council Regulation (EEC) No 1971/83 *Official journal* L195, 1983; Call for tenders *Official journal* C86, 28 March 1983.

[8] For further information see Council Regulation (EEC) 3056/73, *Official journal* L312, 13 November 1973; Calls for tenders *Official journal* C200, 27 July 1983.

[9] *Framework programme for Community scientific and technical activities 1984–1987*, COM(83)260 final.

Eurofi (UK) Limited, 25 London Road, Newbury, Berks., RG13 1JL, Tel: Newbury (0635)31900, is a private company specializing in negotiating EEC and UK government financial incentives for companies investing in the United Kingdom.

11

European Communities information and its use in British universities and polytechnics

MICHAEL HOPKINS

Introduction

It will be evident from the various contributions to this book that British membership of the European Community (EC) has had a significant effect upon the day-to-day information needs of people in many walks of national life. It will also be clear that the nature of the demand for EC information often varies considerably from one user group to another, as does the adequacy of the arrangements made to satisfy that demand. This particular chapter is concerned with the use made of EC information by the academic community, a group of users whose requirements are more easily defined and more generously provided for than most. By way of introduction the chapter opens with a brief review of the place occupied by the European Community in the teaching and research activities of British universities and polytechnics. Consideration is then given to the kinds of information consequently needed by the academic community and the uses to which it is put. The sources of information most suitable for academic purposes are described, with particular emphasis upon the resources of European Documentation Centres (EDCs), established by the Commission of the European Communities in order to encourage the study of European integration.

During the post-war period international organizations have become a prominent feature of the international landscape. They provide member states with a procedural framework within which to resolve their differences and institutional machinery for cooperative action on a wide variety of issues. As a result, they have come to play a key role in debates about such matters as the maintenance of peaceful relations between nations, the preservation of order in the international economic system and the provision of aid to countries in course of development. Moreover, they play a crucial part in sponsoring and conducting large-scale and often highly technical research and development work in many fields of study.[1] It is not surprising, therefore, that the documentation generated by international organizations should constitute a rich source of information for academic study, nor that organizations such as the European Community have become a subject of academic study in their own right.

Indeed, the entry of the United Kingdom (UK) into the European Community has had a considerable impact upon teaching and research activities in British universities and polytechnics. During the early 1970s European studies became a fashionable growth area, boosted not only by the interest provoked by the debate over British membership but also by the trend towards inter-disciplinarity in taught courses, a development which saw the introduction of other umbrella courses such as environmental studies. The European Community became an accepted component of teaching programmes, and research into many aspects of its activities was initiated. New courses which combined language teaching with social science studies and a comparative European element were established, and many existing courses concerned with the systems, processes and issues which characterize contemporary Europe were given a more prominent Community dimension. Inevitably, the initial impetus has slowed, but courses continue to flourish and research activities have been sustained.

SOURCES OF DEMAND

In view of these developments it is not surprising that there is a considerable demand in British universities and polytechnics for information on the European Community. Students following courses on contemporary Europe and academic staff engaged in the teaching of these courses need access to appropriate information. Although undergraduate degree courses centred mainly on the European Community are rare, twenty universities and thirteen polytechnics now offer undergraduate degrees in European studies or in subjects which include a strong European element, such as international relations. Within the overall framework offered by these degrees the European Community forms a subject of study, usually taught in the context of more broadly-based courses such as European integration, European economy or international institutions. European studies courses are also offered as options in other degrees and are a popular subject for taught postgraduate courses. In the case of the latter the EC is studied from different perspectives in such courses as European legal studies, West European politics and European governmental studies.[2]

Postgraduate students and academic staff for whom the European Community is a subject of research constitute a second source of demand. In view of the fact that the level of demand for EC information varies in direct proportion with the relevance of the European Community to the subjects under review, it will be useful to divide academic researchers into two groups. First, there are those for whom the European Community is a principal subject of study. Researchers who fall into this category are drawn from mainly social science disciplines and are often based in multi-disciplinary European studies departments. They study the European Community from a variety of perspectives. There are those, for instance, who see the Community as an instrument of political or economic integration in Europe; their concern is to analyze the overall impact and state of European integration, often by means of national studies or sectoral investigations. There are others whose main interest lies in the role that the EC plays on the international stage, particularly in the context of European political cooperation. Still others are interested in the mechanics of international organization, for whom the unique characteristics of the Community's institutional machinery offer irresistible opportunities for theoretical discussion and debate. Add to these the many legal experts whose attention is drawn by the multitude of legal issues raised by Community law and its national application and it is possible to begin to appreciate the diversity of interests represented in this group. Nevertheless, the group shares interests which cross traditional disciplinary boundaries and it displays a coherence which finds practical expression in the activities of the University Association for Contemporary European Studies (UACES).[3]

The second group of academic researchers from whom significant demand originates is much larger than the first but much less clearly defined. In fact, it is less a single group than a collection of discrete groups each based on an academic discipline but linked at a secondary level by a European Community dimension. For none is the Community the principal subject of study but for all it is a major influence on their work. Clearly, those whose area of study is Europe, and whose interests concern the economic, political and social life of Western European countries, are most directly affected. The agricultural economist, for instance, whose special interest is trends in farm incomes in the United Kingdom must take full account of the impact of the Common Agricultural Policy (CAP); the political scientist working on decision-making at the governmental level must pay due regard to the role played by Community institutions in this process, just as the economic geographer interested in deprivation in the peripheral areas of Europe must consider the contribution of the European Regional Development Fund (ERDF). In such cases the impact of the European Community is just one of a number of factors to be considered, albeit an important one. It is not surprising, therefore, that researchers in this group retain allegiance to their own subject disciplines, work largely within those confines and communicate on a disciplinary basis.

Finally, it should be noted that there is some demand for information from those for whom the European Community is not a subject of academic interest at all. For members of this group it is material 'by' and not 'about' the Community that is significant, and it is significant not because of its provenance but simply because of its information content. The staff of science and technology departments constitute an important component of this group. The

European Community makes a major contribution to scientific and technical research and development in Europe, both directly, through research conducted by its own staff in the Joint Research Centre (JRC), and indirectly through the sponsorship of external research, usually conducted within the framework of multi-annual research programmes. Consequently, researchers in universities and polytechnics must take full note of this work and have access to the voluminous documentation it generates. Moreover, there is a demand not only for research studies and reports but also for information on the availability of research funds. The European Community is a valuable source of research funding; as other sources of finance diminish so enquiries increase about the availability of Community funds and on the procedures to be employed by those who wish to apply for them.

NATURE OF DEMAND

For the most part those who study the European Community for educational purposes need access to literature rather than to information, to documentation rather than to data. Unlike that of applied social scientists and other practitioners, whose principal need is for hard information for practical application, much of the work of both students and staff is book-based. Undergraduates are expected to supplement what they learn in lectures by private reading; lecturers are expected to keep abreast of the literature of their subjects for both teaching and research purposes. Moreover, it is considered to be integral to the education process that members of the academic community learn how to handle printed sources for themselves and how to make best use of the information they contain. This again contrasts with many practitioner groups who see no particular virtue in wasting valuable time in searching for information others can more readily provide.

Consequently, the overriding demand made by the academic community is bibliographical in nature. Staff and students need direct physical access to substantial amounts of documentation for personal use. The type of material required varies according to the purposes for which it is intended. Undergraduate students following courses in European integration generally have reasonably limited and defined literature needs. Their course reading is largely governed by reading lists prepared in advance by lecturers from recently published secondary sources, particularly academic textbooks and journal articles. The constraints of the timetable are such that only those undergraduates who do final-year options on the Common Market usually have an opportunity to make significant use of primary source material. Academic staff and research students, on the other hand, have literature needs which are much more diffuse. They need access not only to the published literature in their own fields of study but also to a wide range of primary source materials often produced over a considerable period of time. In view of the fact that much academic interest centres upon aspects of the relationship between the United Kingdom and the European Community, some of these primary sources are national in origin. British parliamentary papers of the kind described in Chapter 7 of this book provide political scientists investigating the effects of Community membership on the machinery of government with information of considerable value; the official statistics produced by government departments are an indispensable source of information for economic analysts who wish to monitor the performance of the UK within the European economy; British legal texts and national case law constitute the raw data upon which much of the work of legal experts is based. In other fields pressure group literature, newspaper and other media reportage, national archives and private correspondence can yield useful information.

However, the source of much of the information needed by all these scholars to complete their researches and which provides those whose interests focus specifically upon the European Community and its institutions with the bulk of their information is, of course, the organization itself. Just like any other large-scale and complex organization the European Community produces a vast amount of paper during the course of its activities, much of which is internal or administrative in nature but some of which enters the public domain and offers a unique insight into the inner workings of Community institutions. Moreover, in order to improve the public perception of Community ideals and actions the main institutions publish a wide range of literature on their activities and achievements. Documents and official texts, legislative acts and Community case law, statistical serials and scientific reports, together with publications of many descriptions, all form part of a corpus of material which provides academic users with a rich mine of information on Community affairs. It is this material which is described in more detail in the following section of this chapter.

European Community sources of information

The institutions of the European Community recognize that without sustained public support for their policies and actions they can never hope to realise the ideals embodied in the Treaty of Rome. Consequently, they, and especially the Commission, are concerned to keep the citizens of Europe well informed about their activities and achievements so as to increase public awareness of the positive impact made by the Community on daily life and the need for continued support for concerted action to solve Europe's pressing problems. Information is communicated by means that vary according to the needs of the intended audience. In order to ensure daily coverage and comment in the European press, for instance, the Commission's Spokesman's Group provides the accredited press corps in Brussels with information in the form of press briefings and conferences, supplemented by a regular stream of press notices and background notes. In recognition of the powerful influence exerted by radio and television over public opinion, studio and other technical facilities are made available for recording interviews with Community spokesmen and for making short films on

Community subjects. Publicity campaigns, travelling exhibitions and other means are also used, particularly by national information offices, to bring the Community to the attention of the people of Europe.

Notwithstanding these activities, the printed word remains an essential vehicle for transmitting information to both specialized and general audiences. Publications are issued in large numbers for consumption by the general public, informed readers and experts. They explain the nature and aims of the organization; they describe the work of the main institutions, and they disseminate the results of the considerable amount of research carried out by and for Community institutions. In view of their importance for academic study, consideration will be given in the following paragraphs to some of the main types of Community publications and public documents most suitable for educational use. However, it should be noted that in a chapter of this kind individual titles can be cited only as examples of a broad category of material. Reference should be made to Jeffries[4] for more detailed and comprehensive bibliographical descriptions.

INTRODUCTORY TEXTS

Publications are considered to be an integral part of the information policy pursued by the Commission, mainly through Directorate-General X (Information) and its external offices. Attractively designed and skilfully edited publications can reach a mass audience with factual and explanatory information which can do much to improve the quality of public debate on European affairs and enhance the public perception of Community institutions. Consequently, the Commission issues a constant stream of topical, glossy and usually free leaflets, pamphlets, booklets and magazines which aim to project a positive image of the European Community and its actions in a lively and popular style. Although many are too lightweight for academic study some of the more substantial publications are, in fact, ideal introductory texts for undergraduate course use. Two prolific series are worthy of special attention. Firstly, the *European documentation* series, which consists of forty to sixty page booklets each of which provides a clearly written and well organized introduction to a main Community policy area such as regional policy or transport policy or to such administrative topics as the Community budget and the operation of the various Community funds. Liberally provided with graphs, tables and charts where appropriate, and invariably with bibliographies of further reading, these excellent publications, mostly written by senior Community officials and regularly updated, are certainly worthy of inclusion on student reading lists. Between six and eight booklets are issued each year.[5] The second series is *European file*, a collection of eight-page leaflets prepared by Directorate-General X (Information) and issued on a fortnightly basis. Each leaflet is devoted to a single topic, which might be a broad policy sector, such as competition policy or external relations, or just one aspect of sectoral policy, such as state aids or enlargement. Less comprehensive, of course, than equivalent booklets in the *European documentation* series, these brief articles nevertheless provide useful résumés of the main issues and problems raised by the topics under review, succinct accounts of what has been achieved so far and an indication of what, in the eyes of the Commission, remains to be done. Regularly updated, these leaflets quickly build up to a handy reference source when kept together in a loose-leaf binder. *European file 20/83*, published in December 1983, consists of a numerical and subject list of those leaflets published during the period 1979–1983. Individual titles in both series are also listed by subject in *The European Community as a publisher*, an abridged version of the annual catalogue of publications, which lists the main publications issued over the past five years or so, with particular emphasis upon general interest titles.

PROGRESS REPORTS

During the course of the academic year it is likely that students and particularly their lecturers will need more information than is provided in the general introductions referred to in the previous paragraph. There may be need for more facts on a new policy initiative, an important piece of legislation or a significant event; alternatively, there may be call for an in-depth study of the evolution of policy in a particular sector or a review of the activities of a Community institution. In these circumstances recourse may be had to the various annual reports which constitute a significant group of Community publications and which are a rich source of information on most aspects of Community affairs. As digests of information, summaries of main events and accounts of activities, these reports are ideal as source material for teaching purposes or as introductory texts for those about to embark upon academic research into unfamiliar topics. Indeed, the annual report of the Commission, the *General report on the activities of the European Communities*,[6] is a standard source of reference not only on the work and activities of the Commission but also the European Community as a whole. Each annual volume contains the Commission's view on the present state of European integration and a public record of progress achieved and initiatives proposed in each Community sector. The reports of other Community institutions such as the Council[7] and the Economic and Social Committee[8] and more specialized bodies such as the European Investment Bank,[9] are less comprehensive but still provide a concise account of the achievements of the parent body during the previous twelve months. Together with the annual reports published on such individual policy sectors as agriculture,[10] social affairs[11] and competition,[12] these publications are particularly well suited for academic use. Each volume contains a wealth of information on the past year's achievements. Successive issues consulted together become a continuous narrative of the gradual unfolding of Community policy objectives. Liberal use of footnote references to legislative texts and other Community publications enhance their value and make them valuable points of departure for more detailed study.

Annual reports have the disadvantage, of course, of appearing only once a year. Provision is made for keeping the public informed about current events by the publication of more frequent news reviews and accounts of Community developments. The most important of these is the *Bulletin of the European Communities*,[13] edited by the Commission's Secretariat-General and published monthly except in August. Each issue contains a number of brief reports upon topics of current concern, perhaps an important new Commission policy proposal or the most recent meeting of the European Council, together with a detailed survey of activities and progress in the main Community policy sectors during the month under review. In terms of scope and treatment the *Bulletin* complements the *General report on the activities of the European Communities* and, like it, contains numerous references to documents, legislative texts and publications which can be followed up if appropriate. It also contains as an appendix a catalogue of publications issued during the month under review. Separately published Supplements to the *Bulletin* usually consist of published versions of important policy documents submitted by the Commission to the Council. More selective and popular in its coverage is *Europe*,[14] published monthly free of charge by the London Office of the Commission. This attractive illustrated magazine contains short articles on topics of interest to the British public, general Community news and reviews.

LEGAL TEXTS

However, as descriptive publications compiled after the event, progress reports cannot satisfy all the information needs of the serious researcher. Such is the nature of Community policy formation that ready access to legislative texts is necessary for those who wish to undertake thorough investigations of specific Community policies. The Treaty of Rome[15] was concerned primarily with the definition of fundamental principles, broad objectives and the basic institutional machinery. It was left to Community institutions to give practical effect to the obligations entered into by member states by using their designated powers to make Community law. In the event, during the early years when enthusiasm for European ideals was widespread and the economic situation promising, considerable progress was made in the implementation of treaty obligations, sometimes ahead of schedule. However, as the Community has grown older, become larger and had to exist in a harsher economic climate, so it has become increasingly difficult to translate treaty objectives into practical policies. Progress in many sectors has been slow and spasmodic; positive measures have been implemented often only after protracted negotiations and their impact has usually been incremental rather than dramatic.

The substantial corpus of legislation created by Community institutions reflects the nature of the Community legal order and the way in which treaty provisions have been implemented. It also reveals characteristics that can pose problems for academic study. The most obvious of these is the volume of legislation, the sheer number of legislative texts adopted each year. In 1983 alone more than 3,700 regulations were adopted together with more than 650 other legal instruments. The researcher tracing policy development over a number of years can easily be faced with the prospect of searching a body of legislation consisting of many thousands of individual texts. The fact that the vast majority of these texts are administrative instruments adopted by the Commission in conjunction with the day-to-day management of the Common Agricultural Policy and the Customs Union and are quickly superseded, serves only to obscure the more significant texts and make them difficult to identify. A second and related characteristic is that at any given time Community law is embodied in a large number of texts. At the end of 1982, for instance, all or part of more than 4,000 separate pieces of legislation were in force, excluding purely administrative measures. This may be explained by the gradual and often piecemeal way in which progress has been made and by lack of consolidation in Community law. Although some acts are subsequently replaced in their entirety by others, still more are only partially superseded, thus increasing the number of acts in force and thereby making it difficult to establish the precise state of the law on a particular subject. Indeed, part of some legal acts adopted many years ago are still in force. At the end of 1982, for instance, more than 20 instruments adopted in the 1950s were still in force, in part or in full, together with more than 350 adopted in the 1960s.

The consequence for academic study is that researchers who wish to trace the evolution of sectoral policy must examine large numbers of legislative texts promulgated over a considerable period of time in order to construct an accurate representation of the subject under review. Unfortunately, the sources at their disposal do not make it particularly easy to identify, locate and consult the myriad separate pieces of legislation that make up each policy area. The principal source of information on Community legislation is, of course, the *Official journal of the European Communities*,[16] the official gazette of the organization in which the authentic texts of Community laws are formally published. Indeed, Article 191 of the Treaty of Rome requires that regulations be published in the *Official journal* and that they 'shall enter into force on the date specified in them or, in the absence thereof, on the twentieth day following their publication'.

Although the Treaty does not make similar provision for directives and decisions, in practice these too are published in the *Official journal*. In fact the *Official journal* is a mine of information on the work and activities of Community institutions. In addition to the legislation itself, published in the *Legislation* or 'L' series, many other types of official text are given publication in the *Official journal*. The separately published *Information and notices* or 'C' series (from the French title *Communications et informations*) contains such diverse texts as Commission legislative proposals, European Parliament resolutions, Economic and Social Committee opinions, Court of Justice judgements and much more besides. A third section, the *Supplement* or 'S' series, contains invitations to tender for public works and supply contracts. The

Official journal is a unique publication, an indispensable source for anyone undertaking serious research into Community affairs. It is also a complex publication and one which can be difficult for the uninitiated to use. Consequently, it is important to be familiar with both its internal organization and with the range of official texts it contains. Greer[17] provides a useful introduction to the bibliographical characteristics of the *Official journal*, which is also described by Kearley[18] in his extensive review article on European Community law and legal literature. In Chapter 12 of this book Jeffries not only describes the *Official journal* itself but also the *Special edition* that was published in 1973 containing the English texts of secondary legislation adopted between 1952 and 1972 and still in force on 1 January 1973. He also refers to a number of alternative sources of the texts of Community legislation, including the widely used *Encyclopedia of European Community law*.[19]

The key to successful use of a publication as complex and prolific as the *Official journal* is a sound and detailed index. If the academic researcher is to search systematically the contents of 381 issues of the 'L' series published in 1983 for relevant information or to undertake a retrospective search through back volumes published over a thirty year period, then highly detailed and specific indexes are vital. Unfortunately, the monthly and annual indexes to the *Official journal* are woefully inadequate. They are neither consistent from one year to another nor are they compiled in such a way as to allow direct access by specific subject.[20] Indeed, for academic staff undertaking retrospective subject searches it is usually more profitable to use alternative sources. Although many of the progress reports mentioned in the previous section do not themselves have indexes, their arrangement by policy sector makes them useful sources of information on important legislation. Attention should also be drawn to the *Register of current Community legal instruments*,[21] an index to secondary legislation in force, produced as a by-product of the CELEX system,[22] which, together with other helpful Community publications such as *Europe today*,[23] is also described by Jeffries.

Academic lawyers need access not only to the texts of Community legislation but also to the substantial body of case-law built up by the Court of Justice of the European Communities since the inception of the organization. It is characteristic of the academic treatises which have been written on Community law and on the role of the Court of Justice in ensuring the lawful interpretation and application of the treaties, that they depend heavily upon the judgements of the Court for their basic raw material. The principal source of this information is *Reports of cases before the Court*,[24] although extensive and often preferential use is made of commercial services such as *Common Market law reports*.[25] These and many other sources of information on Community law and the work of the Court of Justice are referred to both by Jeffries in Chapter 12 of this book and by Kearley in the article mentioned above. It should also be noted that both authors also describe the important online services available to academic lawyers, with particular reference to CELEX, which contains among other things the full texts of Community treaties and secondary legislation and EUROLEX[26] which includes *Common Market law reports*. Finally, attention should be drawn to the authoritative and extremely comprehensive publication entitled *Thirty years of Community law*[27] which contains a series of detailed chapters written by a group of legal experts. Together, they add up to a wide-ranging review of the development of the Community legal order over the past thirty years.

COMMUNITY DOCUMENTS

Community legislation itself is, of course, just the tip of an iceberg. The promulgation of Community law represents the culmination of an often tortuous legal process whose main features are laid down in the Treaty of Rome. Although it is not always possible for the main actors in this process to agree on the adoption of Community law, the process, once set in motion, never fails to generate a great deal of documentation. This is largely explained by the fact that Community law-making is characterized on the one hand by shared responsibility and constant interaction between Community institutions and on the other hand by almost continuous consultation with member states and interested third parties. Each time the Commission wishes to exercise its right of initiative it conveys its proposals to the Council in document form; each time the European Parliament is asked by the Council for an opinion on a Commission proposal, documents are drafted by the appropriate parliamentary committee. At this level, documents constitute an initial and formal channel of communication between institutions. The sentiments they express will themselves have been the subject of much scrutiny within the institution's own administrative machinery before their adoption as official policy and will inevitably have been preceded by internal documents of many descriptions. Moreover, in view of the fact that successful Community law-making depends upon the identification of common ground and the achievement of consensus, the official viewpoints expressed in formal documents often become little more than negotiating positions. During the course of negotiations numerous modifications, amendments, redrafts and new proposals emerge, all of which mean, of course, yet more documents.

Clearly, documents have high potential value for academic research. Unlike publications such as the *Bulletin of the European Communities* they are not compiled after the event or primarily for an external audience. They form a first-hand, contemporary record of the inner workings of the organization. Individually they can provide a glimpse of policy in the making; as a corpus of material they can provide a unique insight into the gradual evolution of Community policy. Of course, some classes of document are confidential, such as those which originate in the Council and its subordinate organs; others are of little external interest, such as the numerous administrative documents dealing with internal management and personnel matters. However, there remains a considerable number of documents which enter the public domain and which provide invaluable raw material for academic research. These documents emanate from two principal sources, the Commission and the European Parliament.

Undoubtedly, the most valuable class of public document for academic use is COM documents, so called because they bear document numbers which begin with the prefix COM for Commission.[28] They reflect the responsibilities and functions allocated to that institution and may be divided into three main groups. First, there are the many hundreds of proposals for legislation submitted to the Council each year in fulfillment of the Commission's role as the initiator of Community policy. Each document usually falls into two parts, an explanatory memorandum in which the Commission explains why the legislation is necessary, and a draft legal instrument, be it a draft regulation, directive or decision. Although many of these documents are concerned with the day-to-day administration of the Common Agricultural Policy and the Customs Union and have little academic significance, others represent important legislative initiatives in specific Community sectors and can provide valuable information which is not available elsewhere. It should be noted, for instance, that although the texts of draft instruments appear in the 'C' series of the *Official journal* once they have been submitted by the Council to the European Parliament, the explanatory memoranda, which are often the most illuminating sections of the documents for academic purposes, are not. They are available only as part of the original Commission documents.

Communications and memoranda in which the Commission conveys to the Council its general views on matters of policy form the second group of COM documents. Rather than practical proposals for specific pieces of legislation these documents contain the Commission's sentiments on how policy should be evolved in particular sectors and what complexion it should take. Some are discussion documents in which a range of options is considered; others outline a broad strategy and overall framework within which subsequent legislative proposals can be placed. Although a number of these documents have become landmarks in the evolution of policy in almost every Community sector very few attain the status of publication and can therefore be consulted only in document form. They are not published in the *Official journal*, and although a very small number are given wider publicity by virtue of their publication as Supplements to the *Bulletin of the European Communities*, the vast majority remain in their original form as COM documents. In his book on the subject Hopkins[29] lists and describes more than 600 such policy blueprints prepared by the Commission during the period 1958–1978.

The third group of COM documents reflects the Commission's role as the executive arm of the Community. They consist of reports to the Council on the implementation of policy. They take stock, for instance, of progress in the application of Community rules and regulations, or report upon the current state of affairs in areas of Community activity. Very often they consist of annual reports prepared in compliance with the provisions of individual pieces of legislation. Such reports often make available a wealth of factual and statistical information which is not published elsewhere in such detail. For this reason they also constitute a rich source of raw data for academic use.[30]

Despite their undoubted potential for academic research, however, COM documents have yet to be fully exploited by the academic community. The reasons for this are various but include problems of both physical and intellectual access. Such is the nature of their work that, more so than any other user groups, academic researchers need to consult numerous documents issued over a long period of time. Unfortunately, COM documents have been regularly distributed to selected institutions of higher education only since 1974, and available on public subscription only since May 1983.[31] For those many researchers whose work concerns the 1960s and early 1970s the London Office of the Commission[32] is the only place in the United Kingdom where they can feel any confidence in finding the material they need. Moreover, the problem of physical access is exacerbated by the fact that neither the collections made available to European Documentation Centres (see below), nor those available on public subscription, are complete. The fact that many documents are deemed to be confidential and are withheld is not in itself particularly surprising. What is much more disruptive of academic research is the element of uncertainty introduced by the seemingly arbitrary way in which exclusions are made. If the exclusion criteria were explicit and publicly stated then the frustrations caused by fruitless searches for material would be reduced and greater confidence stimulated in COM documents as a primary source for academic research.

Academic users need not only physical access to long runs of documents but also the means of making systematic use of collections which may contain many hundreds of separate items. The sheer quantity of documents issued every year is intimidating and can be a severe deterrent to use unless there are bibliographical tools which can be easily and quickly used to identify individual documents by number and by subject. However, the range of tools provided by the European Community is limited. There is no internal pressure upon the Commission to produce lists and indexes to COM documents because Commission staff have at their disposal a sophisticated online information retrieval system which can satisfy all their documentation needs.[33] Unfortunately, external groups are not allowed access to Commission data bases, although it is intended that CELEX will eventually include COM documents. There are also well-advanced plans for private publishers to cooperate with the Office for Official Publications of the European Communities in the creation of an extensive online data base which would include COM documents and would generate a number of hard-copy by-products.[34]

In the meantime, academic users must rely on the printed sources of information presently available. These may be considered to fall into two groups. Firstly, there are the current awareness tools which provide information on new COM documents. The most recent and potentially the most useful of these is *Documents: monthly catalogue*,[35] first published in 1983 by the Office for Official Publications of the European Communities in conjunction with the launch of its new COM documents subscription service. Divided into nineteen broad subject categories its intention is to list and index all publicly available COM documents. Although it is a welcome innovation, judgement upon it must be reserved until it has established a clear identity, and questions of comprehensiveness, timeliness and quality of indexing have been resolved. Another source of information on recent COM documents is the *Documentation bulletin*,[36] prepared weekly by the Commission's Central Documentation Service (SCAD). Series 'A' consists of a weekly list of documents including not only COM documents but also the documents of other institutions like the European Parliament and the Economic and Social Committee, legislative texts, Community publications and articles on Community affairs appearing in academic journals, all grouped under broad subject headings. In the past its major fault has been the lack of an index. However, since October 1983 production of the *bulletin* has been computer-based and an index has been added, with the result that in future the *Documentation bulletin* will become easier to use and more valuable for academic purposes, even if the index is still available only in French and is not cumulative. Finally, attention should be drawn to the *House of Commons weekly information bulletin*[37] as a source of information on recent COM documents and to the *List of additions to the Library*,[38] compiled by the Central Library of the Commission. The former lists all COM documents received in the House of Commons Library during the week under review. The latter includes COM documents selectively, along with other acquisitions to the Library stock.

The second group of bibliographical aids are those which allow retrospective subject searches to be undertaken. Academic users need to be able to find out what important documents have been issued on a particular topic over a period of time and, ideally, to be provided with references that will help them to trace the passage of these documents through the legislative process. In this respect the subject bibliographies published irregularly as Series 'B' and 'C' of the *Documentation bulletin* are particularly useful. Each issue is devoted to one particular subject, listing all the major public documents prepared by Community institutions on that topic, linking them with subsequent legislation and including references to relevant publications and journal articles. Excellent though they are, these bibliographies do not cover all Community topics and there is often considerable delay before issues are updated.

Apart from the index to COM documents compiled annually since 1981 by Giancarlo Pau[39] and the guide to policy documents by Hopkins already mentioned (see note 29), there are no other basic finding tools to provide ready and systematic access to this valuable material. Of course, bibliographical information may be gleaned from many other sources which report on Community affairs; from, for instance, the very useful *Background reports* issued free by the London Office of the Commission, to such Community publications as the *General report on the activities of the European Communi-*

ties, and from such weekly newspapers as *British business* to more specialized alerting services as *Europe* and *European report*.[40] However, until there are radical improvements in bibliographical access to COM documents, probably in conjunction with the use of information technology, the value of COM documents for academic research will remain more potential than real.

The second major source of public documents is the European Parliament. Legislative proposals from the Commission are invariably sent by the Council to the European Parliament for its consideration. Copies of the original COM documents are circulated to Members and referred to specialized parliamentary committees for detailed examination. Committee deliberations are private. No record of their proceedings is made public. However, a rapporteur is appointed to draw up a report on the committee's findings for consideration by the European Parliament in plenary session. It is these *Working documents*[41] that are made publicly available. They each usually consist of a motion for the resolution of the European Parliament embodying an opinion on the original COM document and an explanatory statement explaining the position adopted. The latter, which can be quite lengthy, often provides a useful summary of the history of the Commission proposal and an insight into parliamentary thinking on the issue. Subsequent discussion and debate of the report in plenary session can be followed through the pages of the *Debates of the European Parliament*, published as an *Annex* to the *Official journal of the European Communities*.[42] The texts of resolutions adopted by the European Parliament, together with minutes of proceedings of part-sessions and parliamentary questions and answers, are published in the 'C' series of the *Official journal*. A *Numerical list of working documents* is published by the European Parliament and *Working documents* are listed and indexed in the sessional *Index* to the *Debates*. They are also listed in the *Documentation bulletin*, and important parliamentary reports are cited in *Europe today*. Many parliamentary reports are indexed by rapporteur in a book edited by Neilson,[43] and sources of information on the European Parliament are described in a leaflet also written by Neilson[44] and by Reid in Chapter 5 of this book.

STATISTICAL DATA

If Community institutions are to make correct decisions about the measures needed to achieve Community goals then they must have ready access to large amounts of statistical data. Such information can often highlight trends in the European economy that might not otherwise be apparent; they can bring into sharp relief differing conditions in member countries and they often lend weight to arguments for or against various policy options.

It is the function of the Statistical Office of the European Communities (SOEC) to provide the facts and figures that are needed and to present them in such a way as to facilitate international comparisons. Data are mostly received from national statistical offices and processed in house for use on a comparative basis, but can sometimes derive from statistical inquiries conducted directly at

Community level. Such data as are collected are made publicly available by SOEC in two main ways. First, regular statistical serials are published covering the main economic and social sectors, together with special statistical studies on specific subjects. Secondly, statistical data are increasingly made available in the form of online data banks such as CRONOS and COMEXT.[45]

In view of the fact that Chapter 13 of this book is devoted specifically to statistical sources and that both Ramsay[46] and Krucoff[47] provide further information, no mention will be made here of individual titles. Suffice it is to say that statistical serials form one of the most heavily used categories of Community publication and that they probably attract use from a more diverse group of academic users than any other category of Community material.

REPORTS AND STUDIES

Just as Community institutions need facts and figures at their disposal for decision-making purposes so they also need more general guidance, advice and background information to assist their deliberations. Reports, reviews, studies and appraisals of many descriptions are compiled by and for Community institutions, most notably the Commission. During the early stages of policy formation, particularly when breaking new ground, the Commission often calls upon external experts for an objective assessment of the present state of integration in a particular area or for independent advice upon the direction in which Community policy should move. Numerous studies of differing types are produced. They include assessments of alternative policy options, reviews of policies pursued in member countries and elsewhere, comparisons of conditions obtaining in different parts of the Community and collations of statistical data. In view of the fact that many are written by academic specialists, often of international repute, it is not surprising that they constitute a valuable source of information for the academic community. Indeed, some such studies have made major contributions to the literature of their subject fields. Works of considerable merit or general interest are often given full publication in one of the several monograph series which have the common title *Studies*, followed by a sub-heading to denote the subject series, e.g. *Studies: energy series*. Many others, it should be said, are not formally published. They are not necessarily confidential and can often be acquired from their originating directorate-general if their existence is known. Some are listed in the *Documentation bulletin* and in the *List of additions to the Library*, but generally they are given no positive publicity, are printed in small numbers and are generally difficult for external users to trace and obtain.

The reports and studies mentioned in the previous paragraph represent an input into the Community decision-making process; they are prepared in order to facilitate the work of Community institutions. Many publications, however, represent an output of Community activity in the sense that they are the products of actions undertaken by or for Community institutions. They are usually produced in order to give wider dissemination to the results of

Community actions. Scientific and technical reports published in the EUR series are perhaps the best and certainly the most numerous examples of this type of material. Each year several hundred highly specialized and technical research reports are published in order to make publicly available the results of work undertaken by the Community directly through its Joint Research Centre and indirectly through the sponsorship of external research, often in the context of multi-annual research programmes. Chapter 4 of this book is devoted to scientific and technical publications so no further comments will be made here. However, it is clear that for academic scientists and research staff working in fields in which the Community has an active interest EUR reports are an invaluable source of specialist information.

The principal source of information on the individual titles which make up the various monograph series is *Publications of the European Communities*, published monthly by the Office for Official Publications of the European Communities as an insert in the *Bulletin of the European Communities*. Monthly issues eventually cumulate into an annual catalogue of the same title. Jeffries[48] describes these catalogues and other sources of bibliographical information in some detail, and Hopkins[49] outlines some of the problems concerning their use. Although significant improvements have been made in the presentation of information the scope of the catalogues has remained largely unaltered. For academic users there are still significant amounts of material which are not recorded, which are difficult to trace and which consequently receive much less use than the quality of their contents deserve. Moreover, there is also a need in academic circles for a single, comprehensive source of information on publications issued over a number of years. One such retrospective catalogue covering the years 1952–1971 was published in 1972[50] but has never been updated.

In some fields these general catalogues can be supplemented by more specialized bibliographical aids. Details of EUR reports, for instance, may be obtained not only from *Publications of the European Communities* or from *Euro abstracts* (described in Chapter 4), but also from the very useful compilation *Catalogue EUR documents 1968–1979*.[51] EUR reports prepared by the Joint Research Centre are listed along with other publications in its *Publications bulletin*.[52] Similarly, other Community agencies sometimes issue their own publications catalogues and lists. The European Foundation for the Improvement of Living and Working Conditions issues a *Catalogue of publications in print*[53] and the European Centre for the Development of Vocational Training issues a publications list.[54] However, despite the availability of these catalogues and other sources such as the helpful *Publications and documents of the EC received by the Library*, which is published as a supplement to the *List of additions to the Library*, it is still all too easy for recent publications to slip by unnoticed and all too difficult to find bibliographical details of publications for which no precise date of publication is known.

European Documentation Centres

Academic libraries traditionally constitute a principal source of information supply in higher education. Members of the academic community are library-oriented and much of their work is literature-based; they expect to find a good deal of the information they require in their local university or polytechnic libraries and for it to take the form of printed sources for personal use. Clearly, if teaching and research into Community affairs are to thrive, then there must be ready physical access to substantial collections of the publications and documents described in the previous section of this chapter. To its credit, the Commission of the European Communities has long since recognized this fact. It has made practical and exceedingly generous provision for those academic institutions whose teaching and research programmes include the study of European integration to receive automatically and free of charge a full range of Community publications together with an extensive collection of documents prepared by Community institutions, notably the Commission and the European Parliament. Institutions which attain this status are called European Documentation Centres (EDCs). In return for their privileged position EDCs must agree to make the documentation freely available to all members of the parent institution and must nominate a senior member of academic staff to assume responsibility for the collection. Institutions are urged to house the material separately and as far as possible to make material available to outside users.

The academic community receives the benefit of this generous gesture because in the eyes of the Commission's Directorate-General for Information (DG X) it is one of a number of groups who have a particularly important influence upon the formation of public opinion. Substantial resources have been invested in the EDC network not primarily for the advancement of scholarship and learning but for the purpose of promoting the study of European integration, on the assumption that this would in turn encourage the intellectual appreciation of the ideals embodied in the Treaty of Rome. Responsibility for executing this policy rests with the University Information Division of DG X, whose work takes on a number of additional aspects. In order to stimulate interest in European studies, conferences and seminars are organized or sponsored which are intended to stimulate interest and foster international collaboration. Their proceedings are often published.

In addition, each year research grants are made to individual researchers, subsidies are provided for the publication of doctoral theses on European themes, and individual or group visits to Community institutions are arranged. The University Information Division also acts as a clearing-house for information on European studies. It publishes *European university news*,[56] a modest but useful news and information bulletin which provides details of new courses in European studies, research grants and prizes, conferences and meetings in member countries and elsewhere. It also includes brief reviews of recent books, theses and journal articles on relevant subjects. Each year *Summer courses on European integration* is published as a separate supplement, principally for the use of students and young people who wish to attend short courses and seminars on European themes. *Postgraduate degrees in European integration* is another occasional supplement, in which are listed the postgraduate European studies courses available in member countries and elsewhere. The University Information Division also sponsors a regular survey of research activity in the area of European integration. This survey is mentioned later in this chapter.

However, it is undoubtedly the EDC system which is the most ambitious instrument of information policy for higher education. The Commission has so far created more than 200 EDCs in member countries, 44 of which are in the United Kingdom, and over 100 in other parts of the world. A number of British EDCs date from the 1960s, but the majority were created during the early 1970s when the membership debate was in full flood. Indeed, such was the demand for EDC status that demand soon outstripped resources, with the result that no new EDCs have been created in the United Kingdom since 1974.[55] Of the 44 EDCs in the United Kingdom 35 are located in university libraries, 8 in polytechnic libraries and 1 in a research institute. A full list appears as an appendix to this book.

The resources made available to EDCs are extensive. They include all the categories of Community material described in the previous section of this chapter, with the exception of EUR reports, which are supplied only on demand. Particularly valuable are the sets of COM documents regularly distributed to EDCs since 1974. Until May 1983, when the Office for Official Publications commenced its subscription service, COM documents were nowhere else generally available outside the depository libraries (DEPs),[57] Community institutions and their external offices. Of course, the extent to which individual EDCs are able to satisfy academic needs for access to material, particularly to long and complete backruns of important titles such as the *Official journal*, depends partially upon their date of origin and the assiduousness with which material has been collected. Such is the history of EDCs in the United Kingdom that their strength lies generally in material issued during the 1970s and later. Although local circumstances can vary considerably, academic staff and research students whose work has an historical dimension find it increasingly difficult to obtain material as they go back in time into the 1960s and earlier. Problems occur not with major titles such as the *Official journal*, of which there are a good number of complete sets available as well as microform backup, but with the more obscure serial titles, individual monographs and above all with documents. Although both the British Library Reference Division and the British Library Lending Division are Depository Libraries and have surprisingly good historical collections of Community publications, the only substantial — but by no means complete — collection of documents in original paper form dating from the 1960s and earlier is at the London Office of the Commission. If existing resources in British academic and national libraries are to be effectively exploited by academic researchers, an inventory of library holdings is required similar to that conducted by Pemberton[58] in 1972 but never updated.

It must also be said that academic use of the resources of EDCs is sometimes inhibited by deficiencies in the administration of the system, poor organizational arrangements in host libraries and a certain reluctance on the part of many academics to venture beyond such basic sources as the *General report* and the *Bulletin of the European Communities*. Problems concerning the exact entitlement of EDCs to publications and documents and difficulties over distribution sometimes make it difficult for librarians to provide an efficient service. A reluctance on the part of some host libraries to divert scarce resourses, particularly senior staff time, to the organization and exploitation of EDC collections means that library users who are intimidated by this sometimes complex and inhospitable material do not receive the guidance and advice that is required. Hopkins[59] describes some of the problems associated with the EDC scheme. Similar sentiments are expressed in a list of recommendations[60] sent to Brussels by the Association of EDC Librarians, a professional organization established to represent the views and promote the interests of those librarians in charge of EDCs.[61] However, despite the fact that all three partners in the scheme — the European Communities, host libraries and academic users — can each improve their contribution, the EDC system has been an undoubted success in both facilitating and stimulating academic activity in the field of European studies.

Scholarly literature on European integration

Much of the educational demand for information on the European Community is satisfied by a substantial and expanding body of literature produced by the academic community itself in the form of theses, scholarly monographs and articles in learned journals. This literature, which often depends for its raw material on the Community publications and documents described earlier, represents both an end-product of scholarly activity and a source of information to fuel new scholarly activity. In view of the fact that such material is written by academics mainly for the use of other academics it is often more suitable for educational use than original Community publications. This is particularly true in the case of undergraduate teaching, where prescribed readings take the form of textbooks and journal articles whose contents not only record significant actions and events but also provide commentary and interpretation at the appropriate intellectual level. Community publications feature occasionally on reading lists, particularly such encyclopedic titles as the *General report on the activities of the European Communities* and the *Bulletin of the European Communities*, but documents feature rarely, except when dissertation work encourages greater reliance on primary sources.

It is not appropriate in a chapter of this kind to undertake a detailed bibliographical survey of the mass of literature now available on the European Community. Instead, some cursory comments will be made on the characteristics displayed in this literature and attention drawn to some sources of further information. Firstly, however, it might be useful to begin with reference to a number of useful guides and bibliographies to the literature of European integration. Particularly valuable as a guide to recent undergraduate readings on mainly political issues is *The European Community: bibliographical excursions*, edited by Lodge.[62] In each of three parts dealing with integration theory and institutional matters, internal policies and external relations, academic specialists contribute a total of twenty-two essays each of which combines an introduction to the subject with a detailed review of its literature. More traditional bibliographies are also available but are now somewhat dated. Collester's *The European Communities: a guide to information sources*[63] is a useful annotated bibliography of the monographic literature on the political aspects of European integration in general and the European Communities in particular. Kujath's *Bibliography on European integration*[64] is more wide-ranging in its subject coverage and is international in its scope. Although published a considerable number of years ago, *A reader's guide to Britain and the European Communities* by Cosgrove,[65] is still a useful guide to the book and journal literature of the 1960s for those researching the entry of the United Kingdom into the European Communities. Finally, Twitchett provides a brief commentary on recent British books in his article *Britain and the European Community: the first ten years*.[66]

THESES

Theses and dissertations are one of the yardsticks that can be used to measure the level of academic activity in a subject field such as European integration. In view of the fact that most do not achieve full publication they represent not only the fruits of endless hours of toil on the part of their authors but also an important and often ignored body of literature. This fact has been recognized in the field of European integration. In addition to such standard sources of information as *Dissertation abstracts international* and *Index to theses*, which provide information on theses in all subject fields, there are a number of more specialized sources that conveniently bring together works on European integration which are scattered in the more general sources. A useful retrospective record of academic research is presented by Siemers and Siemers-Hidma in their book *European integration: select international bibliography of theses and dissertations 1957–1980.*[67] More than 2,200 theses and dissertations from universities and other institutions in twenty-eight countries are listed. Information on more recent theses and on research in progress is provided by *University research on European integration*,[68] prepared on behalf of the University Information Division of DG X by the Centre for European Studies at the Catholic University of Louvain in Belgium. In view of the fact that it lists not only doctoral theses but also papers prepared for conferences and published works, it is just as valuable as an international register of institutions and individual researchers active in European studies as a source of bibliographical information. The data contained in all twelve issues so far published have been entered into a data bank called EUREKA, which now contains details of more than 8,000 research works prepared over a thirty year period.[69] Research undertaken in the United Kingdom alone is also recorded in a similar *Register of current research into European integration* compiled by UACES.[70]

SCHOLARLY MONOGRAPHS

It will be apparent from cursory examination of the bibliographical guides mentioned at the beginning of this section that there exists a substantial and diverse body of literature on European integration. The subject remains buoyant, and writings on the subject have been sustained by the fact that at no time in the past ten years has Community membership ceased to be a political issue in the United Kingdom. The prolonged and often passionate debate on Community membership provoked not only a rash of polemical and partisan literature but also more balanced and informative texts for public consumption as well as more reflective academic evaluations. Specific events such as direct elections to the European Parliament and continuing differences of opinion on such matters as the Community budget and the Common Agricultural Policy have stimulated the interest of academics and produced a market for their publications. Indeed, advantage was taken of the tenth anniversary of British membership to make 1983 a vintage year for monographs on the European Communities. Authors such as Bailey,[71] Cohen,[72] El-Agraa,[73] Gregory,[74] Jenkins[75] and Willis[76] all took the opportunity afforded by this milestone to consider aspects of Britain's relationship with the European Communities.

Monographs published during 1983 are illustrative of another characteristic of the literature on the European Communities — the popularity of collections of essays as a form of publication. Books published in 1983 by Coffey,[77] Cohen,[72] El-Agraa,[73] Jenkins,[75] Lodge,[62] Lodge,[78] Tsoukalis[79] and Wallace[80] all conform with this pattern. There are obvious advantages in having specialists to contribute chapters to books whose scope is too wide to fall within the competence of a single author. However, the genre also provides a convenient format on which to base undergraduate texts; each chapter in books such as those by Lodge and El-Agraa in a sense represents a lecture in which a distinguished contributor provides an authoritative overview of the subject and summarizes the main issues it raises. Indeed, books such as that by Coffey are in fact direct products of existing lecture programmes. Other collections, such as those by Hill,[81] Jenkins and Tsoukalis, represent the published proceedings of conferences. Here again the contributors are leading scholars, but in this case the emphasis is upon analysis and interpretation rather than factual recapitulation. Collections are also popular because aspects of European integration lend themselves to a case-study approach, particularly when the focus of attention is the implementation rather than the evolution of policy.[82]

Many of the research monographs published on European integration come from academic activity initiated by the various professional bodies active in this field. On a national level there are, for instance, organizations such as UACES, the Federal Trust,[83] the Policy Studies Institute[84] and the Royal Institute of International Affairs;[85] on an international level organizations such as the Trans-European Policy Studies Association (TEPSA)[86] are active. These associations organize conferences and seminars, undertake research investigations, support research and sponsor the publications which often result from these activities. In some cases important research is carried out and published by staff of the organization; more often it is done voluntarily by researchers and academics. Small study groups are convened to discuss particular issues; their members are drawn from home and abroad and from backgrounds in academia, politics, the civil service and the professions.

JOURNAL ARTICLES

For those engaged in the academic study of the European Communities journal articles constitute a highly important source of information. In Lodge,[62] for instance, the total number of references to journal articles (712) is only marginally less than the number of citations to monographs (747). Mainly factual and descriptive articles are common, but the contributions of more lasting value are usually those whose approach is more analytical or interpretive. Case studies of specific Community events, policies or decisions, often viewed in the context of the impact they make in one member country, are also numerous. They constitute invaluable additions to the literature and enhance understanding of the wider issues they raise.

As in most fields of scholarship there are a small number of pre-eminent academic journals which constantly attract articles of the highest standard on a wide variety of topics concerning European integration. This may be illustrated by the fact that no less than 35% of the 712 articles cited in Lodge come from just 7 journals. Not surprisingly, the *Journal of Common Market studies* is most heavily cited (63), followed by *World today* (44), *Common Market law review* (38), *European law review* (36), *International organization* (35), *Government and opposition* (20) and the *Journal of European integration* (19). Although a much more broadly based survey and more rigorous investigation would be needed in order to produce an accurate rank list of journals covering the whole field of European integration, this example does show how articles tend to cluster around a limited number of titles.

However, Lodge is also illustrative of an equally important characteristic. Despite the dominant position occupied by the titles listed in the previous paragraph, the 712 articles cited in Lodge come from no less than 186 different journals. In other words, in addition to articles which appear regularly in a small number of core journals the literature is made up of many more articles which appear infrequently in a large number of additional journals, many of which are not normally associated with the subject of European integration. This phenomenon may be explained in several ways. Relatively few journals are in fact concerned predominantly with the European Community or are truly interdisciplinary in their scope. These are the strengths of the *Journal of Common Market studies*, although even this journal has a wider remit than its title suggests. The consequence is that many articles on the broader issues of European integration form part of the periodical literature of their parent subject disciplines. In some disciplines, such as law, articles tend to gravitate towards specialized titles such as the *Common Market law review* and the *European law review*; more usually, however, they are scattered throughout the mainstream titles in a particular subject field. Articles on the role of the European Community in world politics, for instance appear in such esteemed journals as *International affairs*, *Foreign affairs* and *Orbis*; articles which are more concerned with the economic issues raised by Community actions appear in such journals as *World economy* and the *Economic journal*. Frequently, articles appear in well-established journals whose focus is on one aspect of a broad subject discipline, particularly if it coincides with a sector of Community policy. Articles on the Common Agricultural Policy, for instance, are published in standard sources such as the *European review of agricultural economics*, and on regional policy in *Regional studies*. Moreover, in reflection of the considerable interest in the external relations of the European Community, numerous articles appear in journals that specialize in particular parts of the world and which do not always have widespread circulation in the United Kingdom. Journals that fall into this category include *African review*, *Asian survey* and *Australian outlook*. The nature of the subject is such that a wide scatter of periodical literature is inevitable. The consequence is that considerable reliance must be placed on indexing and abstracting services for identifying relevant articles; libraries have to depend on the considerable resources of the British Library Lending Division in order to satisfy many of the resultant requests for material.[87]

Conclusion

In conclusion, one can say that European studies has established itself as a valid and valued part of the curriculum in higher education and that academic interest in the subject of European integration is likely to be sustained. As in the past, areas of particular research attention will no doubt continue to be determined largely by political events. It is not difficult to imagine, for instance, that the Community budget and the disbursement of resources will remain subjects of both public controversy and academic interest. The probable accession of Spain and Portugal will focus attention not only on the economic consequences of enlargement but also on such matters as the Community decision-making process. The foreign relations of the Community will probably remain a buoyant area, with renegotiation of the Lomé Convention attracting extra attention to relations with developing countries. International events, new initiatives and significant progress in individual policy sectors will stimulate academic involvement, as has recently been the case with the common fisheries policy. Conversely, lack of initiative and progress will mean that academic activity in other Community sectors will remain relatively dormant.

Sustained interest in the subject of European integration means, of course, continued demand for access to information about the European Community. Such are the characteristics of official publications that some users will always find it difficult to exploit to the full the documents and publications made available by Community institutions. However, developments are already in train that will bring considerable benefits to academic users and make systematic use of Community documentation easier in future. Firstly, developments in information technology wil provide new opportunities for improved bibliographical services. The Office for Official Publications of the European Communities has already made impressive use of the computer to improve its sales catalogues, to develop the electronic journal and to construct a common indexing language. There are firm plans to create an extensive and sophisticated data base of public documents and publications which in terms of scope and comprehensiveness will solve many of the the present problems of bibliographical access. Secondly, the growing involvement of private publishers in the provision of EC information will have beneficial effects. The Office for Official Publications is actively seeking cooperation with private enterprise in the construction of the online documentation service mentioned above and Commission support has already been given to a project to investigate the possibilities of electronic transmission of documents and data. Moreover, commercial publishers are likely to improve significantly the physical availability of Community material. There are plans, for instance, for a commercial publisher to reproduce in microfiche a complete set of publicly available COM documents. Finally, ten years' experience of organizing and using Community documentation means that both librarians and academic users are better placed to make best use of the rich resources made available for academic use by the institutions of the European Community.

References and notes

[1] C. Archer, *International organizations*, Allen & Unwin, 1983, describes the growth and role of international organizations in the international political system and reviews the literature.

[2] Further information on both undergraduate and postgraduate courses on European studies may be obtained from the *Register of courses on European studies in British universities and polytechnics 1982/83*, University Association for Contemporary European Studies, 1982.

[3] Further information on the aims and activities of UACES may be obtained from the UACES Secretariat, King's College, London, WC2R 2LS.

[4] J. Jeffries, *A guide to the official publications of the European Communities*, 2nd edn., Mansell, 1981. Brief but useful overviews of Community publishing are also provided by T. Kearley, 'Official publications of the European Community: a valuable resource for U.S. libraries', *RQ*, vol. 22, no. 1, Fall 1982, pp. 58–69 and M. Hopkins, 'The bibliographical resources of European Documentation Centres', *Journal of librarianship*, vol. 7, no. 2, April 1975, pp. 84–99.

[5] Booklets published in 1983 include the following: 1/1983, *The European Community and the energy problem*; 2–3/1983, *Wine in the European Community*; 4/1983, *The Court of Justice of the European Communities*; 5/1983, *The social policy of the European Community*; 6/1983, *The Customs Union*; 7/1983, *Europe as seen by Europeans: ten years of European polling — 1973–1983*.

[6] Commission of the European Communities, *General report on the activities of the European Communities*, Office for Official Publications of the European Communities, 1968–date. The *General report* is presented to the European Parliament each February by the Commission in accordance with Article 18 of the Merger Treaty. Previously separate reports were published by each of the three former Community executives. From 1970 to 1976 the *General report* contained the address given by the President of the Commission to the European Parliament on the occasion of the presentation of the report and an annexed memorandum setting out the Commission's programme for the coming year. Since 1977 that address and memorandum have been published separately in a booklet called *Programme of the Commission for …* .

[7] Council of the European Communities, *Review of the Council's work*, Office for Official Publications of the European Communities, 1960–date.

[8] Economic and Social Committee, *Annual report*, Office for Official Publications, 1973–date.

[9] European Investment Bank, *Annual report*, European Investment Bank (100 bd K. Adenauer, L-2950 Luxembourg), 1958–date.

[10] Commission of the European Communities, *The agricultural situation in the Community*, Office for Official Publications of the European Communities, 1975–date.

[11] Commission of the European .Communities, *Report on social developments*, Office for Official Publications of the European Communities, 1979–date. Previously published from 1958 to 1978 as *Report on the development of the social situation in the Communities*.

[12] Commission of the European Communities, *Report on competition policy*, Office for Official Publications of the European Communities, 1972–date.

[13] Commission of the European Communities, *Bulletin of the European Communities*, Office for Official Publications of the European Communities, 1968–date. Previously published as the *Bulletin de la Communauté européenne du charbon et de l'acier*

(1956–1967) and the *Bulletin de la Communauté économique européenne* (1958–1967).

14 Commission of the European Communities (London Office), *Europe*, Commission of the European Communities (8 Storey's Gate, London, SW1P 3AT), 1981–date. Previously published as *European Community* (1957–1980).

15 European Communities, *Treaties establishing the European Communities, treaties amending these treaties, documents concerning the accession*, Office for Official Publications of the European Communities, 1978, contains the text of the Treaty of Rome.

16 European Communities, *Official journal of the European Communities*, Office for Official Publications of the European Communities, 1973–date. Previously published as the *Journal officiel de la Communauté européenne du charbon et de l'acier* (1952–1958) and the *Journal officiel des communautés européennes* (1958–1972). The *Official journal* split into two separate sections for *Information and notices* and *Legislation* in January 1968.

17 H. Greer, *Using the Official journal of the European Communities*, Association for EDC Librarians (available from Mrs A. Ramsay, Hon. Sec., Association of EDC Librarians, The Library, Newcastle Polytechnic, Newcastle upon Tyne, NE1 8ST), 1982, ('How to' leaflet, no. 4).

18 T. Kearley, 'An American researcher's guide to European Communities law and legal literature', *Law library journal*, vol. 75, no. 1, 1982, pp. 52–97.

19 *Encyclopedia of European Community law*, Sweet & Maxwell, 1973–date. Volume A, United Kingdom Sources (2 volumes), covers the European Communities Act 1972 with up-to-date annotations and other legislation. Volume B, European Community Treaties (3 volumes), contains the official texts, in up-to-date and amended form, of all the basic Community treaties. Volume C, Community Secondary Legislation (6 volumes), contains annotated texts of Community secondary legislation.

20 M. Hopkins, 'Gaps and inadequacies in the bibliographic control of the publications of the European Communities', *Aslib proceedings*, vol. 32, no. 9, September 1980, pp. 350–356, has more to say on this subject.

21 European Communities, *Register of current Community legal instruments*, 4th edn., Office for Official Publications of the European Communities, 1983. Volume 1: Analytical register. Volume 2: Chronological index. Alphabetical index. The *Register* appears annually with six-monthly updates.

22 CELEX is the computerized documentation system for European Community law and is described in Chapter 12 of this book. CELEX is publicly available through the Euronet host service EURIS (5 square de Meeus, B-1040 Brussels), from where further information may be obtained.

23 European Parliament, *Europe today: state of European integration 1982–1983*, Office for Official Publications of the European Communities, 1983. Two commercially published handbooks which also provide details of important legislation are B. Morris, P. Crane, K. Boehm, *The European Community: the practical guide for*

business and government, Macmillan, 1981, and D. Overton, *Common Market digest: an information guide to the European Communities*, The Library Association, 1983.

[24] Court of Justice of the European Communities, *Reports of cases before the Court*, Office for Official Publications of the European Communities, 1954–date.

[25] *Common Market law reports*, European Law Centre (4 Bloomsbury Square, London, WC1A 2RL), 1962–date.

[26] Further information on EUROLEX, the online legal service offered by the European Law Centre, may be obtained from EUROLEX, 4 Bloomsbury Square, London, WC1A 2RL.

[27] Commission of the European Communities, *Thirty years of Community law*, Office for Official Publications of the European Communities, 1983 (European perspectives series).

[28] Other classes of Commission documents, particularly 'SEC' and 'C' documents, are briefly described in M. Hopkins, *Publications, documentation and means for their dissemination in the Commission of the European Communities*, British Library Research and Development Department, 1981 (BLRD report No. 5618).

[29] M. Hopkins, *Policy formation in the European Communities: a bibliographical guide to Community documentation 1958–1978*, Mansell, 1981.

[30] M. Hopkins, *How to find out about Commission documents*, Association of EDC Librarians, 1982 ('How to' leaflet, No. 2), provides a brief introduction to Commission documents and sources of information about them.

[31] COM documents are available on annual subscription in either paper or microfiche form from the Office for Official Publications of the European Communities. In 1983 the annual subscription was £535 for the paper version or £95 for the microfiche version, both including indexes, which may also be purchased separately at an annual cost in 1983 of £38.

[32] Commission of the European Communities, 8 Storey's Gate, London, SW1P 3AT.

[33] The Commission's internal data bases are run by DG IX/E/4 Integrated Information Systems (IIS). The main files include ECO/1, the largest and most general file; PRC, which follows the progress of Commission proposals, recommendations and communications; ASMODEE, which deals with the application of directives in member states; and ACTU, which covers documents sent by the Secretariat-General to members of the Commission. The documents to which these files refer are stored on microfiche.

[34] See *Official journal of the European Communities*, S 188, 30 September 1983, p. 31.

[35] Commission of the European Communities, *Documents: monthly catalogue*, Office for Official Publications of the European Communities, 1983–date.

[36] Commission of the European Communities, *Documentation bulletin*, Office for Official Publications of the European Communities, 1973–date. Until 1977 it was called the *Bulletin on documentation*.

[37] House of Commons Library, *House of Commons weekly information bulletin*, HMSO, 1978–date.

[38] Commission of the European Communities, *List of additions to the Library*, Office for Official Publications of the European Communities, 1959–date. Entries for Community publications and documents are periodically brought together in special supplements under the title *Publications and documents of the EC received by the Library*.

[39] G. Pau, *Index to documents of the Commission of the European Communities 1982*, Eurofi (UK) Ltd. (25 London Road, Newbury, Berks., RG13 1JL), 1983.

[40] Further information on *Europe*, published by Agence Internationale d'information pour la presse, and on *European report*, published twice weekly by European Information Service, may be obtained from *European Communities publications: a guide to British Library resources*, British Library, 1983, which lists more than thirty similar alerting services.

[41] *European Parliament working documents* are placed on annual subscription (March to February) by the Office for Official Publications of the European Communities. The 1983/84 subscription was £24.

[42] European Communities, *Official journal of the European Communities. Annex. Debates of the European Parliament*, Office for Official Publications of the European Communities, 1968–date. Previously published separately by the European Parliament as *Débats du Parlement européen*, from 1952 to 1967/68.

[43] J. Neilson, *Reports of the European Communities, 1952–1977: an index to authors and chairmen*, Mansell, 1981.

[44] J. Neilson, *How to find out about the European Parliament*, Association of EDC Librarians, (available from Mrs A. Ramsay, Hon. Sec., Association of EDC Librarians, The Library, Newcastle Polytechnic, Newcastle upon Tyne, NE1 8ST), 1982 ('How to' leaflet No. 5).

[45] CRONOS contains economic time series arranged in separate files which include foreign trade, agriculture, industry, energy and development. COMEXT contains foreign trade statistics of member countries both with each other and with the rest of the world. Both are available online in the United Kingdom through SIA Computer Services, Ebury Gate, 23 Lower Belgrave Street, London, SW1W 0NW, from whom further information may be obtained.

[46] A. Ramsay, *How to find out about the statistics of the European Communities*, Association of EDC Librarians, 1982 ('How to' leaflet, No. 3). Available from Mrs A. Ramsay, Hon. Sec., Association of EDC Librarians, The Library, Newcastle Polytechnic, Newcastle upon Tyne, NE1 8ST.

[47] E. Krucoff, 'European Community publications: a statistical abundance', *Government publications review*, vol. 9, no. 3, May–June 1982, pp. 189–193.

[48] J. Jeffries, 'Problems of bibliographic control: the main bibliographic sources and publications catalogues', *Aslib proceedings*, vol. 32, no. 9, September 1980, pp. 345–349.

[49] M. Hopkins, 'Gaps and inadequacies in the bibliographic control of the publications of the European Communities', *Aslib proceedings*, vol. 32, no. 9, September 1980, pp. 350–356.

[50] European Communities, *Catalogue des publications 1952–1971*, Office for Official Publications of the European Communities, 1972.

[51] Commission of the European Communities, *Catalogue EUR documents 1968–1979*, Office for Official Publications of the European Communities, 1983 (EUR 7500).

[52] Available from the Joint Research Centre, Publications Service, Bldg. 36, Ispra Establishment, I-21020 Ispra, Italy.

[53] Available from the European Foundation for the Improvement of Living and Working Conditions, Loughlinstown House, Shankill, Co. Dublin, Ireland.

[54] Available from the European Centre for the Development of Vocational Training (CEDEFOP), Bundesallee 22, D-1000 Berlin 15.

[55] Commission of the European Communities, *European university news*, Office for Official Publications of the European Communities, 1965–date.

[56] In view of the fact that in late 1983 the Polytechnic of Central London withdrew from the scheme it is possible that a new EDC will be created in 1984.

[57] Depository Libraries are intended to serve the needs of the general public. They are generally placed in large public, usually national, libraries. Approximately 100 DEPs have been created throughout the world, of which 4 are located in the United Kingdom. These are the British Library Reference Division; the British Library Lending Division; Liverpool and District Scientific, Industrial and Research Library Advisory Council (LADSIRLAC); and Westminster City Library.

[58] J. E. Pemberton, *European materials in British university libraries*, UACES, 1972.

[59] M. Hopkins, *Publications, documentation and means for their dissemination in the Commission of the European Communities*, British Library Research and Development Department, 1981 (BLRD report No. 5618).

[60] 'Recommendations to the institutions of the European Communities concerning the future development of the EDC/DEP system', *Government publications review*, vol. 9, No. 5, September–October 1982, pp. 513–517.

[61] Further information on the aims and activities of the Association of EDC Librarians may be obtained from the Honorary Secretary, Mrs A. Ramsay, The Library, Newcastle Polytechnic, Newcastle upon Tyne, NE1 8ST.

[62] J. Lodge, *The European Community: bibliographical excursions*, Pinter, 1983.

[63] J. B. Collester, *The European Communities: a guide to information sources*, Gale, 1979 (International relations information guide series, 9).

[64] K. Kujath, *Bibliography on European integration*, Europa Union Verlag, 1977.

[65] C. A. Cosgrove, *A reader's guide to Britain and the European Communities*, Chatham House: PEP, 1970 (European series, 14).

[66] K. J. Twitchett, 'Britain and the European Community: the first ten years', *British book news*, March 1983, pp. 148–152.

[67] J. P. Siemers and E. H. Siemers-Hidma, *European integration: select international bibliography of theses and dissertations 1957–1980*, 2nd edn., Nijhoff, 1981.

[68] Commission of the European Communities, *University research on European integration*, Office for Official Publications of the European Communities, 1963–date.

[69] Further information on EUREKA may be obtained from the Centre for European Studies, Catholic University of Louvain, 1 place de l'Université, B-1348 Louvain-la-Neuve, Belgium.

[70] E. Evans, *Register of current research into European integration 1983*, UACES, 1983 (UACES information guides, 13).

[71] R. Bailey, *The European connection: implications of EEC membership*, Pergamon, 1983.

[72] C. D. Cohen, *The Common Market: ten years after*, Allan, 1983.

[73] A. M. El-Agraa, *Britain within the European Community*, Macmillan, 1983.

[74] F. E. C. Gregory, *Dilemmas of government: Britain and the EEC*, Robertson, 1983.

[75] R. Jenkins, *Britain and the EEC*, Macmillan, 1983.

[76] V. Willis, *Britons in Brussels: officials in the European Commission and Council Secretariat*, Policy Studies Institute, 1983.

[77] P. Coffey, *Main economic policy areas of the EEC*, Nijhoff, 1983.

[78] J. Lodge, *Institutions and policies of the European Community*, Pinter, 1983.

[79] L. Tsoukalis, *The European Community: past, present and future*, Blackwell, 1983.

[80] H. Wallace, W. Wallace and C. Webb, *Policy-making in the European Community*, 2nd edn., Wiley, 1983.

[81] C. Hill, *National foreign policies and European political cooperation*, Allen & Unwin, 1983.

[82] H. Wallace (op.cit.) and D. Allen, *European political cooperation: towards a foreign policy for Western Europe*, Butterworth, 1982, are good examples of how a case study approach can be more effective than a straight narrative.

[83] Further information may be obtained from the Federal Trust for Education and Research, 12a Maddox Street, London.

[84] Further information may be obtained from the Policy Studies Institute, 1–2 Castle Lane, London, SW1E 6DR.

[85] Further information may be obtained from the Royal Institute of International Affairs, Chatham House, 10 St. James's Square, London, SW1Y 4LE.

[86] Further information may be obtained from TEPSA, 11 rue d'Egmont, 1050 Brussels, Belgium.

[87] British Library, *European Community publications: a guide to British Library resources*, British Library, 1983, lists Community serial titles held by the British Library.

Note added in proof

Since this chapter was originally drafted Europe Data, an electronic publishing company based in Maastricht in The Netherlands, has announced the publication of the *EC index*, comprehensive indexing and abstracting service covering Community documents and publications. A 1984 annual volume will be followed in 1985 by monthly issues, cumulated quarterly and annually.

12

Sources of Information on
the Law of the European Communities

JOHN JEFFRIES

Introduction

The purpose of this chapter is to survey the various sources of legal information available to the user and to indicate some of the problems involved in understanding the law of the European Communities. It is also intended to highlight strategies for tracing legal information on the European Communities, although it must be recognized that information about information dates notoriously quickly, and that the range of tools available is continually changing.

It is through the legal order of the European Communities that the impact of membership on the national life of individual member countries, and hence on the lives of citizens, is at its most pervasive. Further significance can be attached to the fact that there is such a large and growing body of literature published in the United States, providing texts and commentaries on European Community (EC) legal instruments. As the world's largest trading bloc the Community has a potent influence over world trade, including that of the United States. The complexity of international business transactions is such that a need for European Community legal information exists throughout the world. It is not simply a domestic issue for the member countries themselves.

Granted that the law of the European Communities affects the life of every citizen in the member countries, it is also clear that it is the sphere in which people seem worst informed and understand least. There is a general lack of awareness in society at large of the rights and obligations implicit in membership. Moreover, membership itself is not a politically neutral issue. There is no particular reason why an individual in society should feel profoundly motivated towards some abstract ideal of European unity. In the United Kingdom (UK) a number of opinion leaders have objected to a legal order which they see as externally imposed. If the EC has failed to win public sympathy for Community policies then the institutions themselves must share some of the blame for not placing sufficient emphasis on the significance of action taken at Community level to harmonize the national laws of member countries in order to facilitate economic progress. What could be seen as excessive regulation can equally be seen as a means of breaking down artificial and technical barriers to trade and hence of achieving greater economic prosperity. Thus, anyone who has an interest in the economic progress of Europe ought to be informed of the legal measures which accompany it. One is not speaking solely of matters arising in the context of dispute and litigation.

The popular equation of law with crime and punishment does not help matters either. One has to look very hard for any criminal dimension to European Community legal activity. It is hard to convey to the layperson the idea of a legal system almost wholly geared towards economic regulation. In the minds of many the issue has been further obscured by the tendency for politicians to concentrate on the constitutional significance of membership, so that debate on ideological issues has concealed the immediate practical implications for daily life of the citizen. Indeed, European Community law seems to become a matter of debate only in terms of horror stories in the press about what Brussels is about to perpetrate upon the unsuspecting British public. The grosser popular misconceptions about Community policies are themselves a barrier to understanding the policies. Nowhere is this more true than in the case of EEC draft directives, a problem which will be dealt with later in this chapter.

Although the issues involved are complex and the volume of legal materials is great, a number of helpful tools have been developed to assist the researcher. One significant area of development has been online information retrieval and there are now several services worth mentioning, of which CELEX and EUROLEX are the most notable. Whereas the scale of the problem gets larger, the range of research tools available makes answers easier to find.

The treaties

The treaties are important because they set out the scope of Community activity. The secondary legislation gives flesh to the bare bones of Community policies as laid down by the treaties. The treaties are the 'fundamental' or 'primary' materials of European Community law. It is true that there are many conventions and agreements involving the Community countries, as well as third countries, but it is to the treaties that the researcher must first look for the basic legal principles of the European Communities.

Although the term 'European Community' has a general currency, and is indeed used in some of the official publications, it is really an abstract concept, like the ideal of European unity itself. There are in fact three European

Communities, each with a separate legal identity and each established by founding treaties.

The first treaty of all was designed to pool the coal and steel resources of Europe in an attempt to overcome the devastation of the Second World War and to foster the concept of European unity. The 'Treaty establishing the European Coal and Steel Community' (ECSC) was signed in Paris on 18 April 1951 by Belgium, France, the Federal Republic of Germany, Italy, Luxembourg and the Netherlands. It came into force on 23 July 1952.

An attempt to create a European Defence Community came to nought, but it was clear that there was much to be gained from further cooperation in the economic sphere. So it was that the same six countries signed two treaties in Rome on 25 March 1957. These treaties established the European Economic Community (EEC) and the European Atomic Energy Community (EAEC). It is the European Economic Community or EEC which is popularly referred to as the Common Market. The European Atomic Energy Community is referred to invariably as Euratom. The Treaties of Rome came into force on 1 January 1958.

As well as having three separate legal identities (and these separate identities remain) the three Communities had separate institutions, except that the Court of Justice and the Assembly or Parliament were common to all three from the outset. It was thought appropriate that the three Councils of Ministers should be merged and that the High Authority of the ECSC should be merged with the Commission of the EEC and the Commission of Euratom. So it was that on 8 April 1965 the six signed a treaty in Brussels establishing a single Council and a single Commission of the European Communities. This is sometimes called the 'Merger' Treaty and it came into force on 1 July 1967.

On 10 July 1975 another treaty was signed amending certain provisions of the protocol on the Statute of the European Investment Bank. This came into force on 1 October 1977.

In order to create a new institution, the Court of Auditors, a sixth treaty was signed on 22 July 1975. This is the 'Treaty amending certain financial provisions of the Treaties establishing the European Communities and of the Treaty establishing a single Council and a single Commission of the European Communities'. It came into force on 1 June 1977.

Any European country is eligible for membership of the Communities but it must join all three. When new member countries join there has to be an accession procedure. Documents concerning the accession of Denmark, Ireland and the United Kingdom in 1973, and Greece in 1980 should be read alongside the founding and amending treaties.

TEXTS OF THE TREATIES

The current official edition of the treaties was published by the Communities in 1978.[1] It is available in all the official languages, including Irish. It replaces an edition published in 1973 but omits some of the annexes to the Act concerning the conditions of accession and the adjustments to the treaties. The documents concerning the accession of Greece to the European Communities were published in the *Official journal* in 1979.[2]

Texts of the treaties can also be found as Command papers, published by Her Majesty's Stationery Office (HMSO) in the United Kindom Treaty Series. There are also a number of well-known commercial sources, of which perhaps the most generally useful is Sweet and Maxwell's *European Community treaties*,[3] which has become a standard work in its own right. In addition to the basic treaties it also includes such elusive texts as the 'Luxembourg accords'[4] and the documents relating to the accession of Greece. The texts of Community treaties also appear in Volume B of the *Encyclopedia of European Community law* and may be searched online through CELEX.

Secondary legislation

The treaties define the scope of European Community law and also establish the procedure by which the secondary legislation is made. In view of the existence of a number of excellent Community publications on the subject, particularly those by Noël[5] and Louis,[6] only brief mention will be made here of the legislative process. Put simply, it is the Council of Ministers which enacts legislation upon proposals made by the Commission, though certain administrative regulations can be made by the Commission acting alone. The European Parliament or Assembly is a consultative body: its opinion on Commission proposals is sought by the Council of Ministers but such opinions are not binding. Only the Commission can make proposals for new legislation to be laid before the Council of Ministers. There is a large and complicated committee structure within the Council at the apex of which is the Committee of Permanent Representatives (COREPER), which prepares the agenda for meetings of the Council. The activity of the Council is described in an annual *Review of the Council's work*.

The significance of the secondary legislation of the European Communities is embodied in the doctrine of 'direct applicability'. This means that the rules of law of the European Communities must be fully and uniformly applied in the member countries from the date of their entry into force and for so long as they continue in force. This doctrine was elaborated in a case brought before the Court of Justice of the European Communities.[7]

Although the structure of the legislative activity of the Council is sometimes difficult to follow, a path can be cut through the maze. A number of distinctions can be drawn, some of which are of more significance than others. In the first place, there are four main categories of acts, each of which is described below.

REGULATIONS AND GENERAL ECSC DECISIONS

Regulations relate to EEC and Euratom matters (see Article 189 of the EEC Treaty and Article 161 of the Euratom Treaty). They have general application, are binding in their entirety and are generally applicable in all member countries. Although Article 14 of the ECSC Treaty speaks only of general ECSC decisions being binding in their entirety, the Court of Justice has ruled that they are generally and directly applicable in the member countries as well.

Whereas there is a detailed process to be gone through before a regulation is enacted by the Council of Ministers, as mentioned above, there is provision in the treaties (Article 155 of the EEC Treaty and Article 124 of the Euratom Treaty) for the Council of Ministers to confer powers on the Commission to take 'implementing measures' under the Management Committee procedure. This is simply a means whereby rapid action can be taken in the agricultural market for reasons of day-to-day administration. It is improbable that many issues of principle would be involved in such measures. There are a great many of these Commission made regulations but the bulk of them remain in force for only a very short time. In any event most of the EEC regulations are concerned with the implementation of the Common Agricultural Policy and are not of wide interest.

DIRECTIVES AND ECSC RECOMMENDATIONS

Directives relate to EEC and Euratom matters (see Article 189 of the EEC Treaty and Article 161 of the Euratom Treaty). ECSC recommendations are provided for in Article 14 of the ECSC Treaty. These acts are binding upon a member country or, in the case of a recommendation, upon an individual as well. What this usually means is that it is up to the government of a member state to decide how to implement a measure. It is used as a device for achieving the approximation of legislation. In other words, there is a systematic attempt to bring the social and economic law of the individual countries into harmony, though the actual means whereby this is done can differ in each case. For example, the Commission has made a series of proposals for the harmonization of the law relating to company accounts. These have been enacted as EEC directives and have been embodied in successive United Kingdom Companies Acts.

There are several stages in the life of a directive. It becomes a matter for general discussion first in draft form, though it is probable that some discussions will have taken place when an idea is under consideration within the Commission but before it is submitted to the Council of Ministers as a COM final document and published in the 'C' series of the *Official journal*. To take a well-known example. The so-called draft 'fifth directive' on company structure began its life in 1972.[8] As a result of objections to the suggestions that companies over a certain size should make provision for worker representation on their boards of directors, the Commission brought out a 'green paper' in 1975 on employee participation and company structure in the European Community.[9] Subsequently, the Commission put forward the controversial 'Vredeling proposal' on procedures for keeping employees informed about company performance,[10] so named after the Commissioner then responsible for social policy. This proposal also attracted opposition and was amended in

1983,[11] when a new version of the draft 'fifth directive' was also presented to the Council.[12] And so the discussion of these measures goes on.

When the Council of Ministers does finally reach an agreement on a new directive the member countries are given a time limit for the introduction of the laws, regulations and administrative provisions necessary to comply with the terms of the directive. The Commission has a data base known as ASMODEE designed to monitor the progress of directives. This is in itself an indication of the extent of the difficulty in tracing the effect of EEC directives. The Council of Ministers publishes a *List of laws and regulations adopted in the member states of the Communities in application of acts adopted by the Communities*, but frankly it is of little use. ASMODEE is unlikely to be made available to the public.

DECISIONS

EEC and Euratom decisions and individual ECSC decisions are binding upon those to whom they are addressed. They may be addressed to individuals, groups of individuals or even governments, but they are binding in their entirety. They comprise a convenient way of dealing with individual cases.

RECOMMENDATIONS AND OPINIONS

The EEC and Euratom Treaties provide for recommendations. All three treaties provide for opinions. They are usually addressed to governments and for the most part can be regarded as a means of giving advice: opinions if the advice is solicited, and recommendations if it is not. This last category of acts differs from all the others in that there is no question of binding force.

TEXTS OF THE SECONDARY LEGISLATION

Legal acts are always published in the 'L' series of the *Official journal*. In the format of this publication can be seen other means of categorizing the secondary legislation, though on the whole such distinctions are not as useful as the distinction by legal form mentioned above. Each issue of the 'L' series *Official journal* is divided into two parts, of which the first comprises those acts for which publication is obligatory. The second includes those acts for which publication in the *Official journal* is not obligatory — usually decisions. Also, on the title page of each issue the entries for the more ephemeral acts are printed in lighter type to distinguish them from the more important acts which appear in heavy type with an asterisk against them.

A *Special edition* of the *Official journal* was published in two series in 1973 and gave an English and Danish text of the secondary legislation enacted between 1952 and 1972 and still in force on 1 January 1973. It represents only about 10% of the legislation actually passed in that period, the remainder having lapsed, and much of it is 1972 legislation that by now will also have largely lapsed. The first series of the *Special edition* includes 'binding acts of general application throughout the Community' and the second series is for those acts which, though in force, would not have had obligatory publication in the *Official journal*. In other words, the organization of the *Special edition* follows the same pattern as the 'L' series of the *Official journal* itself.

Up to 1972, the secondary legislation had been reprinted in 108 loose-leaf volumes, in the original four languages, known as *Recueil d'actes*. Publication of this work has long since been abandoned and there are no plans to revive it.

In 1970, the Foreign and Commonwealth Office published an unauthenticated translation of the secondary legislation which was issued through HMSO. The subject arrangement of this series was used when the Statutory Publications Office undertook to produce an authentic work which was designed to be rather more useful to the reader than the *Special edition*. The official texts which appeared in the *Special edition* were rearranged into forty-one subject volumes and published by HMSO under the title *Secondary legislation of the European Communities: Subject edition*. An index was added as Volume 42, which the *Special edition* had never had, and the work was kept up to date by the publication of monthly *Subject lists and table of effects* and annual cumulations. Using this publication it was possible to discover how an act had been subsequently amended — which was not evident from the *Special edition*. Unfortunately, publication of the *Subject lists and table of effects* ceased in 1979.

There are a number of other comprehensive sources from commercial publishers. Butterworths published a Volume 42A of the third edition of *Halsbury's Statutes of England* in 1975, which digests the secondary legislation in force at the end of 1972 under the headings used in the main part of the work. Supplements have been published subsequently. This is a useful service for those who already have access or subscribe to *Halsbury's*, especially if what is required is a conspectus of English law. Sweet and Maxwell have produced the multi-volume loose-leaf *Encyclopedia of European Community law*. Volume A consists of United Kingdom sources. Volume B contains the treaties. Volume C contains annotated texts of the secondary legislation. At present there are eleven binders in the set. This work is particularly valuable because it shows how directives have been incorporated into English law, which no text published by the Communities themselves will do. It is also useful as a statement of the secondary legislation in force. The penalty is the very high cost of purchase and upkeep, but as a single comprehensive work it is the one which can be most highly recommended.

Common Market reports, known formerly as *Common Market reporter* is another loose-leaf service which contains some of the secondary legislation; it contains a legal commentary. Published by Commerce Clearing House, it is not a comprehensive work but is usually found to be current; it contains most of the acts of significance, especially those relating to business and commerce. It seems to find particular favour in law firms, possibly because of its currency and the way it is angled towards the commercial world.

TRACING THE SECONDARY LEGISLATION

Index to the Official journal

One annual index covers both the 'L' (*Legislation*) and the 'C' (*Information and notices*) series of the *Official journal of the European Communities*. It is divided into two parts which are now usually issued as separate volumes. The 'Alphabetical index' is not a conventional chain index, as one might expect in a work of this kind, but is arranged in a form alleged to conform 'generally to the structure of the Treaties and the organization of Community institutions'. This is by no means an easy tool to use. One example may illustrate the point. Take Council Directive 82/606/EEC of 28 July 1982 relating to the organization by the Member States of surveys on the earnings of permanent and seasonal workers employed in agriculture. To trace this act in the 'Alphabetical index' one has to turn first to the section entitled 'Social policy'. The fourth second-level heading under this term is 'miscellaneous'. The seventh entry under this term is 'organization by the Member States of surveys on the earnings of permanent and seasonal workers employed in agriculture'.

So, how one finds the appropriate section of the index in which to start searching seems to be largely a matter of guesswork. There is an alphabetical 'List of keywords' which directs the reader to sections of the 'Alphabetical index', but no word in the title of the above act would appear to be a key word.

The second volume of the *Index* is a 'Methodological table' which simply lists the acts in number order.

The *Index* to the *Official journal* has not been compiled in such a way that would make it possible to produce a cumulation, and it would be laborious to search on a subject basis over a number of annual volumes. One needs to have fairly precise information to begin with in order to retrieve documents using the *Index*. The 'Methodological table' is convenient enough if the user has the official number of an act already. General or speculative searches are not likely to prove particularly fruitful.

Register of current Community legal instruments

So far there have been four editions of this work, each published in two volumes with an updating supplement by the Office for Official Publications. It is the official annual cumulative index to the secondary legislation, as published in the *Official journal*. The fourth edition gives the situation as at 1 January 1983. It is an attempt to provide a finding list of the secondary legislation in force, and is a by-product of the online information system CELEX. Its method of arrangement is remarkably similar to that of the *Index* to the *Official journal*, except that the provision of subject index entries in the second volume is rather more generous. This work is a qualified success. It requires a great deal of patience to use, particularly because the heading for each act is the CELEX field number, which has to be decrypted. With more forethought, the *Register* could have been a very valuable tool, especially with more subject headings in the main body of the work. Although it has been improved through various editions, it is open to further improvement.

Europe today

This single volume produced by the European Parliament is extremely helpful. It was originally conceived as a loose-leaf work that would provide an overall picture of the development of Community policies to make it possible to trace the policy formation process through all its stages. The current edition was published in 1983 and the loose-leaf format has been abandoned. It follows the now familiar arrangement of a sort of classification by area of Community activity. Unfortunately it lacks an index. On the other hand, one gains an impression of the way the policies of the European Communities are developing which is not so readily apparent from other official publications.

Review of the Council's work

If one knows the approximate date of an act the *Review* is sometimes a convenient supplementary aid to tracing secondary legislation, though it is intended to be an annual summary of the Council's activities. It is more current than *Europe today* and is helpful whenever precise details of an act are lacking.

Commercial publications

As well as the four official publications noted above, there are several commercial publications which can be used for tracing secondary legislation. The *Guide to EEC-legislation*[13] consists of two volumes plus supplements and is intended to be a key to current and lapsed secondary legislation excluding most of the regulations relating to agriculture. The *Register*, described above, gives similar information at less cost for current acts. The *Guide to EEC-legislation* would be most useful to those who need current awareness information because it has microfiche supplements on a regular basis together with a telex updating service. Commercial organizations may wish to consider the benefits of this service. Having a reasonably detailed subject index, the Sweet and Maxwell *Encyclopedia of European Community law* is useful for retrieving information by subject. And, of course, it includes the full text. *Policy formation in the European Communities: a bibliographical guide to Community documentation 1958–1978* by Hopkins[14] is a valuable tool. It is well indexed and intelligently arranged indicating all the documentation associated with the policies it describes, within its self-imposed limits. *The law of the European Economic Community*, by Smit and Herzog[15] is published in six loose-leaf volumes and follows the order of the EEC Treaty article by article. For each one it provides a commentary, a list of secondary legislation, Court cases and a bibliography. Its value is clear for those who need to know what litigation has occurred in connection with either treaty provisions or the secondary legislation.

Online sources

CELEX

CELEX is now an inter-institutional service of the European Communities, having been developed by the Legal Service of the Commission. It is also available in all the member states on a commercial basis from the Euronet-Diane host EURIS, a subsidiary of Honeywell-Bull.

It is intended that CELEX should include all the legal documents of the European Communities in full text, in all the official languages. It is an extremely sophisticated system with a wide range of search facilities. But the degree of sophistication, combined with the fact that the command protocol is unfamiliar, means that users need even more training than is common with full text online systems. It is not a particularly 'user friendly' system, but might turn out to be essential for those who make heavy use of European Community legal materials. It includes all the treaties, secondary legislation and case law, and it is proposed that other material such as draft legislation and the decisions of national courts will be loaded as well. Further information on CELEX is available from EURIS.[16]

EUROLEX

The *Legislation* series only of the *Official journal* is being loaded by EUROLEX (at the moment for the period 1980 to date). In addition, since its inception EUROLEX has contained *Common Market law reports*. EUROLEX may be more useful to the organization which makes use of legal information of which the European law is only a part. Further information is available from EUROLEX.[17]

Court of Justice of the European Communities

The judicial arm of the European Communities is the Court of Justice, which should not be confused with the Council of Europe's European Court of Human Rights. The Court of Justice of the European Communities functions in several areas: reviews of the legality of Community acts; proceedings brought against states failing to fulfil their obligations under the treaties or the secondary legislation of the European Communities; disputes involving the liability of the European Communities; cases relating to failure to comply with the anti-trust legislation; disputes between the Communities and their officials; and interpretation of the rules of law of the European Communities.

It is the individual member state which has the obligation under the treaties to enforce Community law in each country, but national courts can and do apply to the Court of Justice for a preliminary ruling. The Court of Justice is, as it were, the 'supreme court' for the law of the European Communities.

THE WORK OF THE COURT OF JUSTICE

A calendar of public hearings is drawn up each week, in French, and is available from the Court Registry. Actions and judgements are reported in the 'C' series of the *Official journal*. The Court issues a quarterly *Information on the Court of Justice of the European Communities*, which summarizes the more important cases before the Court as well as significant cases involving the law of the European Communities before national courts. Also, there is a short annual *Synopsis of the work of the Court of Justice of the European Communities in …* . The rules of the Court, together with other constitutional provisions and the like, can be found in *Selected instruments relating to the organization, jurisdiction and procedure of the Court*, the third edition of which was published by the Office for Official Publications in 1976.

As well as these official publications, Elsevier Information Services publish a digest of all the decisions and opinions of the Court of Justice in their *European Court of Justice reporter*, which is of value as a current awareness service.

CASE LAW

When case-law is cited in legal argument the most authoritative series for the Court of Justice is its own *Reports of cases before the Court*, published by the Office for Official Publications. It is available in the official languages and there is a retrospective translation of the case law, 1953 to 1972, in twenty volumes. There is always a considerable delay in the publication of *Reports of cases before the Court*, but the judgements and the opinions of the Advocates-General are available to the interested parties soon after the hearing. They are also available on subscription, Hammick, Sweet and Maxwell having taken over the United Kingdom agency in 1980. In the interim, one can consult the weekly *Proceedings of the Court of Justice of the European Communities*, which is available from the Court of Justice.

Common Market law reports has been published by the European Law Centre since 1962. It appears weekly and covers the decisions of national courts as well as those of the Court of Justice itself. Some of the more important cases are published in a much shortened form in *The Times* and the *New law journal*. Subscribers to *Common Market reports*, mentioned above, will also find case-law there.

The Court is issuing a loose-leaf work entitled a *Digest of case-law relating to the European Communities*. It is intended that it should be in four series. The 'D' series is for cases before the Court of Justice and national courts which arise from the Convention of 27 September 1968 on Jurisdiction and the Enforcement of Judgments in Civil and Commercial Matters. Such cases had appeared previously in the *Synopsis of case-law*, which has now ceased publication. The 'C' series is for cases before the Court concerning the officials of the European Communities. The 'B' series is for other cases before the national courts, and the 'A' series for all other cases before the Court of Justice.

Since 1977 the Court has published a *Bulletin bibliographique de jurisprudence communautaire* which continues the *Bibliography of European case-law: decisions relating to the Treaties establishing the European Communities* (and six supplements) 1965–1976. The Legal Service of the Commission issues

National decisions concerning Community law: selective list of references to published cases. Most of the entries which relate to United Kingdom law have been digested from *Common Market law reports.*

Increasing use is being made of online services to search case-law, both in academic institutions and law firms. *Reports of cases before the Court* has been loaded in full text on CELEX and LEXIS. *Common Market law reports,* together with other publications of the European Law Centre, can be searched in full text with EUROLEX.

Other sources of information

There are a number of periodicals and a large and growing number of books relating to the law of the European Communities. The following are among the most important periodicals: the *Common Market law review,* the *European law review,* the *Journal of Common Market studies* and *Legal issues of European integration.* The Office for Official Publications of the European Communities has itself published a number of titles which provide useful starting points for the study of Community law[18] and there is also a chapter on 'Community law' in the Commission's *General report on the activities of the European Communities,* which is also available as a separate pamphlet.

Possibly the best general introduction to the law of the European Communities is that written by Lasok and Bridge.[19] Other major books and articles on Community law are cited in the appropriate chapter of the guide to Community literature edited by Lodge.[20] From a general bibliographical point of view, Kearley[21] has written a comprehensive review of Community law and legal literature. In addition, legal bibliographies have been published by FitzGerald and Emringer,[22] Dahlmanns[23] and Germain,[24] the very size of which indicates the scale of the publications explosion in this area.

References and notes

[1] *Treaties establishing the European Communities, treaties amending these treaties, documents concerning the accession,* Office for Official Publications, 1978.

[2] *Official journal of the European Communities,* L291, 19 November 1979, pp. 1–192.

[3] *European Community treaties,* Sweet & Maxwell, 4th edn., 1980.

[4] The 'Luxembourg accords' may also be found in the *Ninth General report on the activities of the Community (EEC),* Publishing Services of the European Communities, 1966, pp. 31–33.

[5] E. Noël, *Working together: the institutions of the European Community,* Office for Official Publications, 1982.

[6] J. V. Louis, *The Community legal order*, Office for Official Publications, 1979 (European perspectives).

[7] Case 106/77, *Amministrazione delle Finanze dello Strato v Simmenthal S.p.a. (preliminary ruling requested by the Pretore di Susa)*, [1978] ECR 629.

[8] Proposal for a fifth directive on the structure of sociétés anonymes, *Bulletin of the European Communities*, Supplement 10/72.

[9] Employee participation and company structure in the European Community, *Bulletin of the European Communities*, Supplement 8/75.

[10] Proposal for a Council directive on procedures for informing and consulting the employees of undertakings with complex structures, in particular transnational undertakings, *Official journal of the European Communities*, C297, 15 November 1980, pp. 3–8.

[11] Amendment to the proposal for a Council directive on procedures for informing and consulting employees, *Official journal of the European Communities*, C217, 12 August 1983, pp. 3–16.

[12] Amended proposal for a fifth directive founded on Article 54 (3) (g) of the EEC Treaty concerning the structure of public limited companies and the powers and obligations of their organs, *Official journal of the European Communities*, C240, 9 September, pp. 2–38.

[13] A. E. Kellermann, *Guide to EEC-Legislation*, North-Holland, (1979–).

[14] M. Hopkins, *Policy formation in the European Communities: a bibliographical guide to Community documentation 1958–1978*, Mansell, 1981.

[15] H. Smit and P. E. Herzog, *The law of the European Economic Community*, Bender, (1976–).

[16] EURIS, Square de Meeus 5, 1040 Brussels, Belgium.

[17] EUROLEX, European Law Centre Ltd., 4 Bloomsbury Square, London, WC1A 2RL.

[18] These titles include *Thirty years of Community law*, 1983 (European perspectives series), and J. V. Louis, *The Community legal order*, 1979 (European perspectives series). Also useful as introductions to the subject are 'The Court of Justice of the European Communities', *European documentation* 4/1983, and 'The European Community's legal system', *European documentation* 6/1981.

[19] D. Lasok and J. W. Bridge, *Introduction to the law and institutions of the European Communities*, 3rd edn., Butterworths, 1982.

[20] J. Lodge (ed.), *The European Community: bibliographical excursions*, Pinter, 1983.

[21] T. Kearley, 'An American researcher's guide to European Communities law and legal literature', *Law library journal*, vol. 75, no. 1, Winter 1982, pp. 52–97.

[22] F. N. FitzGerald and L. Emringer, 'Principal source material on European

Community legislation: a bibliographical note', *International journal of law libraries*, vol. 3, no. 3, 1975, pp. 208–214.

[23] G. J. Dahlmanns, 'European Communities law', *International journal of law libraries*, vol. 3, no. 3, 1975, pp. 215–272.

[24] C. M. Germain, 'European Community law — a selective bibliography of publications in English, French and German with annotations', *International journal of law libraries*, vol. 8, no. 6, 1980, pp. 239–281.

13

Statistical sources of the European Communities

MARIA COLLINS

Introduction

The purpose of this chapter is to provide an overview of the statistical sources of the European Communities. It concentrates mainly on the data issued by the Statistical Office of the European Communities (known as Eurostat), but is not intended as a comprehensive catalogue of European Community (EC) statistical publications. Rather, the intention is to provide a general introduction to the nature of Community statistical provision. Specific publications are cited either as examples of certain types of publication or to illustrate particular problems or features of development, although naturally the major sources are highlighted. Agricultural statistics are dealt with in Chapter 14 and are therefore only briefly mentioned here.

Most statistics are collected by governments to help in their regional and national planning. In the case of Eurostat the same principle applies. The Commission of the European Communities has a responsibility to formulate and direct policy: it needs statistical data in order to monitor economic and social trends in Community countries and to assist in the decision-making process. However, it is generally recognized both by governments and by international organizations that the statistics they collect have a much wider relevance and can be of value for purposes often far removed from that for which they were first collected. For the business community in particular, statistics can be an invaluable management tool. They provide the essential data upon which to base decisions relating to long-term investment and expansion; they provide a means of measuring and monitoring short-term performance, both internally between departments, and externally with competitors; and they provide much of the raw data upon which marketing strategies and financial decisions are often based. In this context, the statistics produced by Eurostat are particularly important. The member countries of the European Communities attract more than 40% of the external trade of the United Kingdom (UK); if British firms are to exploit further the export potential afforded by the Common Market then they can derive much useful information from the statistical data made available by Eurostat.

Role and work of the Statistical Office of the European Communities

Established initially to serve the High Authority of the European Coal and Steel Community (ECSC) in 1953, the first statistical service of the Community developed a very comprehensive system of statistics, concentrating on coal, steel and the energy sector in general. In 1958 a joint decision was taken by the executive bodies of the European Economic Community (EEC), the European Atomic Energy Community (EAEC or Euratom) and the ECSC to form the Statistical Office of the European Communities. This early history might explain why there are separate detailed series for the industry sectors covered by the ECSC but until recently rather poorer coverage for other industries. In fact, there are three series dedicated to iron and steel statistics. The *Monthly bulletin of iron and steel statistics* (1978–) updates important rapid short-term data; the *Quarterly iron and steel bulletin* (1962–) covers major data, in particular, production, trade and apparent consumption; and finally, the *Iron and steel yearbook* (1964–) gives most detail, including prices and investment. Three other sectors are given special coverage in *Coal: monthly bulletin* (1977–), *Electrical energy: monthly bulletin* (1977–) and *Hydrocarbons: monthly bulletin* (1977–). Each has a regular section giving the principal monthly series and a variable section on important new developments.

Eurostat is housed with other Commission services in the Jean Monnet Building in Luxembourg.[1] It provides Community institutions with the statistics they need for formulating and monitoring policy, demand changing as economic and political interests change. It coordinates statistical activities within the Communities, providing a framework within which the national statistical systems of member states can move towards a more unified system. The work of the Statistical Office is undertaken by six directorates headed by the Director-General who is assisted by a secretariat. Each directorate is responsible for statistics relating to specific policy areas, such as general economic statistics (Directorate B) and energy and industrial statistics (Directorate D).[2]

STATISTICAL PROGRAMMES

Since 1973 the work of Eurostat has been guided by statistical work programmes that provide a general framework and specific targets for the Statistical Office during the period under review. Draft programmes are discussed with the Conference of the Directors of the National Statistical Institutes[3] before submission for approval by the Council of the European Communities. Once approved, numerous working groups and committees, also with representatives from member states, work out the details of implementation. The latest programme is the fifth covering the years 1982–1984.[4] This is likely to be the last presented in this way, as it is no longer considered necessary for the full programme to be produced for the Commission and the Council. Instead, an annual update will be discussed each year with the Directors of the National Statistical Institutes.

The fifth programme places considerable emphasis upon computer applications in the preparation and dissemination of statistical data. It lists the following priorities:

— to reduce duplication in the demand for data by international organizations and to strengthen their links with the European Commission.

— to improve the software, that is, CRONOS (which seems to be the name for both the software and the time series data bank which will be described later), OSIRIS (which is being developed for table generation), SABINE (the data base system for classification) and SIGISE, formerly called AISE (the integrated system for production and dissemination of statistics).

— to look at output technologies and the possibilities being offered by new telecommunications techniques.

— to rationalize the use of computer facilities, optimizing the potential offered by flexible transmission of data online, by magnetic tape or on microfiche. A specific project will look at data delivery from member states to see if the format can be harmonized and the programmes used simplified.

— to provide catalogues designed as an inventory and guide to statistical publications. The list would be automatically updated.

— to provide a new yearbook to complete the programme of key general publications. (This has been promised for some time but has yet to appear).

Programmes such as this enable the Statistical Office to focus its energies on particular issues. The detailed plans provide a yardstick by which achievements may be measured. However, although many projects are usually completed, circumstances and the availability of resources may sometimes cause changes in priorities. The programmes do not represent firm commitments and it must be realized that Eurostat has only a comparatively small staff.

HARMONIZATION OF NATIONAL STATISTICS
The harmonization of statistics at the Community level has been a major concern of Eurostat throughout the thirty years of its existence. As data are received from many different sources, control is essential if the statistics needed to frame new policies are to be comparable. Notable achievements have been made, such as

in the construction of Community nomenclatures, which are the subject of a later section in this chapter, and in the field of national accounts. The European System of Integrated Economic Accounts (ESA)[5] has been devised to give a coherent, quantitative description of the economies of Community countries. It is the Community version of the United Nations System of National Accounts (SNA) but is more precise and rigorous. Additional information can be incorporated so that input–output details and financial accounts taking in the distribution of income can be investigated. A set of uniform definitions and classifications is used to provide a common system to meet the needs of planners of social and economic policies within the European Communities.

Another extremely useful example of harmonized statistics is input–output tables, which give a detailed and consistent description of the flow of goods and services between branches of the economy of a country and between that country and the rest of the world.[6] The tables can be used to compare the economic structures of member states, since a common method is used in their compilation. However, the large amounts of data from different sources needed for their compilation does mean that only broad categories of economic activity can be dealt with and that there are considerable delays in their publication. The latest tables available, for instance, are for 1975[7] and cover only forty-four branches of economic activity as defined by NACE-CLIO.[8] Data for individual products cannot be given. Even so, the complexity of compilation means that one-third of the volume relating to the 1975 tables is needed for explanatory notes. The data are available on magnetic tape or as a computer printout as well as in published form. A series of computer programs have been developed for use with the data, such as a price impact model which calculates the effect on production price of an increase in wages or the price of imported goods. The programs can be run by Eurostat on request from users, whenever resources permit.

Although publications are produced which contain statistics that are clearly not harmonized,[9] constant efforts are being made to improve the situation. Consumer price indexes are a case in point. In 1977 a discussion paper was published in which consumer price indexes used in the nine member states were compared, the differences in the methodologies used to compile them were highlighted and possible approaches to harmonization suggested.[10] As a result of this exercise, there has appeared the *Consumer price index: monthly bulletin* (1982–), which contains a general index whose components correspond to groupings of the national indexes aggregated according to the ESA and calculated on 1975 as the base year for all countries. Methodological notes draw attention to the differences between the indexes compiled in member countries. It should also be noted that this is not an official sales publication; it is available only on demand from Eurostat itself, which is unfortunate in view of the importance of the consumer price index as a short-term indicator.

COMMUNITY SURVEYS

A very high degree of harmonization has been achieved in Community surveys, in particular with social and agricultural statistics. Unlike the United Nations, which has to collect its statistics on a voluntary basis, the European Community can invoke the power of legislation to enable it to lay down the precise manner and form in which statistics are to be collected. Such Community surveys are requested only when the need for comparability is particularly high and national sources cannot be reconciled.

A labour force sample survey has been conducted every two years since 1973, although only results up to 1979 have so far been published.[11] A special regulation empowers the Commission to conduct the survey based on a sample of households in each member state. Different laws, rules and administrative practices in member states would otherwise make it impossible to gain meaningful comparisons. Eurostat is responsible for the content of the survey and the size of the sample, compiles the list of questions and devises the common coding required. The national statistical institutes are responsible for selecting the sample, preparing the questionnaires, conducting the necessary interviews and forwarding the results to Eurostat. Analysis of the results and their publication is, naturally, the responsibility of Eurostat. It is laid down that the survey must take place in the spring of the designated year; only private households (using the definition in force in each respective country) are to be included, although information on individuals is to be used only for compiling statistical aggregates. In addition to standard questions the opportunity is usually taken to add supplementary questions on subjects of current Community concern. In 1977, for instance, pensioners and retirement conditions were singled out and data provided which was subsequently published separately.[12] Complete comparability is still not possible and care must be taken in particular when comparing the results of successive surveys.

Another important Community survey is the annual inquiry into industrial activity. Lack of detail in the industrial statistics of the Community as a whole has been a long standing problem; national sources vary and are each based on different survey methods. The standard annual inquiry was set up by Council Directive No. 72/221/EEC of 6 June 1972,[13] which placed on member states an obligation to achieve uniformity. Unfortunately, the ease with which member states could comply varied greatly; some were already carrying out regular surveys, others had to start from scratch or make major changes. There is still only two-thirds implementation of the directive, although this is enough to make the survey reasonably useful.

The survey covers enterprises which employ over twenty people and concentrates on the principal activity of these enterprises. Since in some countries small firms occupy a significant place in the economy, every five years a special supplementary inquiry covering firms with less than twenty employees is held. Further, to document the diverse activity within individual firms, a special unit, the kind of activity unit (KAU), has been created. Collection of information at KAU has been fragmentary so far; only Italy, the Netherlands, Belgium and Denmark are fully covered. Early surveys of industrial activity were considered to be unreliable and results were given only limited distribution. The year 1980 saw the publication of the 1975 survey in sixteen volumes.[14] The main results of surveys for subsequent years up to 1978 have been published annually as single volumes.[15] Efforts are being made to speed up publication. Although problems with data processing have now been solved, Eurostat is still dependent for data on the national statistical institutes which actually carry out the surveys.

Community surveys have also been conducted in other sectors. A considerable amount of time has been invested, for instance, in the design of surveys to assist decision making in relation to the Common Agricultural Policy (CAP). These range from the large-scale survey on the structure of agricultural holdings[16] to more specialized studies concentrating on one aspect, such as the survey of orchard fruit trees conducted in 1977.[17] Some surveys are conducted only on a one-off basis and quickly become out of date. Examples of these are the surveys on the structure and distribution of earnings in industry conducted in 1972[18] and on earnings in wholesale and retail distribution, banking and insurance, conducted in 1974.[19]

CLASSIFICATIONS

Two types of classifications are used to facilitate the compilation of economic statistics; commodity classifications, and classifications of industries (or activities). Most countries devised their own schemes well before they joined the European Community — the United Kingdom first started to divide trade figures into economic classes in 1920[20] — although in practice most national classifications were based on existing international schemes. As early as the late 1950s work was started on the creation of special nomenclatures to meet the needs of the Community. Since that time the Statistical Office has produced several classifications, of which the most important are NIMEXE, NACE and NIPRO.

NIMEXE

NIMEXE, the Nomenclature of Goods for the External Trade Statistics of the Community and Statistics of Trade between Member States, was devised in order to facilitate the presentation of comparable statistics on intra- and extra-Community trade. It has been applied since 1966 and is revised annually by a special committee. The revised version is published each December in the *Official journal*. Care should be taken to consult the correct version when using trade figures.

NIMEXE is a commodity classification based on the Customs Cooperation Council Nomenclature (CCCN),[21] previously known as the Brussels Tariff Nomenclature (BTN). The CCCN provides standard headings for the whole range of products entering world trade and was specifically constructed to aid customs officials when assigning duty rates. Products from the same raw material are grouped then subdivided according to stage of fabrication. Classes are fairly broad so that individual countries can assign their own tariff categories while still maintaining agreed headings. Eurostat's own tariff, *Nomenclature of the Common External Tariff of the European Communities* or Common Customs Tariff (CCT), is so developed from and consistent with CCCN. Eurostat has built on this structure by adding two digits to the four CCCN digits, thus allowing more precise commodity differentiation. There is no alphabetical approach to the NIMEXE code. However, it is possible to use the alphabetical index to the Brussels Nomenclature and its explanatory notes[22] or the guide to the classification of United Kingdom overseas trade statistics.[23] Although the latter refers to Standard International Trade Classification (SITC)[24] codings, it also lists tariff numbers that are related to NIMEXE. In order to classify and code the countries engaged in international trade the Statistical Office uses its own geonomenclature.[25]

Eurostat has participated actively in the work being carried out by the Customs Cooperation Council in Brussels to produce a new, harmonized commodity description and coding system. The Harmonized System (HS) is effectively an update of CCCN and work has already commenced on the adaptation of both NIMEXE and the CCT to the new HS framework. It is hoped that the system will be operative from 1985.

NACE

Emphasis in the collection of industrial statistics is on the production unit — usually at enterprise or company level, which may be the output of several factories. In order to facilitate the compilation of comparable data on economic activity in the Community as a whole the Statistical Office devised the General Industrial Classification of Economic Activities within the European Communities (NACE). First published in 1970[26] NACE is more detailed than the International Standard Industrial Classification of all Economic Activities (ISIC)[27] produced by the United Nations, but its classes can be amalgamated to make the schemes compatible. With its revised Standard Industrial Classification,[28] now used in the *Business monitors*, the United Kingdom has brought its own industrial activity classification into closer correspondence with NACE.

NIPRO

The Common Nomenclature of Industrial Products (NIPRO) is a classification of industrial products constructed according to the NACE framework. As such it further refines NACE by assigning the products associated with each industrial branch. An excellent summary of this classification, and of both NIMEXE and NACE, appears in the introduction to the published version of NIPRO.[29]

Eurostat publications

Eurostat places considerable importance on the dissemination of the statistics it produces. Statistical data are made available not only in published form but also in microform, on magnetic tape, as computer printout and by direct access to online data banks. However, it is in published form that data still receive most widespread dissemination and it is Eurostat publications that are described in this section.

Material formally published by Eurostat can be of three types:

(i) Regular series, which can be subdivided into those giving time series (showing fluctuations in key economic and social data) and those giving the results of regular surveys.

(ii) Special studies, either one-off surveys or specially commissioned work intended to give insight into a particular Community problem or to serve as a basis for discussion.

(iii) Methodologies and definitions. Every care is taken to ensure that the statistics are accompanied by the necessary notes and explanations. Where it is impractical to include these in the publication a separate volume is produced.

Slight blurring of this pattern occurs when results of the surveys are included in the regular series, but this happens only occasionally.

In 1980 a scheme was introduced to place each publication within one of seven subject themes. Reference is normally made within each publication to other publications in the same theme. In view of the fact that regularly produced Community surveys have already been dealt with, the following section covers time series periodicals published in each of the subject themes.

THEME 1 — GENERAL STATISTICS

There are at present three main general titles, each one containing a wide range of statistical information. *Eurostat review* (1981–), published annually, provides a broad economic overview of the Community. Ten-year runs of figures are included, highlighting trends and making comparisons possible. *Basic statistics of the Community: comparison with some European countries, Canada, United States of America, Japan and the Union of Soviet Socialist Republics* (1958–) has the longest title but is only pocket-sized. It also appears annually and is especially useful for one-off, factual enquiries about the Community on such topics as population, gross national product, number of television sets, etc. Separate language editions are published for each of the six main languages; figures for Greece are included, but there is as yet no Greek version. *Eurostatistics: data for short-term economic analysis* (1979–) has its purpose explained in its sub-title. Each monthly issue is divided into four parts. A short text on the latest economic trends is followed by a graphic illustration of the figures. The third section gives fully harmonized Community data on employment, production, trade, etc. In the last section each country's most commonly used indicators are presented, using their own national definitions. Cross-country comparisons within this section are not possible. *Eurostatistics* was published up to December 1981 in two versions. The Danish, English and Italian version and the German, French and Dutch version were published on alternate fortnights. Each one contained the latest available figures as it went to press. Now a single edition appears monthly with its text in German, English and French. If other languages are needed, a supplement with translations of the headings and with explanatory notes can be provided. Figures for Greece have been included since January 1982. Since 1980 a fourth publication, *Eurostat yearbook*, has been planned but has not yet appeared. The *Yearbook of regional statistics* (1981–) also appears in this theme.

THEME 2 — NATIONAL ACCOUNTS, FINANCE AND BALANCE OF PAYMENTS

National accounts are classified within the framework of the European System of Integrated Economic Accounts mentioned earlier. The flows of the economy are divided into a small number of fundamental categories so that the whole economic system can be represented in a way that is suitable for analysis, forecasting and policy making. Data are collected annually from member countries using a standard questionnaire sent out nine to twelve months after the end of the year. An aggregates volume, *National accounts: ESA aggregates* (1974–), is then quite speedily produced. Aggregates, which are sum totals of data used to express particular concepts, are quite closely defined, e.g. national disposable income or change in stocks are expressed in national currencies, European Currency Units (ECU), purchasing power parities, and as volume and price indices. Subsequently, two further annual publications appear, *National accounts ESA: detailed tables by branch* (1980–) and *National accounts ESA: detailed tables by sector* (1981–), where branch refers to industry, e.g. fuel and power products, and sectors refers to groups of institutional units having a similar type of economic behaviour, e.g. credit institutions, government or households. In fact the government sector is further developed in a separate annual publication, *General government accounts and statistics* (1980–), in which there are three sub-sections: central government, local government and social security funds.

Balance of payments is defined in the introduction to *Balance of payments — quarterly data* (1981–) as being the record of a country's international transactions with the rest of the world. These transactions can involve merchandise, services, loans, foreign exchange, etc. The items are recorded by a double-entry system of book-keeping. Two annual series, *Balance of payments: global data* (1975–) and *Balance of payments: geographic breakdown* (1975–) complete the provision of data on this topic.

THEME 3 — POPULATION AND SOCIAL CONDITIONS

Publications on a number of topics were once issued under the general title *Social statistics* but now most subjects have their own series. *Demographic statistics* (1978–) appears annually. It contains both Community tables and data for each individual country, including Spain and Portugal. Tables are not equally up to date for all countries but data on population by sex and age group, births, deaths and marriages are given on a comparable basis.

The concern of the Community for education and training is expressed in a publication which brings together information on the topic. First entitled *Education statistics* (1977–1979) its growing tendency to include coverage of aspects of training outside the normal school system is reflected in its more recent title *Education and training* (1980–). However, as education systems vary considerably from country to country, care must be taken in interpreting the figures.

Unemployment figures, which are currently of more concern than those for people in work, are published in the *Unemployment monthly bulletin* (1977–), also known as *Monthly statistics of registered unemployed*, since both titles confusingly appear on its cover. Compiled from figures submitted by national employment offices, the tables show the total number of unemployed and also the proportion as compared with the working population. Separate figures are given for youth unemployment (under twenty-five years of age), new registrations in the month under review, and the number of vacancies. Annual figures are consolidated in *Employment and unemployment* (1978–), which contains recent statistics and retrospective figures which allow trends to be discerned. A table showing the duration of registered unemployment is also now included, as are harmonized data on employees within each industry as defined by NACE. Figures on Spain and Portugal are included but have not been harmonized. For those in work their remuneration is documented on a half-yearly basis in *Hourly earnings: hours of work*, which now includes a table expressing hourly earnings in terms of purchasing power standards so that levels of earnings in each member state can be more meaningfully compared.

THEME 4 — INDUSTRY AND SERVICES

Coverage of much of this theme has been dealt with elsewhere. *Industrial production* (1982–) fills the gap left by the demise of the *Quarterly bulletin of industrial production* (1976–1978). Its content has not yet stabilized and sectors of industry are being added with each new issue. At the time of writing the latest issue covers man-made fibres, leather and footwear, pulp, paper and board, office machines, data processing and domestic electrical appliances. *Industrial short term trends* (1978–) started when the *Quarterly bulletin of industrial production* ceased publication, but was never intended as its successor. It contains brief commentaries on the current industrial scene, presents the main indices under very broad NACE headings and occasionally has special supplements of long time series not suitable for the normal monthly publications. Reflecting the concern about stocks of strategic minerals, *EC raw materials balance sheets* (1981–) appears annually. The balance sheets indicate the degree of dependence on certain imported minerals; common non-ferrous metals, such as lead and tin, and rarer metals, such as titanium and tungsten, are amongst the twenty minerals included.

On a more general level *Annual investment in fixed assets* (1976–) is a useful publication which shows under NACE industry sectors where investment (or lack of it) is taking place. Tables for each country give the amount invested in machinery, plant and vehicles, construction of buildings, purchase of land and disposals. The prevailing interests of the Community are reflected in the existence of two other industry titles, *Energy statistics yearbook* (1964–) and *Operations of nuclear power stations* (1976–), and in *Statistical yearbook transport, communications, tourism* (1976–), all of which appear annually.

THEME 5 — AGRICULTURE, FORESTRY AND FISHERIES

As this theme is dealt with fully in Chapter 14 only the most general publication is mentioned here. The *Yearbook of agricultural statistics* (1970–) contains major agricultural, fisheries and forestry statistics, including tables on production, structure, supply balance sheets and prices.

THEME 6 — FOREIGN TRADE

Detailed statistics on the foreign trade of the Community are vital to any analysis of its economy. The main series published by Eurostat is the *Analytical tables of foreign trade — NIMEXE* (1966–), which is available in both hard copy and on microfiche. The *Monthly external trade bulletin* (1961–) lists commodities according to broad SITC Rev. 2 headings. It is more up to date but far less detailed than the annual NIMEXE tables. Some series are available only on microfiche, such as *Foreign trade — ECSC products*, which shows iron and steel export and import data. It was not until January 1978 that all member states met the requirements laid down by the Community for the submission of trade data; fully comparable figures are not available for the period before then. Moreover, it should also be noted that Eurostat trade figures are recorded on a 'special basis', that is, as goods move across a customs boundary. United Kingdom figures are published on a 'general basis', recording the movement of goods across our frontiers. In the Eurostat system goods in a bonded warehouse are counted only when they leave to enter the market and not at all if they are re-exported directly.

THEME 9 — MISCELLANEOUS STATISTICS

Under this heading comes *Government financing of research and development* (1978–), an annual publication which contains a statistical section giving central government figures as well as those for Community funded projects. *Eurostat news* (1976–) also appears under this theme.

SPECIAL STUDIES

On occasions, Eurostat commissions special studies from external authorities, an example being the report on the social features of households prepared in Rome by the Comitato italiano per lo studio dei problemi della populazione.[31] Social affairs has, in fact, been a particular focus of attention. Although the Commission has championed the cause of women's rights by providing legislation, financial support and information, and has directed that social statistics should be broken down to show separate figures for men and women, data on women were previously scattered and difficult to obtain. A recent study,[32] covering demography, women in relation to work and the training of women, attempts to bring these data together. Other recent surveys, such as those on multiple job holders[33] and vacancies,[34] reflect the need for information on aspects of the job market in the Community.

METHODOLOGIES AND DEFINITIONS

The methodology used in the compilation of most series is usually explained in the introduction to the publication in which they appear. Occasionally, more detail is necessary and a separate volume is published, as in the case of the European System of Integrated Social Protection Statistics (ESSPROS),[35] a system which has been introduced to provide a harmonized framework for national data on social protection. Slightly different, in that it is not linked with statistics used in a particular publication, is a report on multilateral measurements of purchasing power and real GDP,[36] which investigates ways of bringing together the work of the United Nations, the Economic Commission for Europe and Eurostat on international comparisons based on purchasing power parities.

INTERNAL PUBLICATIONS

Prepared primarily for interested official organizations, these publications are available on demand, while stocks last, and at the discretion of the sections responsible for their content. Variously known as statistical telegrams or rapid information, they are additional to or updates of already formally published material. In addition, press releases can often be a source of statistical information on a wide range of topics.

MICROFICHE

Microfiche was first used as a means of publishing foreign trade statistics more speedily and in a more compact form than the multiple volumes of hard copy. It is now used to disseminate data that would be too expensive to publish in a conventional way. The 1978 labour costs in industry survey is published in slim summary volumes[37] but much more detail can be obtained on microfiche. Quarterly data on foreign trade are also restricted to this medium for similar reasons of expense.

MAGNETIC TAPE

For some statistics magnetic tape is available. Foreign trade statistics, various time series from the CRONOS data bank, and input–output tables can all be supplied in this format. Depending on the status of the user, supply can be arranged by purchase, on exchange or free of charge. Sales are made at a fixed cost per reel. A limited selected dissemination of information (SDI) service can be arranged for certain specific categories of foreign trade statistics.

Other Community statistical publications

Statistical publications do not only originate in Eurostat; certain statistical publications are produced by individual directorates-general within the Commission. A notable example is the *Results of the business survey carried out among managements in the Community* (1962–), prepared by the Directorate-General for Economic and Financial Affairs. A monthly sample of about 20,000 enterprises is questioned on such matters as state of order books, expected future production and employment levels, stocks of raw materials, etc. *European economy* (1978–) is another product of the same directorate-general. It is not primarily a statistical publication but its quarterly issues have articles that review the economic situation and discuss current economic problems, backed up in the text by statistical data. Three supplements appear throughout the year which are much more statistical, on recent economic trends,[38] business survey results[39] and consumer survey results.[40] A third example is *Investment in the Community coalmining and iron and steel industries* (1956–), prepared in Directorate-General XVIII (Credit and Investments), which presents the results of an annual survey into actual and intended capital expenditure and production potential in the coalmining and iron and steel industries.

Statistical data banks

CRONOS is the name given to the data base management system designed by the Statistical Office for the compiling, editing and processing of the vast number of time series required by the Commission. Although primarily developed to cope with the magnitude of data, it was also needed to overcome the distance between the service department, Eurostat, and its prime customer, the Commission. In recognition of the potential value of the data to people in government, industry, finance and research organizations it was decided to make the system publicly available through Euronet hosts.[41]

CRONOS consists of time series divided into more than twenty 'domains', each of which corresponds to one principal category of statistics, such as national accounts, energy, external trade. Manipulation of the data online is possible, and personalized tables, graphs and models can be created. In view of the fact that CRONOS now contains more than one million time series, users need guidance in their use of the system. Consequently, CADOS, a documentary statistical catalogue, has been devised to allow users to establish whether data on particular subjects exist in CRONOS, for which countries and for what periods. Metadata, or data about data, (the definitions and methodology) can also be traced through CADOS.

A separate databank, COMEXT, has been devised for external trade statistics of the Community and statistics of trade between member states. This databank contains the external trade statistics for the last three years on a quarterly basis and on a monthly basis for the last eighteen months, stored in accordance with the NIMEXE nomenclature. As with CRONOS, COMEXT is accessed through Euronet hosts.[41]

Sources of information on Community statistics

Eurostat news is the main source of information on the activities of Eurostat. It appears quarterly, with a news section followed by a list of new publications and regular periodicals. Occasionally, special issues are published.[42] Earlier issues contained articles by statisticians but this seems to have been discontinued. If the pattern of the last two years is continued then the fourth issue of the year will provide a list of titles expected for the following year, and the first issue of the year a list of expected internal publications. Although *Eurostat news* is undoubtedly a mine of information, more attention to bibliographical detail would be beneficial. The titles given to forthcoming publications change without apparent reason, proposed publications are often talked about without reference to how or when they will appear, and the cessation of titles is not always reported.

The *Eurostat index*[43] is an invaluable aid, which facilitates the use of Eurostat statistics by providing an alphabetical keyword subject index to their contents. Titles referred to are listed and briefly described; titles that have ceased publication since the first edition and new serial titles are listed in the appendices. A more historical approach is available in Jeffries.[44] A recent newcomer to the scene is the *Index to international statistics: a guide to the statistical publications of international and intergovernmental organisations*,[45] the first issues of which appeared in 1983, first monthly then with quarterly and annual cumulations. Produced by the same publishers as the excellent *American statistics index*,[46] this is an expensive but comprehensive item. It differentiates monographs from serials and provides full details of each title. Indexes provide access to subjects, names, geographic locations and special types of publication or data. Indexing reaches table level in some instances.

Other sources of bibliographical information include the monthly and annual sales catalogues produced by the Office for Official Publications under the title *Publications of the European Communities*. Occasional feature articles on Community statistics and bibliographical information on new publications appear in *Market and statistics news*,[47] whilst both *British business*[48] and *Statistical news*[49] can also be expected to cover topics of relevance. Two other sources of bibliographical information are *Statistics Europe*[50] and the *Subject index to sources of comparative international statistics SISCIS*,[51] although the latter is now rather out of date and somewhat superseded by the *Index to international statistics*.

Availability of Community statistics

Depository Libraries (DEPs) and European Documentation Centres (EDCs) have comprehensive collections of Eurostat publications, although the latter are based in university and polytechnic libraries which grant varying degrees of access to non-members. Information offices of the Commission may also have some or all of the series. Statistical publications may be purchased separately from Her Majesty's Stationery Office (HMSO), although annual subscriptions are recommended. Internal publications must be obtained direct from Eurostat. The *Eurostat index* contains a list of useful addresses.

For the most recent statistics, that is those covering the last ten years, the Statistics and Market Intelligence Library (SMIL)[52] has a comprehensive reference collection. All Eurostat publications are taken. In addition, SMIL has good coverage of statistics produced by member states, which may often be more detailed and up to date. Although provided by the Department of Trade and Industry as a library where exporters can do their desk research prior to entering a new market, SMIL is freely open to members of the public for reference; enquiry staff can advise on relevant sources but cannot undertake any research on behalf of readers. A limited postal and telephone service is provided, confined to simple factual queries. Photocopying facilities are provided and may be used subject to copyright restrictions (Eurostat publications contain the instruction that copying is permitted provided that the source is acknowledged). Backruns of many statistical serials may be consulted in the British Library's Official Publications Library or borrowed from the British Library Lending Division, details of both of whose holdings appear in a recent British Library publication.[53]

References and notes

[1] Statistical Office of the European Communities, Bâtiment Jean Monnet, rue Alcide de Gasperi, L-2920 Luxembourg-Kirchberg.

[2] See the *Directory of the Commission of the European Communities*, Office for Official Publications, irregular, for an organizational chart of the Statistical Office.

[3] The Conference meets every six months. It is an important body whose recommendations and opinions influence the shape of statistical programmes and progress in their implementation.

[4] *Fifth statistical programme of the European Communities 1982–1984*, COM(81)327 final, 28 August 1981.

[5] See the *European system of integrated economic accounts: ESA*, 2nd edn., Office for Official Publications, 1980.

[6] For methodological background see *Community input–output tables 1970–1975 — methodology*, Office for Official Publications, 1976. See also 'The harmonised input–output tables and their uses', *Eurostat news*, 8–10/1979, pp. 7–13.

[7] *National accounts ESA: input–output tables 1975*, Office for Official Publications, 1983.

[8] NACE/CLIO is the branch of NACE (described later in this chapter) which is used in the compilation of input–output tables.

[9] For instance, *Fisheries — quantity and value of landings in the EC*, for which data is obtained directly from various bulletins published by the administrations of member states.

[10] *Consumer price indexes in the European Community*, Office for Official Publications, 1977.

[11] See *Labour force sample survey 1973–1975–1977*, Office for Official Publications, 1980 (Population and social conditions), and *Labour force sample survey 1979*, Office for Official Publications, 1981 (Social statistics).

[12] *Pensioners in the Community 1977*, Office for Official Publications, 1981.

[13] *Official journal of the European Communities*, L133, 10 June 1972, pp. 57–60.

[14] *Structure and activity of industry*, Office for Official Publications, 1980, 16 vols.

[15] *Structure and activity of industry: main results 1976*, Office for Official Publications, 1981. *Structure and activity of industry: main results 1977*, Office for Official Publications, 1982. *Structure and activity of industry: main results 1978*, Office for Official Publications, 1983.

[16] *Community survey on the structure of agricultural holdings 1975*, Office for Official Publications, 1979, 6 vols.

[17] *Community survey of orchard fruit trees 1977*, Office for Official Publications, 1979.

[18] *Structure of earnings in industry 1972*, Office for Official Publications, 1975–1977, (Social statistics: Special series), 13 vols.

[19] *Structure of earnings in wholesale and retail distribution, banking and insurance in 1974*, Office for Official Publications, 1977–1979, (Social statistics: Special series), 10 vols.

[20] M. J. G. Lockyer, 'Commodity classifications and codings', *Statistical news*, 24 February 1974, pp. 24.5–24.8.

[21] *Nomenclature for the classification of goods in customs tariffs*, 5th edn., Customs Cooperation Council, 1976.

[22] *Explanatory notes to the nomenclature*, 2nd edn., Customs Cooperation Council, 1976.

[23] *Guide to the classification of the overseas trade statistics of the United Kingdom*, HMSO, annual.

[24] *Standard international trade classification*, Rev. 2, United Nations, 1975, (Statistical papers, series M, No. 34/Rev. 2). The SITC is produced by the United Nations as an aid to economic analysis of trade statistics. The groupings and ordering of products is completely different from CCCN. Goods are grouped by industries, e.g. transport equipment. Although different in concept, the two schemes have now been rationalized to enable some correlation.

[25] *Geonomenclature 1983*, Office for Official Publications, 1983.

[26] *General industrial classification of economic activities within the European Communities (NACE)*, Office for Official Publications, 1970.

[27] *International standard industrial classification of all economic activities*, United Nations, 1968 (Statistical papers, series 17, No. 4, Rev. 2).

[28] *Standard industrial classification revised 1980*, HMSO, 1979.

[29] *Common nomenclature of industrial products NIPRO*, Office for Official Publications, 1976.

[30] Themes 7 and 8 are not in use at present.

[31] *Economic and social features of households in the member states of the European Community*, Office for Official Publications, 1982 (Population and social conditions).

[32] *Economic and social position of women in the Community*, Office for Official Publications, 1981.

[33] J. Alden and R. Spooner, *Multiple jobholders: an analysis of second jobs in the European Community*, Office for Official Publications, 1982.

[34] K. Walsh, *Vacancies notified: methods and measurement in the European Community*, Office for Official Publications, 1982.

[35] *European system of integrated social protection statistics (ESSPROS)*, Office for Official Publications, 1981.

[36] *Multinational measurements of purchasing power and real GDP*, Office for Official Publications, 1982.

[37] *Labour costs 1978*, Office for Official Publications, 1983, 2 vols.

[38] *Economic trends*, Office for Official Publications, monthly.

[39] *Business survey results*, Office for Official Publications, monthly.

[40] *Consumer survey results*, Office for Official Publications, quarterly.

[41] Further information may be obtained from SIA Computer Services, Ebury Gate, 23 Lower Belgrave Street, London, SW1W 0NW.

[42] For instance, 'Conclusions of the seminar on statistical data banks (Luxembourg, 25–27 May 1981)', *Eurostat news*, special number, 1982.

[43] A. Ramsay, *Eurostat index*, 2nd edn., Capital Planning Information, 1983.

[44] J. Jeffries, *A guide to the official publications of the European Communities*, 2nd edn., Mansell, 1981.

[45] *Index to international statistics*, Congressional Information Service, monthly.

[46] *American statistics index*, Congressional Information Service, annual.

[47] *Market and statistics news*, Warwick Statistics Service, monthly.

[48] *British business*, HMSO, weekly.

[49] *Statistical news*, HMSO, quarterly.

[50] J. M. Harvey, *Statistics Europe*, 4th edn., CBD Research, 1981.

[51] F. C. Piper, *SISCIS Subject index to sources of comparative international statistics*, CBD Research, 1978.

[52] Statistics and Market Intelligence Library, Department of Trade and Industry, 1 Victoria Street, London, SW1W 0ET. Tel: 01-215 5444/5445. Telex: 8811074 (DTHQ G).

[53] *European Communities publications: a guide to British Library resources*, The British Library, 1983.

14

Agricultural policy and its information sources

SIMON D. A. O'SULLIVAN

Introduction

The Common Agricultural Policy (CAP) plays a vital part in the operation of the European Communities. Its significance may be judged by the fact that it takes some 70% of the Community budget, and over 85% of all Community regulations are concerned with agriculture and fisheries. Indeed, it is arguable that until recently the CAP has been the only fully worked out common policy of the European Communities. The accession of the United Kingdom (UK) to the European Communities has therefore meant a radical change in the shape of agricultural policy in this country, since the mechanisms of Community agriculture are markedly different from the deficiency payments system previously in operation in the United Kingdom. Virtually all agricultural activity, and part of the food processing industry, now works within a framework of detailed legislation from the European Communities. Although in other areas of economic activity, Community legislation and policy influences United Kingdom policy, in agriculture the impact is fundamental.

Since the CAP is the one fully developed Community policy, many of its information channels are those of the European Communities in general. So there are numerous inevitable overlaps with other chapters in this book, especially those on statistics and legal and scientific information. This chapter is concerned with the specifically agricultural applications of these general information sources, as well as other sources specially concerned with agriculture.

Because of the complexity of the mechanisms of the CAP, considerable attention is paid to the operation of market and price policy. Only if the user has a clear understanding of how the CAP works can he or she begin to appreciate the information needs that arise. The first sections of this chapter are thus devoted to an analysis of CAP mechanisms and the policy-making process. User studies have shown that the most important kinds of information are statistical data and news services. These are emphasized. A final series of short sections looks at some other sources of information which are important to specific user groups. As the Common Fisheries Policy (CFP) has to some extent developed an independent existence, fisheries are treated in a separate section.

Users of agricultural policy information

A good picture of the users of agricultural policy information and their needs can be gleaned from the AMIS study of agricultural management information systems.[1,2] This broadly divided users according to types of organizations, namely, government; semi-state bodies; private industry and commerce; farmers' organizations; research, university and extension workers; trade associations; credit organizations. Their subject interests give a good idea of the kinds of information required, ranging in ranked order of priority through agricultural policy, economics of production, supply, demand and prices, education, training and advice, marketing and distribution, international trade, co-operatives, rural sociology, financial management, law, and technical innovation. Notably, there were no significant differences in ranking between types of organization. Specific types of information were also ranked according to organization. In the overall ranking the main sources, in order, were statistical information, personal contacts, newspapers and trade journals, grey literature, and conventional literature; the various kinds of secondary information service all ranked lower. Although statistical sources came first or equal first for most organizational types, second choice for researchers was conventional literature, for trade associations grey literature, and for most other organizations newspapers and trade journals. While this analysis gives a good overall picture of information needs, many of the more specific needs must be inferred from the way in which the CAP operates and its policy is formulated.

How the CAP works

THE AIMS AND GENERAL PRINCIPLES OF THE CAP

The Treaty of Rome formally includes agriculture in the European common market for goods and services, defining agricultural products as 'the products of the soil, of stockfarming and of fisheries and products of first-stage processing directly related to these products'.[3] The food industry proper is thus excluded from the CAP. It goes beyond primary processing. The Treaty further provides that the operation of the common market in agricultural products is to be accompanied by the establishment of a common agricultural policy, with five fundamental objectives as set out in Article 39. These are: a) to increase agricultural productivity; b) thus to ensure a fair standard of living for the agricultural community; c) to stabilize markets; d) to ensure the availability of supplies; and e) to ensure that produce reaches consumers at reasonable prices. The Treaty does not lay down the specific form that the common organization of agricultural markets should take, but in practice three underlying principles have been recognised: a) a single market, i.e., free movement of goods in the Community; b) Community preference, i.e., member states give preference to Community production by means of a common external frontier; and c) financial solidarity, i.e., the European Agricultural Guidance and Guarantee Fund (EAGGF) provides common support between the member states for the costs of operating the policy. Although the greater part of activity is accounted for by market and price policy (95% of EAGGF expenditure is taken up by the market guarantee section of the Fund), the common organization of the markets is supplemented by policies for the improvement of agricultural structures, scientific research and veterinary measures.

THE COMMON ORGANIZATION OF THE MARKETS

The CAP operates chiefly by common organization of the markets for individual groups of products, of which the cereals market organization is usually taken as the classic example. The pivot of the system is the 'target price', which is fixed annually at a level considered to provide an appropriate income for growers. As the market will not reach this price if there is an excess of supply over demand, an 'intervention price' is also set as a guaranteed minimum price. At this price Community intervention agencies will buy in surpluses. Because world market prices for cereals are generally below the Community target price, in order to prevent imports undermining internal Community prices, a 'threshold price' is set at a level that will ensure that imported cereals will sell at around the target price after transport costs have been taken into account. An 'import levy' is then charged on the importer's price in order to bring it up to the threshold price. Conversely, for exports, if there is a surplus of cereals in the Community, an 'export refund' can be made to Community producers so that they can sell their produce at the lower prices of world markets.

Although this description may suggest that the CAP is less dauntingly complex than it is often made out to be, each group of products has slightly different arrangements, and terminology differs according to the individual régimes. While some 70% of agricultural production is governed by régimes that are broadly similar to that for cereals, a quarter of production including wine, fruit and vegetables, is covered by arrangements based chiefly on the external protection of Community production from fluctuations on the world market, with a system of 'reference prices' which importers must respect. For other products, such as olive oil, there are supplementary aids to increase production, and certain fruit products benefit from processing aids. Even the basic régimes are not static, but subject to amendment in the light of changing circumstances — for example, with the introduction of a 'co-responsibility levy' in the dairy sector in recent years, whereby producers have to share in the costs of disposing of surpluses.

SOME INFORMATION NEEDS

Clearly, anyone having any dealings at all with the CAP needs a general understanding of how the system works, at a level which is appropriate to their involvement. Students and the general public may be content with an overall appreciation, but the policy-maker and the trader need to have an intimate knowledge of the details of particular régimes. This knowledge needs to be both of how the mechanism works, for example, the precise rules for the calculation of import levies, and, for the trader especially, of how the various prices and levies are moving from week to week or even from day to day, although the policy-maker will also require a view of trends in order to assess what changes may be needed to the régime. The next section discusses a number of guides, both to the CAP as a whole and to its individual commodity régimes, but the ultimate authority lies in the regulations themselves. These are treated in the section on policy making, while the observation of prices, etc., is discussed in the sections on statistics and current awareness.

GENERAL GUIDES TO THE CAP AND ITS RÉGIMES

A number of good introductory guides are available for the CAP as a whole. These range from booklets issued by the Commission of the European Communities,[4, 5, 6, 7, 8] through chapters in studies of the Community in general,[9, 10] to textbook introductions.[11, 12] Of these the standard work is Fennell's study of the institutional and administrative organization of the CAP.[13] The Commission has also produced an audio-visual programme on agriculture and agricultural policy in the Community,[14] and the University of Sussex has joined with the BBC to produce a magazine issue for schools.[15] While these may be adequate for the general reader and for students, users involved in the day-to-day operation of the CAP need more detailed guides. The *CAP monitor*[16] provides a comprehensive picture of the régime for each commod- ity, including practical details of how and when the various prices and aids are calculated, and references to the regulations which govern each aspect of the régime. Each commodity section is updated by loose-leaf amendments as significant changes occur.

For the trader, the Intervention Board for Agricultural Produce issues a comprehensive guide to the trading régimes, both in general and for individual commodities, in a series of 'External market' leaflets.[17] For the livestock régimes, i.e., beef and veal, pigmeat and sheepmeat, the Meat and Livestock Commission has produced explanatory guides for farmers and the trade.[18, 19, 20] For cereals both the Home Grown Cereals Authority and Toepfer International also produce specialist guides,[21, 22] the latter of which is revised annually. However, for many products, unfortunately including the milk and dairy sector, there is a lack of specific guides that treat the régimes in depth. In these cases, the best 'potted guides' are often contained in more general reports, for example by the House of Lords and university departments for the fruit and vegetables[23, 24] and olive oil sectors.[25, 26]

THE PRICE FIXING

The common organization of the markets implies the adoption of common prices across the Community. These are set usually around April at an annual 'CAP price fixing'. This is one of the major events of the agricultural policy year. It determines much of the day-to-day operation of the CAP for the following twelve months. Not surprisingly, the associated documentation is considerable. It is referred to again at several points below because the material forms part of more general series. One of the most important sources, however, is the Commission's annual report on the agricultural situation in the Community,[27] which is a mine of useful detail on developments in agricultural policy and the market situation, including copious statistical data. The full price proposals are issued in the COM series of documents (see below), but summaries of the proposals and the actual agreement on prices are covered by *Green Europe newsletter*.[28, 29]

Prices are determined in the common currency unit of the Community (ECU), as uniform pricing between countries is fundamental to the free movement of goods. However, the ECU is not a currenc used in any member state, so all prices need to be converted into national currencies. This is done at fixed 'green' rates of exchange, which apply only to agricultural products. Because fluctuations in national currencies could lead to distortions in trade flows, a system of monetary compensatory amounts (MCAs) has been developed to bridge the gap between the price converted at the green rate and the price which would be represented by the common price if converted to national currency at actual market rates of exchange. For some countries (the United Kingdom, Italy and Greece), the MCA fluctuates with changes in the weekly market rates of exchange, but for others it changes only when their currencies are realigned in the European Monetary System or their green rates are changed. Green rate changes can happen at any time but are most common at the annual price fixing. The system of MCAs is one of the most complex, and yet operationally most important, aspects of the CAP. Its basic principles are covered by the general works on the CAP already cited, of which the most comprehensive is a section of the *CAP monitor*. Historical studies are also worth examining, as much of the complexity of the system is the result of successive refinements.[30, 31, 32]

STRUCTURAL POLICY, RESEARCH AND VETERINARY ASPECTS

Although market and price policy are the dominant aspects of the CAP, the intention of the Community from the outset has been to complement this with structural improvement of agriculture in the member states. This takes place through a combination of 'horizontal' socio-structural measures for the modernization of farms, encouragement of cessation of farming where appropriate, development of advisory services and training, special measures for defined less-favoured areas, and aid to the processing and marketing of agricultural products. These are supplemented by specific regional measures in a number of individual member states. One of the main features of structural policy is that although action is undertaken in a Community context with Community funds, there is a predominant use of measures tailored to the needs of individual member states, so that much of the documentation needed by farmers and their advisers to take advantage of the aid schemes, grants and subsidies is obtained from national rather than European Community sources. Two issues of *Green Europe* outline the basic features of structures policy[33] and the role of state aids,[34] and this aspect of the CAP is also discussed in the general guides already cited. More specific information on how to find out about the various grants is included in the chapter on grants and loans from the Community.

Closely allied with structural policy, though not strictly part of the CAP, are a number of measures concerning agricultural research and veterinary matters. The current agricultural research programme includes scientific and technical research to improve land use and effluent disposal, eliminate animal disease, improve the technical efficiency of production, and develop alternative products, especially protein plants and animal feeds. On the veterinary side, the main work has been the harmonization of national laws so as to reduce health obstacles to the free circulation of livestock and livestock products. Both these areas of activity have been described in issues of *Green Europe*[35, 36]

FINANCING THE CAP

One of the fundamental operating principles of the CAP is financial solidarity between member states. This has been achieved by the establishment of a common fund, the 'European Agricultural Guidance and Guarantee Fund' (EAGGF, but often referred to by its French initials as FEOGA). The Fund consists of two sections: the Guarantee Section finances the market and price policy of the CAP, and accounts for around 95% of total agricultural expenditure, while the Guidance Section administers the financing of structural policy. The Commission has produced a guide to the functioning and importance of the EAGGF[37] and more recently has devoted an issue of *Green Europe* to the Guarantee Section.[38] For details of its operation from year to year the main source of data is its annual report, published in the COM series of documents (see below) in separate parts for the Guarantee and Guidance Sections.

The legislative process

The aim of this section is to show how the Community legislative process is applied to agriculture, and to point out some of the particular distinguishing features of the CAP in this respect. Further information on Community legislation appears in Chapter 12.

TYPES OF LEGAL INSTRUMENT

Agricultural policy makes use of the three main types of Community legal instrument. Regulations, directly applicable in the member states without further national legislation, are the most important instrument for overall policy, especially for market organization and price policy. The distinction drawn between 'Council' and 'Commission' regulations is especially important in agriculture. Broadly speaking, the former are framework regulations, such as the basic regulations for the common organization of the markets and the annual CAP fixing, within which the Commission exercises delegated powers; the latter are the day-to-day, usually temporary, regulations for the practical management of the CAP, for example the fixing of import levies and export refunds, etc. Decisions, usually taken by the Commission, and concerning specific persons or bodies, for example individual member governments, have been of special importance in the application of structural measures. Directives are also framework acts within which member states are required to enact national legislation conforming to Community objectives, but they allow room for the adaptation of the detailed legislation to specific national circumstances. Prominent examples are again the structural measures, such as those covering the modernization of farms and the less favoured areas.

DRAFT REGULATIONS

Draft regulations are prepared within the Commission, where necessary including consultation with experts from the member states and professional bodies. They are then submitted to the Council in the form of proposals, which are disseminated in two forms: in the 'C' series of the *Official journal*, and as COM series documents.

COM DOCUMENTS

These include an explanatory memorandum which sets out the background of the proposal, and usually also a financial statement of likely budget expenditure. It is worth noting that the COM series of documents goes wider than just the texts of draft regulations. From time to time, when the Commission is unable to make a firm proposal for a regulation because it considers discussion of the general principles to be necessary in the Council of Ministers, it may instead submit a guidelines paper or a situation report. Certain of these reports, such as the guidelines for European agriculture arising from the Council mandate of 1980,[39] have become major landmarks in the documentary history of CAP policy making. So although the series is very much part of the 'grey' literature, it is a vital source of both ephemeral and long standing information. The earlier documents of lasting significance have been analyzed and abstracted in an historical review of Community policy making in different sectors,[40] and from

1981 an annual subject index has been produced.[41] For current proposals, a weekly *Documentation bulletin* of the Commission lists COM documents, and they are also covered by the *House of Commons weekly information bulletin*.

PROCEDURE

Once the draft regulation has been formally transmitted to the Council of Ministers, it is discussed by a working group of experts in the subject from the member states, and by the Special Committee on Agriculture, whose function is to undertake sufficient groundwork where possible so that the regulation can be passed by the Council of Ministers without the need for detailed discussion. In practice, most of the fundamental regulations involve much discussion at political level. Although the records of working groups, the Special Committee on Agriculture, and the Council of Ministers are not available outside government, the general tenor of discussion will be reported in the news services when regulations prove contentious. These services are described later in this chapter.

EUROPEAN PARLIAMENT AND ECONOMIC AND SOCIAL COMMITTEE

For the main Council regulations, the Opinions of the European Parliament and of the Economic and Social Committee are mandatory. The Committee on Agriculture of the European Parliament prepares a report, which is published as a *European Parliament working document* at the stage at which it is presented to the Parliament in the form of a 'Motion for resolution' with accompanying explanation. The Committee from time to time also produces 'own-initiative' reports on subjects of major importance, e.g., in response to the Commission's mandate guidelines referred to above.[42] All these reports are listed in the minutes of the sittings of the Parliament, which are published in the 'C' series of the *Official journal*. The Economic and Social Committee likewise compiles an opinion in the form of a report, which is published in the 'C' series of the *Official journal*, together with rather more occasional 'own-initiative' reports.

UNITED KINGDOM PARLIAMENTARY SCRUTINY

All European Community draft legislation is scrutinized in the United Kingdom by the British Parliament. Many agricultural regulations that raise no points of legal or political importance for the United Kingdom receive no more than a passing mention in the reports of the scrutiny committees. More important draft regulations, especially if they involve new principles or will have a major effect on agricultural policy in the United Kingdom, are reported on in depth by the House of Lords Select Committee on the European Communities and the House of Commons Select Committee on European Legislation. Both of these Committees, along with the House of Commons Agriculture Committee, from time to time produce major reports on new policy developments, which contain the texts of written and oral evidence presented to the Committees, e.g. a response to the Commission's mandate document.[43] Numerous memoranda in such reports offer concise explanations of technical aspects of the CAP in an easily intelligible form. (See Chapter 7 for more information on the work of the scrutiny committees.)

MANAGEMENT COMMITTEES

Commission regulations, concerned with the day-to-day management of market and price policy, are adopted through Management Committees which have been set up for each of the market régimes. Most of these regulations are so routine that they do not give rise to published documentation other than the final version in the *Official journal* and, possibly, a report in one or other of the news services.

LEGISLATIVE TEXTS

The 'L' series of the *Official journal of the European Communities* is the main, and sole authoritative, documentary source of the texts of agricultural legislation. Although it is comprehensive, it is not in a convenient form for specialist users who are concerned with a single sector, for example livestock or cereals. Such users need to have all the legislation relevant to their own sector brought together, especially because so many regulations are amending rather than basic in nature. For livestock, the Meat and Livestock Commission produces an index in three sections (beef and veal, sheepmeat, pigmeat), which includes the texts of the legislation and is updated regularly,[44] and for cereals the Home Grown Cereals Authority produces a similar service.[45] For other sectors, however, there is no such convenient service, and the best that can be used is the CELEX online service of the European Communities, discussed in more detail in Chapter 12.

Agricultural statistics

PROBLEMS

The user of European Community agricultural statistics faces a complex array of organizations which collect and disseminate statistics in a wide variety of printed and microfiche publications and, increasingly, numeric data banks. Although printed publications from the agricultural statistics directorate of the Statistical Office of the European Communities (popularly known as Eurostat) form a kernel of information, they are only a starting point and need to be complemented in several respects. Firstly, even within Eurostat the agricultural statistics directorate does not cover all agriculture related statistics: agriculture within the national accounts, employment and wages in the agricultural sector, and, most important, statistics of trade in agricultural products, are dealt with by other Eurostat directorates. Secondly, not all Eurostat data are published in printed form, as increasingly Eurostat is using microfiche and its CRONOS and

COMEXT data banks to disseminate the more detailed and specialist statistics. Thirdly, Eurostat is not the only source of agricultural statistics at the Community level: the Directorate-General for Agriculture (DG VI) of the Commission of the European Communities also publishes data on certain topics, partly derived from Eurostat and partly obtained from a variety of other sources, and a large number of other official and professional agricultural organizations set up at the Community level also publish such data; in particular, other inter-governmental organizations include the European Communities in their coverage, and are necessary for wider international comparisons. Finally, the delay in publication of statistics by Eurostat requires users to identify either the primary national sources from which Eurostat derives its statistics, or to find alternative more up-to-date sources.

CONCEPTS AND DEFINITIONS

The non-specialist user of agricultural statistics is confronted with the question of concepts and definitions at two levels. Firstly, the overall understanding of statistical concepts in agriculture, such as 'farm income' or 'farm-gate price', necessary in order to determine whether data sources are pertinent in general terms. Secondly, the need to have the precise definitions according to which particular data series have been collected and presented, in order to make meaningful calculations, comparisons, etc.

There are few guides that give a comprehensive set of explanations of the terms and concepts used in agricultural statistics in the Community. The nearest equivalent is the glossary of European Community terms published by the Council of the European Communities,[46] which in effect gives an explanation of many terms in the process of translating them.

Two general introductions to agricultural statistics are available as a background. Fennell[47] offers a concise and readable overview which examines the purpose of agricultural statistics, questions of reliability, interpretation, comparability, continuity, delays, availability, primary and secondary sources, and special studies. A rather fuller textbook, aimed mainly at developing countries, has been compiled by Idaikkadar,[48] including chapters on agricultural statistics in general and individual topics of production, censuses and prices. Although this is not a description of practice in international organizations or European Community countries, it does provide a general background to the principles and organizational structure involved.

The notes and definitions which are necessary to elucidate how particular time series or items of data have been derived can be found, in general terms, from three sources. First, most regular, periodical statistics publications include the relevant notes and definitions either as footnotes to the tables, appendices within the publication, or methodological supplements. Secondly, more complex topics are often the subject of methodological articles and studies, which can usually be traced from references in the actual data publication. Thirdly, when both these sources have failed to elucidate the user's problem, the compiling organization is usually able to help. In the case of publications of Eurostat and similar organizations, which are mainly secondary compilers of primary data provided by national member states, these national organizations will usually be acting according to clear guidelines which include explicit, comprehensive definitions, and will have one section formally responsible for transmitting the data to Eurostat, so that there is a ready contact point for advice.

EUROSTAT AGRICULTURAL STATISTICS DIRECTORATE

The main work of Eurostat on agricultural statistics is carried out by Directorate D, 'Agriculture, Forestry, Fisheries Statistics', which covers the spheres of agricultural accounts and structures, balance sheets and production, and prices. Agricultural accounts include the economic accounts of agriculture, but not the agricultural branch of the national accounts statistics (see next section). Agricultural prices include the purchase prices of the means of production and selling prices, i.e., producer and wholesale prices but not retail prices, of animal and crop products. These are available both as absolute prices in national currencies and the European common currency unit, the ECU, and as price index numbers for both monthly and annual periods. Besides periodic Community surveys on the structure of agricultural holdings, there are regular six-monthly livestock censuses and biennial surveys of cattle and pig holdings. Supply balance sheets include data on the production, stocks, foreign trade, and utilization of the main agricultural products on quarterly and annual bases, but statistics are also available on areas, yields and production of individual fruit and vegetable crops, monthly meat and milk production, and chick hatchings.

The directorate collects statistics from member government departments, usually the statistical services of the ministries of agriculture but also national statistical offices and customs departments. The main data are then published in the agriculture 'theme' of the Eurostat publications series, easily distinguished by their green and white covers. However, there have been considerable changes over the years in the publishing programme, and while an account of titles and changes up to the late seventies has been given by Jeffries,[49] certain more recent changes are worth noting here. The former monthly publications on statistics of eggs, meat and milk have been amalgamated since 1980 into a quarterly publication, *Animal production*. While each issue contains regular updates of the monthly time series, the contents of the main supply balance sheet and survey sections vary from issue to issue, so it is essential to search through several issues to be sure of finding the latest balance sheet for a particular product or the most recent survey results. *Crop production* has also reduced in frequency from monthly to quarterly publication, and similar considerations apply here to balance sheets and surveys. It is in price statistics, however, that the major developments have occurred. The former *Purchase prices of the means of agricultural production, Selling prices of animal products*, and *Selling prices of crop products* are now available only as microfiche. Price index numbers remain available in printed form, as *EC agricultural price indices (output and input)*, quarterly from 1980 to 1981, half yearly from 1982. Moreover, the main vehicle for the dissemination of detailed agricultural price statistics is now the CRONOS data bank (see below).[50]

A general discussion of various aspects of the work of the Eurostat agricultural statistics directorate is available in the proceedings of a conference on agricultural statistics organized by the Centre for European Agricultural Studies.[51] This includes papers on Eurostat as a whole, economic accounts, prices, balance sheets, and structure surveys, as well as two user viewpoints from the Ministry of Agriculture, Fisheries and Food (MAFF) and the Milk Marketing Board. A detailed account of work in progress on agricultural statistics is given in an annex to the *Fifth statistical programme of the European Communities*.[52] Important current projects include the preparation of a manual on the methodology of agricultural price indices and a catalogue of the characteristics of agricultural prices.[53, 54] The publications programme of Eurostat for each year is contained in the final issue of *Eurostat news* for the previous year, and each issue of this quarterly periodical also includes details of the publications of the current and coming quarters, not only in agriculture but also in other spheres.

A detailed keyword subject index of Eurostat series has been compiled by Ramsay.[55] This includes the publications not only of the agricultural statistics directorate but also those of other directorates mentioned in the following section. The user should, however, regard this as a guide only to the likely availability of statistics on broad subjects, not to their specific relevance in terms of detailed definitions.

OTHER EUROSTAT DIRECTORATES

National accounts statistics are handled by Directorate A, 'General Economic Statistics'. Agriculture in the national accounts is taken to include forestry, hunting and fishing as well as agriculture proper, in accordance with the definitions used in the European system of national accounts – an important difference from the economic accounts of agriculture produced by the agricultural statistics directorate. Directorate A is also responsible for general statistical publications such as the monthly *Eurostatistics* and the annual *Eurostat review*, the latter of which presents a ten-year picture of the key agricultural data not only for the European Communities and member states individually, but also where available for Spain, Portugal and the United States.

Agricultural employment and wages statistics are collected and published by Directorate B, 'Demographic and Social Statistics', although the agricultural statistics directorate has a coordinating role. This is a major area in which Eurostat is at present working towards harmonization.[56]

Directorate E, 'External Trade Statistics', is responsible for all external trade statistics, including those of agricultural products, and uses a variety of printed, microfiche and computer data bank forms of dissemination. In order to present a clear picture Eurostat has published a user guide to the various media and presentations of external trade statistics according to tariff classifications and product-by-country/country-by-product breakdowns.[57] This directorate is also responsible for statistics of the African, Caribbean and Pacific countries (ACP countries) which have agreements with the Community, and includes their agriculture because of its importance in these trade agreements.

THE CRONOS AND COMEXT DATA BANKS

Mention has already been made above of the increasing use by Eurostat of numeric data banks as a means of disseminating statistics. The COMEXT data bank contains detailed monthly data on the external trade of the European Communities, from which both printed publications and microfiche tabulations are generated, including agricultural products. Fuller details are given in the user guide to external trade statistics and in an article in *Eurostat news*.[58]

The CRONOS data bank is arranged in a series of 'domains', each of which covers a particular area of statistics. The domains of particular concern to agriculture are PACO (agricultural prices and the economic accounts of agriculture and forestry), ZPA1 (supply balance sheets and production statistics, plus some livestock and crop survey data), SNAG and MICA (both specialized agricultural trade domains). A list of domains and their contents is given in *Eurostat news*,[59] and individual catalogues of the time series contained in each domain are available on application to Eurostat.

Although the institutions of the European Communities and member governments have direct access to these data banks, public access is through Euronet via host computer bureaux. These are CISI and its UK subsidiary SIA Computer Services (COMEXT and CRONOS), Data Centralen (CRONOS) and EURIS (COMEXT). Besides data retrieval facilities these bureaux also offer possibilities of tabulation, manipulation, and in the case of SIA Computer Services, sophisticated economic modelling.

COMMISSION OF THE EUROPEAN COMMUNITIES

Not all agricultural statistics from the European Communities are disseminated by Eurostat. The Commission also publishes a great deal of information, which should not be confused with Eurostat series, although problems can arise for two reasons. First, the *Agricultural markets: prices* series of the Directorate-General for Agriculture (published monthly with annual retrospective volumes) is similar in physical appearance to the Eurostat green publications of its agriculture 'theme'. It must be emphasized, however, that the prices reported by the Commission are fundamentally different from the Eurostat selling prices series. These latter are average producer and wholesale prices, transmitted to Eurostat by the ministries of agriculture of the member states. *Agricultural markets: prices* on the other hand consists of two kinds of prices: the institutional prices fixed in connection with the CAP commodity régimes, and prices on wholesale markets which the Commission believes to be representative and which are provided by trade sources. This is a good illustration of the need in agricultural statistics to take care not only that statistics are about the subject that the user requires, but that they conform to the necessary definitions to suit the purpose for which he intends to use them.

The second aspect of confusion is that many of the statistical tables published in the *Agricultural situation in the Community* are compiled from data sent to the Commission by Eurostat. Much of this data is aggregated or otherwise processed to produce the final tables, and is combined with other data put together by Commission services from a variety of official and unofficial sources, including non-governmental agricultural organizations set up at the Community level.

In addition, a considerable amount of statistical data is published in tables of background information in Commission documents in the COM series. Many of these are *ad hoc* reports as described above in the section on policy formation and legislation, but regular annual series include the *Situation on the agricultural markets* and the *Financial report on the European Agricultural Guidance and Guarantee Fund*. In addition, the results of the Farm Accountancy Data Network, a survey of farm incomes and related data in the Community, were published as COM documents until 1977, but from 1978/79 have been disseminated as microfiche, and there are plans to include part of the data in a CRONOS domain.

OTHER EUROPEAN COMMUNITY SOURCES

A major group of organizations producing statistical data is the group of non-governmental agricultural organizations set up at the Community level. Most of these are professional and trade associations, so the statistical data they produce is directed towards the interests of their members and may only be made available to the Commission. Part of this is published as described above in the *Agricultural situation in the Community*, and in some cases the organizations will also make information available to a wider audience of interested parties. While there is no index to the statistical material they produce, there is a directory of the officially recognised organizations and their national members, including addresses.[60]

A second group of organizations is that of non-official trade associations. This includes the agricultural press, where *Agra Europe* deserves particular mention. It publishes a great deal of statistical information within topical articles, bringing together official European Community and national trade sources. The German *Zentrale Markt- und Preisberichtstelle* includes comparative European Community statistics in its weekly market reports and in its annual analyses of the market situation for various products in Germany.

In the United Kingdom, statutory bodies usually publish some European Community data within their specialism. The Meat and Livestock Commission's weekly European market reports and periodic European booklets include much useful statistical data, and the Milk Marketing Board's *EEC dairy facts and figures*, and the Home Grown Cereal Authority's *Cereals statistics*, are valuable annual sources. Similar organizations in other member states likewise publish data from their own national resources alongside comparative European Community information. Unfortunately, there is no comprehensive guide to such sources.

INTERNATIONAL ORGANIZATIONS

The publications of international organizations are necessary when wider comparisons are being made between the European Community and other countries. Eurostat does publish some data which takes in other countries such as Spain, Portugal and the United States, but generally the user must turn to other sources. These include the Economic Commission for Europe (ECE), Organization for Economic Cooperation and Development (OECD), the Food and Agriculture Organization (FAO) and the United Nations system in general.

The Economic Commission for Europe publishes an annual *Review of the agricultural situation in Europe* and annual statistics on agricultural prices. The OECD publishes annual supply balance sheets for meat, dairy products and eggs, and food consumption statistics, for each of its twenty-four member states. At a world level, the FAO publishes annual data on production and trade in the main agricultural commodities, and the United Nations Conference on Trade and Development (UNCTAD) produces a monthly bulletin of commodity prices. Mention should also be made of the Foreign Agricultural Service of the United States Department of Agriculture. Although this is not an international organization, it publishes data on production, trade and consumption of agricultural products for most countries of the world, including the European Communities as a whole. Finally, there are the international commodity organizations set up to administer commodity agreements, most of which publish monthly and annual statistical bulletins. They include the International Wheat Council, the International Cocoa Organization, the International Coffee Organization, and the International Sugar Organization. These are of particular importance for information on primary commodities which the European Community trades with its ACP partners.

There are several guides to international statistics which can also be used to trace specifically European Communities sources mentioned above. First, from the beginning of 1983, all statistical publications of inter-governmental organizations, including the European Communities, OECD, FAO, ECE and the international commodity organizations, are being abstracted and indexed in detail in the monthly *International statistics index* produced by Congressional Information Service. This provides indexing in detail down to the level of specific groups of tables, and includes both successive issues of periodicals which contain new data, and non-periodical publications. The sister publication, *American statistics index*, covers all material from the United States Department of Agriculture (USDA), including the Foreign Agricultural Service. For the United Nations system there is a directory of international statistics, including agriculture.[61] This is in the form of an index of, for example, activity subdivided by commodity (and also vice versa), so that agricultural statistics may be found not only through the agriculture section but also through, for example, the foreign trade and the prices sections. Sources of commodity price information, both official and in trade publications, have been indexed by the International Trade Centre.[62] Finally, the University of Warwick Statistics Library has compiled a detailed subject index to sources of comparative international statistics.[63]

NATIONAL SOURCES

Should all the above sources of comparable international statistics fail, the user must turn to primary national sources. Much, though not all, of the data sent by member states to Eurostat and other international organizations is published in their own national statistical periodicals, usually prior to the appearance of the data in Eurostat periodicals. It is therefore often possible to update a time series by referring to these publications. Although there is no systematic index of the tables in national sources which correspond to individual Eurostat series, many Eurostat publications indicate which national source organization provides the data. This normally gives a sufficient clue to the required publication if the user is armed with a national statistical office or ministry of agriculture catalogue of publications, so that the continuity of time series can be checked against the appropriate table. For details of the responsibilities of statistical offices and the statistical services of ministries of agriculture, which vary from one European Community country to another, a useful compendium of national methods of collecting and disseminating agricultural statistics has been published by FAO.[64] This is updated by supplements containing revised information on a country-by-country basis. The main guide to the (chiefly) official statistical publications of European countries (both European Communities member states and other Western and Eastern European countries) is one of a series of sources for social, economic and market research published by CBD Research.[65]

Current awareness and news services

These include general European Community news services, specifically agricultural news services and professional periodicals, and, increasingly, viewdata services. They range also from magazines for the general reader to highly specialized press agency material which provides up-to-the-minute information on the latest European Community proposals and developments of importance to the agricultural industry and policy makers.

For the general reader, *Europe*, published monthly by the London Office of the Commission of the European Communities, usually carries one or two articles on some aspect of the CAP which is of current interest. For rather more detail, *Green Europe: newsletter on the Common Agricultural Policy*, published by the Agricultural Information Service of the Commission, treats subjects of topical interest in single subject issues. Many of these have in fact been guides to aspects of the CAP as mentioned above, but recent issues have also included studies of fraud in the EAGGF, trade with developing countries, and so on. A complementary series, *Green Europe newsletter*, concentrates on topical subjects, including the price fixing, and some texts of major speeches by Commissioners. These series are complemented by the more general *European documentation* series, again based on single-subject issues, and by the *Europe information* series. As an example of the need to draw together material from several Community information services, recent studies of wine have been published in three of these series.[66, 67, 68]

The main European news service is that of the European Press Agency, and, confusingly, is also called *Europe*. This appears daily and provides detailed summaries of all current developments in the Community, including new policy proposals and reports from the Council of Agriculture Ministers, the Special Committee on Agriculture, the European Parliament and other major meetings, together with the views of European farmers' organizations. While not an agricultural news service, it is one of the most up-to-date sources of information on agricultural policy developments.

There is a variety of news services of the Commission which, although general in scope, include agricultural and CAP matters in their coverage. The London Information Office of the Commission issues a series of *Background notes* on topics of current interest in the United Kingdom, while the *P notices* of the Spokesman's Group in Brussels are a valuable source of highly up-to-date information on major topical issues. The Commission's monthly *Bulletin of the European Communities* is also useful as a recent historical record, enabling the reader to identify issues for further investigation once they have passed into secondary legislation, and its supplements are valuable because they reproduce some of the major policy COM documents in a more conventional form.

Specifically on agriculture, the weekly *Agra Europe* is the single most important specialist news service, the more so because it is highly readable by comparison with the press agency style of *Europe*. It includes editorial sections on general CAP matters; management committee news; reports of the market situation for individual commodities in the Community, individual member states, and, where appropriate, world markets; topical Community issues, including concise summaries of major reports or academic studies; national developments; and a selection of current statistics. A monthly supplement, *Green Europe* (not to be confused with the Commission series), offers a similar treatment, but with greater concentration on the more substantial issues. A similar reporting journal is *Agriservice international*, which appears fortnightly. Although primarily concerned with European Community matters, it is less specifically oriented in this direction than *Agra Europe*, and reports on related world-wide agricultural policy and trade developments. For those specifically concerned with Mediterranean products and southern European countries, the fortnightly *Telex Mediterranean* offers a specialist news service including a strong emphasis on agricultural matters because of their importance in the economy of these countries.

Most of the farming press includes some reference to European Community topics. *Big farm weekly, British farmer and stockbreeder, Farmers weekly* and *Farming news* all include articles on current aspects of Community agriculture which are likely to affect the decisions of farmers and traders. Nor should specialist farming journals such as *The grower, Fruit trades journal* and *Poultry world* be neglected as these cater for individual farm enterprises.

Both farmers and traders, such as grain merchants, need to have highly current information at their fingertips. Thus viewdata is coming to play an important role in CAP news, particularly for closed user-groups on Prestel. Of these, the most important is that of *Agra Europe*, which includes information on management committee results, prices, levies and refunds, and MCAs. A similar service for the livestock sector is offered by the Meat and Livestock Commission, and open services are also available from *IPC Agriview*.

Information services for special user groups

GOVERNMENT AND POLICY MAKERS

It would be surprising if the UK government, as one of the chief policy makers in the CAP process, were not a heavy user of such information and were not well provided for. By the nature of its work, the UK government, including the UK Parliament, has direct access to Community documentation and makes extensive use of secondary services. While many of its information channels are only for internal use, certain services are open to the public. Of these, one of the most important is the Main Library of the Ministry of Agriculture, Fisheries and Food, which has extensive holdings of published European Communities information on the CAP, together with academic studies and reports.

FARMERS, THEIR ADVISERS AND THE TRADE

Some of the most useful professional journals have already been mentioned. This section therefore considers some of the organizations which can offer information and advice.

First, there is the Ministry of Agriculture, Fisheries and Food itself. Press notices include regular reports of the Council of Agriculture Ministers and of European Community grants for marketing and processing agricultural products. The Ministry's Agricultural Development and Advisory Service (ADAS) offers advice on European Community matters to farmers through a network of regional and divisional offices, including the grants they may obtain through the EAGGF Guidance Section. A booklet, *At the farmer's service*, is available and outlines these services together with European Community aids and, of course, important regulations.[69] Some of the statutory bodies for individual commodities also publish specifically European information, for example the Meat and Livestock Commission's Economic Information Service publishes weekly European market surveys and a series of European booklets covering the operation of the CAP market régimes, prices, and such current topics as the Spanish livestock industry.[70]

One of the most important sources of information for the professional user is the wide range of non-governmental agricultural organizations set up at the European Community level, which have already been mentioned in the section on statistics. Pride of place must go to the Committee of Agricultural Producer Organizations (COPA) of which the United Kingdom member is the National Farmers' Union (NFU). Each of its specialist committees, but especially the Economics and Taxation Committee, is involved in presenting the United Kingdom farmers' viewpoint and in providing information to farmers on Community matters. These activities are described more fully in the NFU annual report. Many of these professional organizations, either through their European Community umbrella organization or in their own right, submit representations on draft Community regulations and directives. A great number of these remain more or less confidential between the professional organization, Community institutions and member governments, but some are made available to interested parties and enter the 'grey' literature. The best source for identifying them is the farming press.

RESEARCH

Information services for researchers cover the great bulk of the primary (both conventional and 'grey') literature and the associated secondary indexing and abstracting services. 'Grey' literature in particular accounts for a great deal of the large number of studies on the CAP. Space here does not permit more than a cursory sampling of the kinds of sources that are available.

While there is no single journal devoted to the CAP, numerous general economics, agricultural economics and European Communities journals include articles on the CAP from time to time. Among general economics journals, the most useful are the bank reviews, particularly the *Three banks review* and the *National Westminster Bank quarterly review*. For European Community matters generally, the *Journal of Common Market studies*, the *European economic review* and the French *Revue du marché commun* are useful also for articles on the institutional framework within which the CAP operates. The *European review of agricultural economics* has regular articles on the economics of the CAP, and there are also fairly frequent articles in the *Journal of agricultural economics*, with an occasional contribution in the *American journal of agricultural economics*, chiefly on matters likely to affect trade between the United States and the European Community. Because there are relatively few articles on CAP and related agricultural policies in the general economics journal literature, one of the best strategies is to scan the weekly *Contents of recent economics journals* and the quarterly *Journal of economic literature*, which reproduce the contents pages of most significant journals.

As with so much else in the CAP information sphere, much of the most useful monograph literature is not exclusive to the CAP, but one major source is chapters in books dealing with wider Community issues. An example is the literature on the enlargement of the Community, where major contributions on agricultural aspects have been included in compendia by Tsoukalis, Sears and Vaitsos, and the College of Europe.[71, 72, 73] General studies of the CAP have already been mentioned, but a recurring theme is its reform, including budgetary aspects. This is characteristic of the range of contributions from conventional publishers,[74] through policy studies and research institutes,[75, 76] government departments such as USDA[77] and university departments in Germany particularly.[78] Not only on reform of the CAP, but on agricultural policy generally 'grey' literature abounds, as much of the research is published in university reports series rather than as articles or monographs. The two main current centres of research in the United Kingdom are the Centre for European Agricultural Studies at Wye College, which holds regular seminars and also produces occasional papers, and the University of Newcastle upon Tyne, where the Departments of Agricultural Economics and Agricultural Marketing have combined to produce a regular series of discussion papers on European Community agriculture. One Commission series also of note is the *Information on agriculture* volumes, which include major sponsored studies carried out by universities and research institutes in the member states, on a range of topics from econometric forecasting in agriculture to studies of land tenure.

Because of the dispersed nature of CAP research, extensive use needs to be made of secondary abstracting services. *World agricultural economics and rural sociology abstracts*, produced by the Commonwealth Bureau of Agricultural Economics, provides excellent coverage, detailed informative abstracts, and comprehensive indexing. It is available in both a monthly hard-copy printed version and online through the hosts Dialog, ESA-IRS and DIMDI. Areas in which its coverage is particularly useful include German research and government literature, and 'related topics' including rural sociology, development aid policy, and general economic material which has a bearing on the CAP. Also useful is the AGRIS data base from the FAO, used in the production of AGRINDEX and of which the European Community input is known collectively as EUR-AGRIS. This is an indexing rather than an abstracting service, and is perhaps more useful for individual country coverage than for the CAP in general. For information on current research in progress on the CAP in government departments, university faculties and specialized research institutes, AGREP is to be recommended. This is the Community's permanent inventory of research in agriculture, both scientific and policy-oriented, and is issued in annual volumes as well as being available online through Data-Centralen.

There are few specifically CAP bibliographies. However, until 1981, Pudoc (the Netherlands centre for agricultural documentation) produced a monthly bulletin on *Agricultural aspects of the Common Market* which included agricultural policy and economics as well as scientific and technical literature of general interest. Unfortunately, this ceased publication owing to lack of resources at Pudoc. The *Documentation bulletin* of the Commission, already mentioned in the context of the COM series of draft regulations and other Commission papers, includes in addition periodical articles; agriculture is naturally one of its major sections. A number of supplements have also been issued which are useful bibliographies on individual CAP régimes, for example wine.[79] The Commonwealth Bureau of Agricultural Economics publishes major searches of its *World agricultural economics and rural sociology* data base as individual bibliographies on, for example, reform of the CAP and enlargement of the Communities. Finally, once-off bibliographies on the European Communities can offer sources on special aspects. For example, the chapters in Lodge's recent volume include not only agriculture but also relations with the ACP and Mediterranean partners and New Zealand.[80]

The Common Fisheries Policy

The Common Fisheries Policy (CFP) is a relatively recent development and to a considerable degree has an independent existence from the CAP, as the Council of Fisheries Ministers meets separately from the Council of Agriculture Ministers. Although a common organization of the market for fish was introduced in 1970, with a similar price support system to the CAP régimes, and the 1970s saw structural measures financed from the EAGGF Guidance Section, it was not until 1983 that final agreement was reached on the proposals for a CFP which the Commission had tabled in 1976. The CFP, besides the price and structural measures already in existence, incorporated provisions for access to Community waters by fishermen from all member states and the conservation and management of fish stocks by the fixing of total allowable catches which are then divided into quotas for each member state. General guides to the CFP are few so far, but include an issue of *European file*[81] and chapters in general introductions to the Community.[82] Annual report information is given in a separate fisheries chapter of the *General report on the activities of the European Communities*.

In many respects documentation on fisheries policy is similar to that for the CAP, and the following notes are confined to some specifically fisheries information sources where these are separate from CAP material already mentioned. The process of fisheries policy making and legislation is the same as that for agriculture, except that COREPER, the Committee of Permanent Representatives, acts instead of the Special Committee for Agriculture, but all the usual documentary sources apply equally to fisheries.

Fishery statistics are the responsibility of a section in Eurostat's agricultural statistics directorate, and so are covered by the agriculture 'theme' of publications. The CRONOS data bank includes a FISH domain, with data on catches and fleet statistics, and the COMEXT data bank covers the external trade statistics of fisheries. For news services all the general newsletters and press agencies include fisheries in their coverage, but there is no 'Blue Europe' equivalent yet to the Commission's *Green Europe* on the CAP. *Agra Europe* tackles fisheries in EUROFISH, which includes a 'Brussels briefing', the fishing scene, information on supplies and prices and the main new legislative texts; it is published monthly. The main specialist body for fisheries in the UK is the Sea Fish Industry Authority, which produces a periodical *Fishery economics newsletter*, abstracting relevant literature worldwide but including CFP matters.

Conclusion

This chapter has attempted to show something of the variety and disparate character of CAP information. For lack of space, numerous aspects of agricultural policy have had to be neglected, such as trade agreements and external relations, enlargement of the Community, primary food processing and the food industry, forestry, food aid to developing countries, and not least the place of the CAP in the Community budget. This is perhaps not too serious a problem once the user is aware that many other areas of Community policy impinge on the CAP, of which regional policy deserves a special mention.[83]

This chapter has presented a snapshot picture of CAP mechanisms and literature as at the end of 1983. It is, however, an open question how the CAP will develop in relation to other common policies such as those being formulated for energy and industry, and in relation to the increasing pressure on the European Community budget. At the time this chapter was written the Commission had presented proposals for adjustments to the market mechanisms,[84] a review of the Community structural funds in general, but including the EAGGF Guidance Section,[85] and a specific revision of the horizontal socio-structural measures.[86]

Nevertheless, whatever specific changes there may be at various times to different aspects of the CAP, European Community agricultural policy will continue to present a challenge to information specialists — not only to understand its intricacies but above all to keep abreast of the wider Community issues which exert an influence upon it.

References and notes

[1] M. J. Harkin and V. S. Reilly, 'Users and their information requirements in respect to agricultural management, policy, economics and rural sociology: results of the AMIS user study', in *European Regional Congress of Agricultural Librarians and Documentalists: modern systems and networks and the reliability of information*, K. G. Saur, 1978, pp. 279–287.

[2] M. J. Harkin and V. S. Reilly, *Agricultural Management Information Systems: a study of users and their information needs in agricultural management, policy, economics, and rural sociology*, Commission of the European Communities, 1978.

³ *Treaties establishing the European Communities*, Office for Official Publications of the European Communities, 1973, pp. 209–210.

⁴ 'Relaunching Europe: agricultural policy, target 1988', *European file*, 4/82, February 1982.

⁵ *The Common Agricultural Policy*, Commission of the European Communities, 1981.

⁶ 'The agricultural policy of the European Community', 3rd edn., *European documentation*, 6/1982.

⁷ 'Mechanisms of the common organization of agricultural markets: crop products', *Green Europe*, 189.

⁸ 'Mechanisms of the common organization of agricultural markets: livestock products', *Green Europe*, 188.

⁹ A. M. El-Agraa, *The economics of the European Community*, Philip Allan, 1980.

¹⁰ J. Lodge (ed.), *Institutions and policies of the European Community*, Frances Pinter, 1983.

¹¹ C. R. Groves, *An EEC agricultural handbook*, 3rd edn., West of Scotland Agricultural College, 1983.

¹² J. S. Marsh and P. J. Swanney, *Agriculture and the European Community*, Allen and Unwin, 1980.

¹³ R. Fennell, *The Common Agricultural Policy of the European Community: its institutional and administrative organization*, Granada, 1979.

¹⁴ *Agriculture and agricultural policy in the European Communities*, Commission of the European Communities, Agricultural Information Unit, 1981.

¹⁵ *Exploring Europe: the Common Agricultural Policy*, University of Sussex, Schools Unit, 1983.

¹⁶ *CAP Monitor*, Agra Europe.

¹⁷ *The Common Agricultural Policy of the European Community: import–export: the system of licences, levies and refunds*, Intervention Board for Agricultural Produce, 1981, Leaflet EM1.

¹⁸ *CAP—beef and veal*, Meat and Livestock Commission, 1st revision, 1981.

¹⁹ *CAP—pigmeat*, Meat and Livestock Commission, 3rd revision, 1982.

²⁰ *CAP—sheepmeat*, Meat and Livestock Commission, 1st revision, 1981.

²¹ *UK grain marketing arrangements under the Common Agricultural Policy*, Home Grown Cereals Authority, 1979.

²² *The EEC grain market regulation*, Toepfer International, annual.

[23] House of Lords, Select Committee on the European Communities, *Fruit and Vegetables*, HMSO, 1981, (1980–81 HL 147).

[24] C. Ritson and A. Swinbank, *The CAP for fruit and vegetables: its impact on the marketing of third country produce within the EEC*, University of Newcastle upon Tyne, 1983.

[25] House of Lords, Select Committee on the European Communities, *Olive oil*, HMSO, 1982, (1982–83 HL 31).

[26] K. Parris and C. Ritson, *EEC oilseed products sector and the Common Agricultural Policy*, Centre for European Agricultural Studies, 1977.

[27] *The agricultural situation in the Community*, Office for Official Publications of the European Communities, annual.

[28] 'European Community Commission proposes agricultural prices for 1983/84', *Green Europe newsletter*, 21, December 1982.

[29] 'Common agricultural prices 1983/84: Council's decisions', *Green Europe newsletter*, 23.

[30] H. A. Fearn, *The evolution and basic concepts of the green currency system*, MAFF, 1978.

[31] R. W. Irving and H. A. Fearn, *Green money and the Common Agricultural Policy*, Centre for European Agricultural Studies, 1975.

[32] *A history of the monetary compensatory amounts*, Commission of the European Communities, Spokesman's Group, 1982.

[33] 'A new common agricultural structures policy', *Green Europe*, 181.

[34] 'State aids and the Common Agricultural Policy', *Green Europe*, 191.

[35] 'Coordination of agricultural research in the Community', *Green Europe*, 183.

[36] 'The development of veterinary legislation', *Green Europe*, 186.

[37] *EAGGF: importance and functioning*, Office for Official Publications of the European Communities, 1977.

[38] 'Financing the market side of the Common Agricultural Policy: EAGGF Guarantee', *Green Europe*, 182.

[39] *Guidelines for European agriculture*, COM(81)608 final, 23 October 1981.

[40] M. Hopkins, *Policy formation in the European Communities: a bibliographical guide to Community documentation 1958–1978*, Mansell, 1981, pp. 159–183.

[41] G. Pau, *Index of Com documents*, Euroinformation, 1981.

[42] 'Possible improvements to the Common Agricultural Policy', *European Parliament working document* 1-250/81, 27 May 1981.

[43] House of Lords, Select Committee on the European Communities, *Guidelines for European agriculture and the 1982–83 farm price proposals*, HMSO, 1981, (1981–82 HL 101).

[44] *EEC legislation service*, Meat and Livestock Commission.

[45] *EEC legislation applicable to the cereals sector*, Home Grown Cereals Authority.

[46] *European Communities glossary: French–English*, Council of the European Communities, 7th edn., Office for Official Publications of the European Communities, 1980.

[47] R. Fennell, 'Statistical sources', *Information sources in food and agriculture*, G. P. Lilley (ed.), Butterworths, 1981, pp. 142–160.

[48] N. M. Idaikkadar, *Agricultural statistics: a handbook for developing countries*, Pergamon, 1979.

[49] J. Jeffries, *A guide to the official publications of the European Communities*, 2nd edn., Mansell, 1981.

[50] F. Pfähler, 'Agricultural price statistics', *Eurostat news*, 1-1982, pp. 4–5.

[51] *EEC agricultural statistics: problems in their interpretation and use*, Centre for European Agricultural Studies, 1977.

[52] *Fifth statistical programme of the European Communities 1982–1984: annex 4: agriculture, forestry and fisheries statistics*, COM(81)327 final, 28 August 1981.

[53] *Catalogue of the characteristics of agricultural price series stored in Cronos*, Statistical Office of the European Communities, 1983.

[54] *Methodology of EC agricultural price indices: output and input*, Statistical Office of the European Communities, 1983.

[55] A. Ramsay, *Eurostat index*, 2nd edn., Capital Planning Information, 1983.

[56] F. Pfähler, 'Improvement and harmonization of agricultural labour force statistics in the Community', *Eurostat news*, 3-1982, pp. 6–8.

[57] *External trade statistics: user's guide*, Statistical Office of the European Communities, 1982.

[58] G. Rambaud-Chanoz, 'The Comext-Eurostat data bank', *Eurostat news*, 1-1982, pp. 7–8.

[59] D. Byk, 'The Cronos-Eurostat data bank now accessible via Euronet/Diane', *Eurostat news*, 4-1980, pp. 7–11.

[60] *Directory of non-governmental agricultural organizations set up at the Community level*, 6th edn., K. G. Saur, 1980.

[61] *Directory of international statistics*, United Nations Statistical Office, 1982.

[62] *Sources of commodity and product price information*, International Trade Centre UNCTAD/GATT, 1981.

[63] F. C. Pieper, *SISCIS: subject index to sources of comparative international statistics*, CBD Research, 1978.

[64] *National methods of collecting agricultural statistics*, FAO, 1974.

[65] T. M. Harvey, *Statistics Europe: sources for social, economic and market research*, 4th edn., CBD Research, 1981.

[66] 'Wine in the eighties', *Green Europe*, 172.

[67] 'Community wine imports', *European information: development*, April 1980.

[68] 'Wine in the European Community', *European documentation*, 2-3/1981.

[69] *At the farmer's service*, MAFF, 1983/1984 edn.

[70] *The Portuguese meat and livestock industry*, Meat and Livestock Commission, European booklet 83/2.

[71] L. Tsoukalis, *European Community and its Mediterranean enlargement*, Allen & Unwin, 1981.

[72] D. Sears and C. Vaitsos (eds.), *The second enlargement of the European Community: integration of unequal partners*, Macmillan, 1980.

[73] W. Wallace and I. Herreman (eds.), *A community of twelve? The impact of further enlargement of the European Communities*, De Tempel, 1978.

[74] A. E. Buckwell and others, *The costs of the Common Agricultural Policy*, Croom Helm, 1982.

[75] J. Pearce, *The Common Agricultural Policy: prospects for change*, Routledge & Kegan Paul for Chatham House, 1981.

[76] T. E. Josling, M. Langworthy and S. Pearson, *Options for farm policy in the European Community*, Trade Policy Research Centre, 1981.

[77] T. E. Josling and S. Pearson, *Future developments in the Common Agricultural Policy of the European Economic Community*, United States Department of Agriculture, Economic Research Service, 1982.

[78] H. Dicke and H. Rodemer, *Das Finanzproblem der EG und die Reform der gemeinsamen Agrarpolitik*, Kiel University, Institute for International Economics, 1982.

[79] 'Bibliography on the Common Agricultural Policy by product: wine', *Documentation bulletin* B30/A.

[80] J. Lodge (ed.), *The European Community: bibliographical excursions*, Frances Pinter, 1983.

[81] 'The Common Fisheries Policy', *European file*, 11/83, June/July 1983.

[82] See notes 9 and 10.

[83] P. Henry, *Study on the regional impact of the Common Agricultural Policy*, Office for Official Publications of the European Communities, 1981 (Studies: regional policy, 21).

[84] 'Adjustment of the Common Agricultural Policy, *Bulletin of the European Communities*, Supplement 4/83.

[85] 'Increasing the effectiveness of the Community's structural funds', *Bulletin of the European Communities*, Supplement 3/83.

[86] 'Improving the efficiency of agricultural structures: proposal for a Council regulation', COM(83)559 final, 10 October 1983.

List of addresses

Agra Europe (London) Ltd., Agroup House, 16 Lonsdale Gardens, Tunbridge Wells, TN1 1PD.

Agricultural Development and Advisory Service (ADAS), Great Westminster House, Horseferry Road, London, SW1P 2AE.

Centre for European Agricultural Studies, Wye College, Ashford, Kent, TN25 5AH.

CISI, 35 Boulevard Brune, 75680 Paris–Cedex 14, France.

Committee of Agricultural Producer Organizations in the European Communities (COPA), rue de la Science, 23–25, B-1040 Brussels, Belgium.

Commonwealth Bureau of Agricultural Economics, Dartington House, Little Clarendon Street, Oxford, OX1 2HH.

Data Centralen, Retortvej 6–8, 2500 Valby, Denmark.

Euris, Square de Meeus 5, 1040 Brussels, Belgium.

Home Grown Cereals Authority, Hamlyn House, Highgate Hill, London, N19 5PR.

Intervention Board for Agricultural Produce, Fountain House, 2 Queen's Walk, Reading, RG1 7QW.

Meat and Livestock Commission, PO Box 44, Queensway House, Bletchley, MK2 2EF.

Ministry of Agriculture, Fisheries and Food (MAFF), Whitehall Place, London, SW1A 2HH.

National Farmers' Union, Agriculture House, Knightsbridge, London, SW1X 7NJ.

Pudoc, PO Box 4, 6700 AA Wageningen, Netherlands.

SIA Computer Services, Ebury Gate, 23 Lower Belgrave Street, London, SW1W 0NW.

University of Newcastle upon Tyne, Departments of Agricultural Economics and Marketing, Newcastle upon Tyne, NE1 7RU.

Zentrale Markt- und Preisberichtstelle, Godesberger Allee 142–148, 5300 Bonn 2, West Germany.

List of European Documentation Centres and Depository Libraries in the United Kingdom

European Documentation Centres (EDCs)

ABERDEEN
University of Aberdeen
University Library
New Library
Meston Walk
Aberdeen AB9 2UB

BATH
University of Bath
University Library
Claverton Down
Bath BA2 7AY

BELFAST
Queen's University
The Library
Belfast BT7 1NN
Northern Ireland

BIRMINGHAM
Birmingham Polytechnic
Main Library
Perry Barr
Birmingham B42 2SU

University of Birmingham
Main Library
PO Box 363
Birmingham B15 2TT

BRADFORD
University of Bradford
The Library
Richmond Road
Bradford BD7 1DP

BRIGHTON
University of Sussex
University Library
Falmer
Brighton BN1 9QL

BRISTOL
University of Bristol
Law Library
Wills Memorial Bldg
Queens Road
Bristol BS8 1RJ

CAMBRIDGE
University of Cambridge
University Library
West Road
Cambridge CB3 9DR

CANTERBURY
University of Kent
The Library
Canterbury CT2 7NU

CARDIFF
University College, Cardiff
Arts & Social Studies Library
PO Box 78
Cardiff CF1 1XL

COLCHESTER
University of Essex
Library
PO Box 24
Colchester CO4 3UA

COLERAINE
New University of Ulster
The Library
Coleraine
Londonderry BT52 1SA
Northern Ireland

COVENTRY
Coventry Lanchester Polytechnic
The Library
Priory Street
Coventry CV1 5FB

University of Warwick
The Library
Coventry CV4 7AL

DUNDEE
University of Dundee
Law Library
Scrymgeour Building
Park Place
Dundee DD1 4HN

DURHAM
University of Durham
University Library
Palace Green
Durham DH1 3RN

EDINBURGH
University of Edinburgh
Centre of European Governmental
Studies
Old College
South Bridge
Edinburgh EH8 9YL

EXETER
University of Exeter
Faculty of Law Library
Centre for European Legal Studies
Amory Building, Rennes Drive
Exeter EX4 4RJ

GLASGOW
University of Glasgow
The University Library
Hillhead Street
Glasgow G12 8QE

GUILDFORD
University of Surrey
The Library
Guildford GU2 5XH

HULL
University of Hull
Brynmor Jones Library
Cottingham Road
Hull HU6 7RX

KEELE
University of Keele
University Library
Keele ST5 5BG

LANCASTER
University of Lancaster
The Library
Bailrigg
Lancaster LA1 4YX

LEEDS
University of Leeds
Faculty of Law Library
20 Lyddon Terrace
Leeds LS2 9JT

Leeds Polytechnic
The Library
Calverley Street
Leeds LS1 3HE

LEICESTER
University of Leicester
University Library
University Road
Leicester LE1 7RH

LONDON
British Library of Political and Econo-
mic Science
(London School of Economics and
Political Science)
10 Portugal Street
London WC2A 2HD

University of London
Queen Mary College
The Library
Mile End Road
London E1 4NS

Polytechnic of North London
The Library
Kentish Town
Prince of Wales Road
London NW5

Royal Institute of International Affairs
The Library
10 St. James' Square
London SW1Y 4LE

LOUGHBOROUGH
Loughborough University of Tech-
nology
The Library
Loughborough LE11 3TU

MANCHESTER
University of Manchester
John Rylands University Library
Oxford Road
Manchester M13 9PP

NEWCASTLE
Newcastle upon Tyne Polytechnic
The Library
Ellison Place
Newcastle upon Tyne NE1 8ST

NORWICH
University of East Anglia
University Library
University Plain
Norwich NR4 7TJ

NOTTINGHAM
University of Nottingham
University Library
Nottingham NG7 2RD

OXFORD
University of Oxford
Official Papers
Radcliffe Camera
Bodleian Library
Oxford OX1 3BG

PORTSMOUTH
Portsmouth Polytechnic
Frewen Library
Cambridge Road
Portsmouth PO1 2ST

READING
University of Reading
University Library
Whiteknights
Reading RG6 2AE

SALFORD
University of Salford
The Library
Salford M5 4WT

SHEFFIELD
Sheffield City Polytechnic
The Library
Pond Street
Sheffield S1 1WB

SOUTHAMPTON
University of Southampton
Faculty of Law Library
Highfield
Southampton SO9 5NH

WOLVERHAMPTON
Polytechnic of Wolverhampton
The Robert Scott Library
St. Peter's Square
Wolverhampton WV1 1RH

WYE
University of London
Centre for European Agricultural
Studies
Wye College
Wye
Ashford TN25 5AH

Depository Libraries (DEPs)

BOSTON SPA
British Library Lending Division
Boston Spa
Wetherby
West Yorkshire
LS23 7BQ

LIVERPOOL
Liverpool and District Scientific, Industrial and Research Library
Advisory Council (LADSIRLAC)
William Brown Street
Liverpool L3 8EW

LONDON
British Library Reference Division
Department of Printed Books
Overseas English Section
Great Russell Street
London WC1B 3DG

City of Westminster Libraries
Central Library
St Martin's Street
London WC2 7HP

Indexes

The following pages contain two separate indexes: a Subject Index and a Title Index. The Subject Index is intended to provide no more than a general indication of the broad subjects dealt with in the chapters of this book. The Title Index includes references to works quoted in the text. It does not list works which appear only in the References and Notes sections of each chapter.

Subject Index

Title Index

302 *Title Index*